QUILTS 1700–2010

Hidden Histories, Untold Stories

QUILTS 1700–2010

Hidden Histories, Untold Stories

edited by Sue Prichard

V&A Publishing

For Linda Parry, mentor and friend

First published by V&A Publishing, 2010

V&A Publishing
Victoria and Albert Museum
South Kensington
London SW7 2RL

Distributed in North America by Harry N. Abrams, Inc., New York

Paperback edition ISBN 978 1 85177 608 5

10 9 8 7 6 5 4 3 2
2014 2013 2012 2011 2010

Hardback edition ISBN: 978 1 85177 595 8
Library of Congress Control Number 2009932293

10 9 8 7 6 5 4 3 2
2014 2013 2012 2011 2010

A catalogue record for this book is available from the British Library.

Designed by Nigel Soper

New V&A photography by Pip Barnard and Richard Davis, V&A Photographic Studio

Front jacket/cover illustration: At the End of the Day, Natasha Kerr. London, 2007.
V&A: T.43–2008 (cat. no.66)
Back flap and endpapers/inside cover illustration: Bedcover (details). English, dated
1797. V&A: T.102–1938 (cat. no.16)
Frontispiece: Quilted bedcover. English, 1830s. V&A: T.154–1964 (cat. no.30)

Printed in Singapore by C.S. Graphics

V&A Publishing
Victoria and Albert Museum
South Kensington
London SW7 2RL
www.vandabooks.com

Contents

Quilts for the Poor – We are requested to insert the following: 'Delta' would feel much obliged to any lady who could supply her with old muslin or cotton grenadine dress skirts for making into quilts for poor people. Those entirely past wear quite answer the purpose. [We shall be happy to forward letters to 'Delta.' – Ed.]

The Queen, The Lady's Newspaper and Court Chronicle, 25 MAY 1867

Director's Foreword

QUILTS 1700–2010 is the V&A's first major exhibition to focus on British patchwork and quilt-making, exploring over 300 years of production within the context of both the domestic interior and fine-art practice. Drawing on the rich resources of the Museum's textile collection and including loans from some of the UK's finest regional museums and private collections, the exhibition seeks to reveal the hidden histories and untold stories of the makers whose vision, creativity and skill continue to resonate across the centuries. The five thematic displays take an innovative approach to the history of patchwork and quilt-making, juxtaposing stunning historical examples with new commissions from some of Britain's leading artists and practitioners working in both the fine-art and textile fields. Working closely with contemporary artists has ensured that the legacy of the past continues to have relevance in the future. Each new work explores or subverts the skills and traditions of the past in a celebration of the hand-made.

The contributors to this publication bring new insights into the social and cultural trends that influenced three centuries of quilt production and the sources of inspiration for the eclectic designs that provide a window into the maker's world. By engaging with both the oral narratives and personal histories handed down with everyday objects, the contributors reveal why quilts continue to be seen as 'objects of emotion', which remain an integral part of familial heritage.

The investment of time and the innovative use of materials, both new and recycled, within the context of the domestic interior is being rediscovered and re-evaluated. The current economic climate and concerns about the effects of capitalism and globalization have created a new appreciation of the importance of individuality and the hand-made. One of the V&A's key aims is to promote, support and develop creativity; this exhibition is designed both to inspire a new generation of artists and practitioners and to provide a platform for continuing research into objects that provide a rich resource of references to both the private and public world.

MARK JONES,
Director of the Victoria and Albert Museum

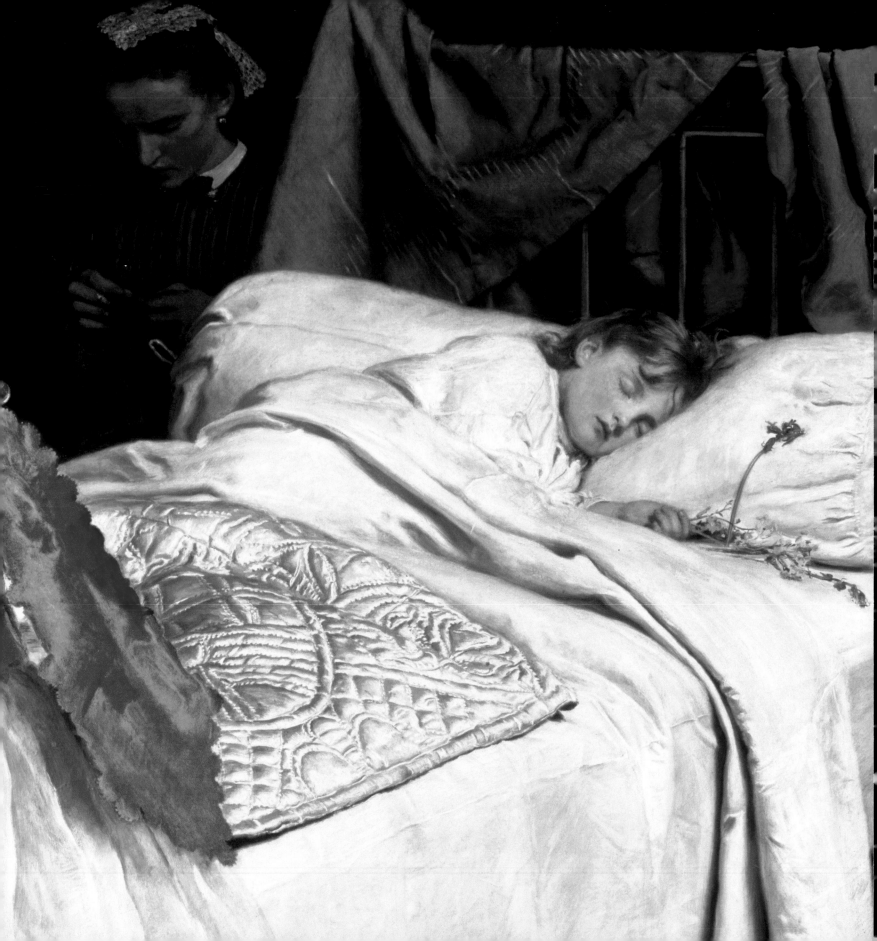

Introduction

Sue Prichard

Print for patchwork is sold by weight, in small bits such as I have sent you. I purchased it in Prescot market … The piece of patchwork is out of an old Quilt I made above 20 years ago …The Hexagon in the middle was a shred of our best bed hangings; they were Chintz, from the East Indies, which my father brought home with him from one of his voyages.

Miss Weeton: Journal of a Governess 1811–1825, 9 September 1824

Quilts stimulate memories of warmth, security and comfort (pl.1). They are also inexorably linked with the feminine. Ellen Weeton's letter to her daughter Mary was accompanied by a parcel containing not only the piece of patchwork, but also a ribbon belonging to her Grandmother Weeton. In her letter Ellen explains the importance of these textiles with reference to Mary's female heritage and sense of kinship.[1] Contrary to popular belief, however, Ellen Weeton is probably one of the few women to document the history of her quilt-making in writing. Many quilts are passed down through the generations undocumented, although some are accompanied by oral histories and personal narratives; over the years names and dates become confused and stories are embellished. Yet the potency of the voice from the past is sometimes more powerful than the evidence revealed by close examination of the textiles used by the makers. The purpose of this book is to navigate a path between the myths and misconceptions and the actual histories surrounding quilt production in Great Britain since the eighteenth century.

Histories of the domestic interior and the objects that have been used within the home have been a popular area of study for art and design historians, socio-economic historians and scholars specializing in the fields of architecture, material culture and gender history.[2] To date, little academic research has been carried out on the significance of patchwork and quilting within the context of the British domestic interior. The British Quilt Study Group[3] is redressing this; however, the ordinariness of the quilt and its utilitarian function have served to marginalize it from the gaze of many historians (pl.2).

Quilts 1700–2010 does not set out to create a seamless history of British quilt-making. Nor does it intend to provide a definitive catalogue of changes in textile design and manufacture over the last 300 years. Instead, this book aims to expand current thinking and approaches to quilt study, presenting material that reflects the period under discussion, from eighteenth-century inventories to contemporary feminist criticism. The four broadly chronological chapters have been approached within the context of their historical framework, whether drawing on the rich resources of the Victoria and Albert Museum's eighteenth- and nineteenth-century textile collections or the archives of some of the country's finest regional museums. Each essay

1 Sir John Everett Millais, *Sleeping.* (detail). Oil on canvas, *c.*1865

9

focuses on a particular period of quilt production, analysing the social and economic factors behind the rise and decline in popularity of the craft within the context of the domestic interior, and its adoption and reinvention within contemporary art practice. In addition to the four main chapters, a series of feature spreads provide a different type of approach to individual quilts and coverlets within the V&A's collection, adding to our understanding of the context of production. To take one example, the intricate piecing of fabric into pictorial representations of domestic scenes and heroic battles illustrates the maker's highly complex and sophisticated engagement with a world beyond the confines of the domestic landscape.

Quilt exhibitions draw enormous audiences and generate thousands of pounds in revenue. Yet the intimate nature of the experience that quilts represent sets them apart from bigger, more newsworthy events, their importance instead being relegated to that of family heirloom or souvenir that represents 'the yesterdays of us all'. The social significance of quilts rests on 'their association with either a single person and his or her life

2 Eric Ravilious, *RNAS Sick Bay, Dundee.* Watercolour, 1941. The Imperial War Museum

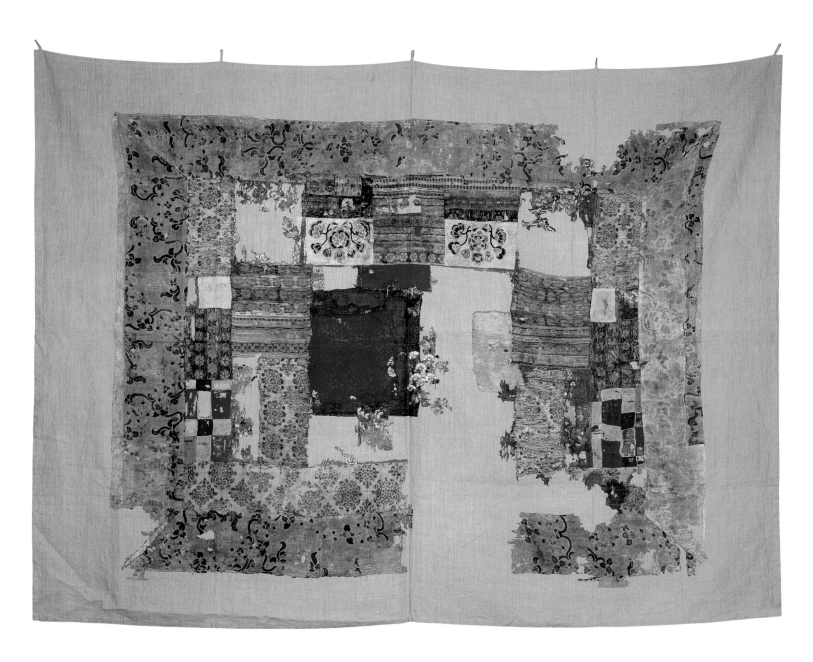

history, or a group of people like a married couple, a family'.[4] Because of this, and within some museum collections, historical quilts are sometimes categorized as memorabilia, or discussed within the context of British cultural production defined as 'folk art' or 'naive art'.[5] All the essays and feature spreads in *Quilts 1700–2010* offer the opportunity to move across interdisciplinary boundaries and widen the audience for further research and collaboration.

'I am assured … Charles II slept under it as he fled to the Isles of Scilly': V&A archive

Archaeological remains, sculptures and paintings testify to the very long history of patchwork and quilting (pl.3).[6] Two distinct crafts with their own separate histories, patchwork was based on a functional need to extend the working life of clothing and domestic goods, whereas quilting provided both warmth and protection. The V&A's collection of patchwork was initially formed

3 Patchwork of silk, probably a *kasaya* (a Buddhist monastic robe), from Cave 17, Mogao, near Dunhuang, Gansu province, China. Tang Dynasty, 8th–9th centuries AD. British Museum: AC MAS.856

4 Walter Langley, *Tender Grace of a Day that is Dead.* Oil on canvas, *c.*1880s. Gallery Oldham

5 Bedcover. Silk patchwork, quilted. English, 1690–1720. V&A: T.201–1984 (see also pp.22–3 and cat. no. 11)

because of the significance of the component fragments of textiles, as opposed to the importance of the personal histories of the makers. Thus the collection reflects the great diversity of fabrics available during three centuries of textile trade and production: from the fine silks and velvets of the seventeenth and eighteenth centuries through to the cheap cottons manufactured during the Industrial Revolution. This collecting policy has been criticized for not encompassing utilitarian production: the quilts and rough patchworks that populate eighteenth- and nineteenth-century representations of poor domestic interiors (pl.4). The harsh reality of poverty, however, dictates that these objects, along with the histories of their makers, are unlikely to survive. One notable exception is to be found in the archives of the London Foundling Hospital. The scraps of textiles left by impoverished mothers who abandoned their babies include a small strip of silk and cotton patchwork

6 William MacDuff, *A Country Auction.* Oil on canvas, 1845–75. Private Collection

embroidered with a heart. A symbol of kinship, should the distressed woman ever have the means to reclaim her child, one half was pinned to the babe, while the other half would have been retained by the mother.[7]

Occasionally, some of the stories handed down with quilts and coverlets have passed into Museum documentation. An early eighteenth century patchwork bedcover (pl.5, cat. no.11 and pp.22–3) was acquired in 1984, accompanied by an assertion that the fugitive second son of Charles I (and future King Charles II) slept under the quilt in Bishops' Court, a medieval manor house, en route to the Isles of Scilly during the height of the Civil War (1642–51). Examination of the component textiles in the quilt reveals that most of the silks post-date the Civil War, and the silk velvets originate from the 1670s and '90s; this story therefore embraces an element of myth-making. Both women and men of the late seventeenth and early eighteenth centuries readily made connections between their family and the state, declaring political allegiance to a king or a patron via objects such as domestic bedcovers. The actual chronology of the 'Bishops' Court' quilt may never be revealed, but by contextualizing its oral narrative we may interpret such myth-making as the manifestation of one family's loyalty to the King and the Royalist cause. In this case, 'what people imagined happened, and also what they believed might have happened … may be as crucial as what did happen',[8] particularly in terms of the survival of the quilt.

Despite extensive research into the V&A's collection, some questions remain unanswered. Frustratingly, even when quilts are signed and dated, it has often proved impossible to trace the personal histories of their makers. Developments in genealogical research (most notably via online archives) can help, but often a name and a date are simply not enough evidence to yield fruitful results. Realistically – particularly with unsigned and undated quilts and coverlets acquired at auction or in antique shops – the identity of the makers of some of the most stunning examples will never be known. Nevertheless, the complexity of design, the skill in piecing and making and the creativity of the maker speak across the centuries. It is hoped that the bringing-together and close study of some of the best examples in the Museum's collection will inspire a new generation to take up their needles and create their own personal heirlooms for the future.

'Quilt – For exchange, a beautiful figured silk amber wadded quilt for largest bed, quite new; both sides alike. Wanted, dark sable muff, and border for jacket; sealskin hat. Offers requested': S.D.L.,

THE QUEEN, 2 January 1869`

In the first chapter of this book, Clare Browne places the terms patchwork and quilt within their historical contexts. Drawing on both the V&A's collection and historical inventories, she discusses the importance of the bed as the focus of both elaborate decoration and considerable expenditure. The eighteenth century witnessed a period of rapid economic growth; affluent consumers were increasingly able to exercise choice in the type of domestic goods they acquired. However, the rapidly growing textile industry fed what contemporary writers criticized as a particularly feminine vice – 'mindless materialism and uncontrolled love of ostentation'.[9] Textiles were both fashionable and desirable, particularly imports from East Asia, whether purchased new or recycled via second-hand dealers and pawnbrokers. As Browne points out, fashions in interior furnishings filtered down through the social ranks, with high-quality chintz appearing in the estates of the middling classes as well as those of the more affluent, in servants' quarters as well as the best bedrooms.

At this period women rarely made their own clothes, and bed hangings and quilts provided an opportunity to showcase their skills to family and friends, transforming what we now consider private into public space. Their role was clearly defined, and in creating and acquiring soft furnishings they were 'expected to exercise taste and to respond to fashion'. The gregarious diarist Mrs Lybbe Powys appears to have been a particularly favoured female house guest, embarking on what was in effect a 'grand tour' of fashionable bedrooms. Her journals (1756–1808) recount a visit to the best bedroom of Mrs Freeman of Fawley Court, Buckinghamshire, and seeing the new bed commissioned for the Queen's bedroom at Windsor.[10]

Popular narratives suggest that the makers of complex pieces of patchwork were the daughters or wives of drapers, who provided them with access to a vast range of fabrics. By examining insurance records and trade cards, both Clare Browne and Linda Parry reveal that major towns and cities were centres of professional patchwork and quilt production. London, Canterbury and Exeter have all been linked with quilts in the Museum collection; the quality of piecing and stitching, and the variety of materials used, suggest professional practice, perhaps a local workshop. Certainly the number of sumptuous jackets, petticoats and gowns that survive in museum collections, as well as exquisitely worked bed hangings and covers, testify to the level of skill required by such workshops. However, the market

7 After Walter-Dendy Sadler, *Nearly Done*. Aquatint, published 1898. Stapleton Collection

for second-hand clothes, furnishings and furniture also flourished during the eighteenth century. Quilts were bought and sold as commodities, even if they had been given as gifts or inherited (pl.6). Nicholas Blundell, a resident of Liverpool, recorded his visit to a house sale in June 1717 where he itemized his purchases. 'I went to the Sail [*sic*] of Goods at Croxtath':[11]

	£	s.	d.
Press for hanging in my Wife's Cloths	01	10	00
Plod [plaid] for Window Curtons	00	06	06
A Sedar Chest of Drawers	01	10	00
Ovell Table	00	01	06
Under Quilt	00	03	00
Frame for warming plates	00	02	06
Pictures three	00	04	06

House sales and auctions were not the only methods of acquiring second-hand furnishings. John Styles' analysis of the use of the term 'patchwork' in eighteenth-century print includes research into the published transcripts of the Old Bailey criminal trials. As he concludes, stolen patchwork was as much a commodity as other domestic goods, and larceny could be a lucrative means of acquiring bedcovers and selling them on in the 'Rag fairs' of the metropolis.

Domestic patchwork epitomized practicality within the home, and the recycling of household furnishings bore witness to a wife's expertise as keeper of the purse strings. However, the production of large-scale patchwork projects, the intricate piecing over papers, and the complex geometric arrangements of minute pieces of fabric are, in written and visual accounts, attributed to middle-class women with sufficient free time to undertake such large projects (pl.7). Making for pleasure, rather than of necessity, is reflected in the vast number of decorative patchwork coverlets in museum collections. However, middle-class women did perform other roles within the domestic sphere. Although these duties might vary from household to household, women were on the whole responsible for all aspects of home-based entertainment, for their children's dress and education, and for the provision and upkeep of soft furnishings and

linen. Joanne Bailey discusses stitching within the context of women's daily lives, when responsibilities within the home and towards the extended family were juxtaposed with periods of leisure. Her examination of the domestic landscape suggests that stitching provided a refuge from the day-to-day operation of the household, a momentary pause for quiet reflection and rare seclusion.

The study of women's diaries reveals their firm grasp of domestic management, from household accounts to information regarding the suitability and foibles of local tradespeople. However, as Claire Smith makes clear, women also went to great lengths to document political instability and intrigue. Smith has undertaken new research into a silk-and-ribbon cot quilt (cat. no.2) made in the first decade of the eighteenth century, uncovering a personal history that reveals the turbulent and sometimes violent landscape of a small fishing village. Life in Deal, which was notorious as one of the smuggling routes on the Kent coast, is revealed via Priscilla Redding's diary, which, rather than documenting her needlework, narrates the multitudinous experiences of her family, including the imprisonment of her father and the almost-fatal accident that befell her child.

'He has taken loving care of it and the love letters in the patchwork …': V&A archive

Paper templates remaining within examples of patchwork document their own history, providing information regarding dates and sometimes a geographical location, although this information needs to be treated with caution: paper was a valuable commodity and, as such, was recycled in the home. In some cases, papers have been discovered in the course of conservation treatments. Joanne Hackett, the V&A's textile conservator, worked extensively on the collection during preparation for the 2010 exhibition and describes the latest technology used to reveal the variety of papers employed in the making of an early eighteenth-century coverlet (1475–1902, cat. no.15). However, papers have also been used as a tool in the construction of stories surrounding individual quilts. Angela McShane has drawn on her expertise of print culture to examine the oral history accompanying the V&A's

'Chapman coverlet' (cat. no.21). Examining the layers of paper and fabric, she separates myth from fact; and, in an unexpected twist to the narrative, for the first time uncovers the origins of what was believed to be a love poem written by Elisabeth Chapman for her husband, John.

Recent research has focused on the role of women as consumers and collectors, and on the use of objects 'to convey a multitude of meanings, from fashion, taste and style to wealth and status, history and lineage, and from science, education, political allegiance and religious conviction to personality, relationships, memory and mortality'.[12] Jacqueline Riding takes up this theme in her discussion of the George III coverlet (cat. no.23). Drawing on classical texts and eighteenth-century popular-print culture, she explores how the unknown maker of the coverlet created a narrative that transformed herself into both observer and chronicler of the cycle of life and death, love and loss. Riding's interpretation of the George III coverlet illustrates how these objects might be used to understand the breadth of women's engagement with the wider world during a period of intense social upheaval and instability. In the second chapter of this book, Linda Parry discusses in greater detail the enormous technological, social and economic changes that took place in the nineteenth century. Britain's unrivalled position as the world's most successful mercantile and manufacturing economy created unprecedented wealth, but also enormous hardship – the effects of which were to be felt in both urban and rural areas. She analyses how these changes affected quilt production and, in a particularly revealing case study, illustrates how one quilt can shed new light on traditional patterns of migration.

The largest number of patchwork quilts and coverlets in museum collections tend to date from the nineteenth century, many of them reflecting the fashion for bold geometric patterns. However, the inspiration for patchwork came from many sources, with some of the most inventive – and, indeed, eclectic – examples produced by both men and women. Jenny Lister explores the rich secular and religious images in the extraordinary wool coverlet attributed to Ann West

(cat. no.35), while in 'Sewing Soldiers' Chris Breward discusses a unique chapter in the history of British patchwork. Appropriated by the Temperance movement in India, patchwork was promoted as a 'self-help' method of resisting the lure of the canteen during long periods of inactivity. Patchwork played a major role in the nineteenth-century campaigner Elizabeth Fry's prison- reform movement. Bags of fabric, needles and thread were distributed to female convicts on board transportation ships, and this practice has been the inspiration for a new commission for the V&A from the prison charity Fine Cell Work. The relationship between stitching and imprisonment has been the subject of myth and literature,[13] while the occupational benefits of craftwork during the long hours of incarceration formed the subject of an article in the V&A's online journal.[14] During the course of this unique collaboration, many of the men in HMP Wandsworth described the benefits of stitching – both physical and emotional – with one of them adding that 'perfection is not usually what's expected in prison'.

'Oh, mother,' said Maggie, in a vehemently cross tone, 'I don't want to do my patchwork.'
'What! Not your pretty patchwork, to make a counterpane for your aunt Glegg?'
'It's foolish work,' said Maggie, with a toss of her mane, 'tearing things to pieces to sew 'em together again. And I don't want to do anything for my aunt Glegg. I don't like her.'
GEORGE ELLIOT, *Mill on the Floss*, 1860

The beginning of the twentieth century witnessed a marked decline in the variety and vitality of patchwork. Quilting, however, survived in some localized areas and was subject to various strategies to ensure that the craft did not completely die out. Dorothy Osler assesses the influential role that the Women's Institute (WI) and Rural Industries Bureau (RIB) played in attempting to safeguard or resurrect skills that had declined since the nineteenth century. Drawing on the archives of both the WI and the RIB, but also on the testimony of two of the

Enid Marx

8 Eric Ravilious, *Enid Marx standing next to a quilt in The Little Gallery, Sloane Street*. Sketch, 1938, in Eric Ravilious, *The Story of High Street*, ed. Tim Mainstone (Norwich, 2008)

most prominent women in twentieth-century quilt literature, she paints a vivid picture of the dedication and
energy of both Mavis FitzRandolph and Muriel Rose, and
of their role in promoting traditional rural crafts (pl.8).

Concern regarding the gradual erosion of traditional
skills and regional designs prompted the first system-
atic attempt to record surviving examples and the oral
histories of the women who made them. Elizabeth
Hake's *English Quilting Old and New* (1937) focused on
West Country quilting and emphasized the importance
of direct contact with makers. In her preface, Hake
acknowledged the help of Mavis FitzRandolph, who
published her own account of the work that she had
undertaken for the RIB in *Traditional Quilting* (1954).

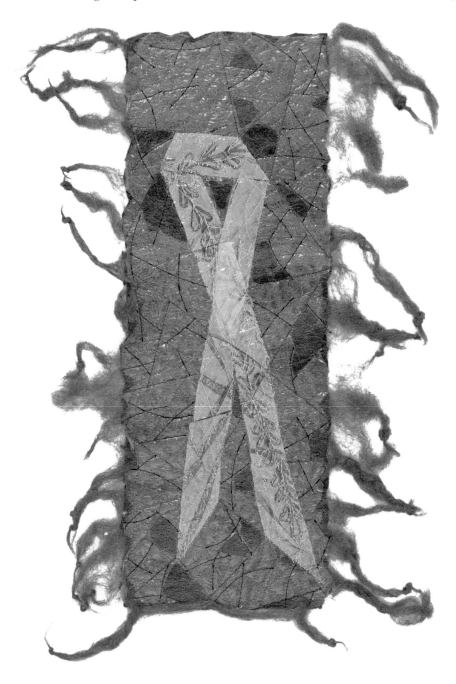

9 Michele Walker, *Study for Memoriam*. Plastic, steel wire wool and lace, 2002. V&A: T.6:2–2009

The next stage in the history of British quilting came nearly 20 years later. Averil Colby had concentrated on the technique, design and history of British patchwork in *Patchwork* (1958), and *Quilting* (1972) followed a similar format, providing diagrams and drawings of patterns and notes on setting up a quilting frame. Hake, FitzRandolph and Colby are still referenced in contemporary accounts of the development of patchwork and quilting, and their seminal work in documenting and recording regional patterns and designs ensured a legacy for later researchers. Latterly, Dorothy Osler's *Traditional British Quilts* (1987) and Janet Rae's *The Quilts of the British Isles* (1996) offered new perspectives on the tradition, illustrating examples from both public and private collections. However, the V&A's extensive collection has never been comprehensively catalogued and published. In 1987 this situation was partially remedied by the publication of *A Guide to Practical Patchwork from the Victoria and Albert Collection* (1987) by Linda Parry, which illustrated a small selection of the Museum's collection, together with technical instructions on how to make some of the best examples. One of the most ambitious projects undertaken in recent years has been the three-year documentation project carried out by the Quilters' Guild of the British Isles (1990–3). The aim of the project was to create the first national database of quilts made before 1960, and *Quilt Treasures: The Quilters' Guild Heritage Search* (1995) illustrates some of the quilts discovered during the project including those with special associations, such as soldiers' quilts and signature quilts. *Quilt Treasures* also focused on the histories of some of the women who made the quilts, in one case revealing an almost magical remedy for removing blood from a pricked finger:

'What you do is spit on the spot and rub it in.
Then you get a bit of white cotton thread and
rub the spot. When this has soaked up the blood
you get a clean piece and rub some more,'
explained one. The 'magic', it seems, is in the
spit – and it has to be spit from the person who
pricked her finger in the first place.[15]

The Guild's documentation days, and the number of quilt exhibitions and competitions held both nationally and internationally, testify to the success of a quilting revival that has attracted growing numbers of contemporary quilt-makers across the globe. Despite this success, however, women artists who choose to work with fabric and stitch often find themselves marginalized in the fine-art arena. 'Negotiating space: fabric and the feminine 1945–2010' discusses the issues surrounding contemporary artistic practice, taking as its platform for debate an article written by the journalist Germaine Greer. Since the late 1960s, feminist artists have provided new perspectives on the role and status of patchwork and quilts, drawing on traditional skills, but also subverting the domestic context. Despite the diversity of approaches to contemporary practice (pl.9), however, many women who work with fabric and stitch continue to face obstacles when seeking to exhibit their work. Chapter Four explores this issue in dialogue with some of the leading practitioners currently working in the textile field.

The historian Raphael Samuel has written that 'memory and history are so often placed in opposite camps'.[16] Memories, particularly those of the home, are often awakened by the sensory triggers of sight, smell and touch. They are embellished by the oral histories handed down with each generation. These memories are uniquely individual – focusing on the intimate rather than the worldly, constructing a patchwork of narrative that is neither true nor false, but an amalgam of the two. History, on the other hand, relies on tangible evidence, most notably the written word, to explain and expand our knowledge of the world. Our intention has been to bring these two camps together, to analyse both the myths and the evidence in order to understand more about the making and meaning of quilts. We hope that this body of research will provide a platform for future scholarship, highlighting the importance of patchwork and quilts as multi-layered, complex signifiers of personal and collective narratives and experiences.

This book is published in conjunction with the exhibition *Quilts 1700–2010* at the V&A (20 March–4 July 2010).

Making and using quilts in eighteenth-century Britain

Clare Browne

What was a quilt in the eighteenth century?

IN EIGHTEENTH-CENTURY HOUSEHOLDS, at all levels of income above the most modest, there was a variety of possibilities for making and dressing the bed. A newspaper advertisement in 1752 laid out some of the choices:

> B Caldwell, at the Blanket Warehouse, almost opposite Chancery Lane, in High Holborn, has made up for the Summer season, a choice collection of washing bed furnishings, both of checkes and fine flower'd cottons, of various patterns, & different prices as well as other beds of Morines, Harrateen, Cheney, Linsey etc, amounting to about 50 in 100, several of which may be seen standing. Likewise just received out of the country, a large cargoe of blankets, quilts, down & feather beds (warranted sweet and fit to use immediately), mattresses, cotton counterpanes, ruggs, coverlets, bedsteads, bed-ticks, & floor carpets of every size & very beautiful. Patterns, all fresh & new.[1]

Eighteenth-century customers would have understood the distinction being made between quilts and other bedding in such a list. But the variety of terms used historically for bedding lying both under and over the sleeper can be confusing today. A modern understanding of an eighteenth-century hand-made quilt encompasses both form and function: bed coverings that were quilted for warmth and decoration, using the techniques of wadded, stuffed, cord and flat quilting; and patchwork bedcovers, pieced together from different fabrics for decorative effect, with or without a filling layer quilted in.

Quilts in Britain before the eighteenth century

Quilted or patchwork bedcovers made in Britain do not survive in their original form from much before the start of the eighteenth century. But it is possible to establish, and visualize, what was available before then. In the previous two centuries decoration, colour and comfort within the home had been encouraged by increasing access to new sorts of textiles for those who could afford them, and beds were often the focus of elaborate decoration – and of considerable expenditure – in both domestic and grander settings. Typically the textile furnishings of a bed would be worth substantially more than the bedstead itself, and their decoration could be complex. Using a single type of fabric for the hangings and covers limited the possibilities of pattern and colour, and so more ornate decoration might be created in a layered process, involving such techniques as embroidery, appliqué (applying pieces of fabric onto the ground material) and paning. 'Panes' and 'paning' were terms used for the joining up of pieces of fabric of different type or colour, applied to bed furnishings from at least the early sixteenth century. Paned bed hangings and bedcovers were a precursor to what became patchwork in the eighteenth century, in their juxtaposition of different coloured and patterned textiles, for visual effect, in a geometric arrangement.

Evidence for the use of quilted or paned covers on beds before the eighteenth century comes in the first place from written records, mostly inventories, which show their existence going back hundreds of years, and their condition ranging from luxurious through to strictly functional. At the luxurious end, many are noted in the inventory of King Henry VIII, taken in 1547: for example, 'a Counterpointe of tawney [yellow/brown] and redde Taphata [taffeta] paned together quilted Lozenged allover with a cordaunte [outlining thread] of veanice [Venetian] golde bordered rounde abowte withe an embraudery of yellowe satten with rooses and Lettres in it'.[2]

As well as using 'newmaking' silk, paning would undoubtedly have encompassed the recycling of valuable older textiles into new use. In the inventory of the possessions of Elizabeth Talbot, Countess of Shrewsbury, taken in 1601, a servant's chamber in Hardwick New Hall had 'a tester, bedes head and double vallans of grene white and yellowe velvett Cutt and paned'.[3] Silk velvet was among the most expensive of textiles, and this use of it as pieced bed hangings for a servant's room suggests that it may have become well worn since its original use. At the utilitarian end, quilts could be purely functional. In the inventory taken of the Tower of London in 1547 there were listed a 'quilte of Lynnen Clothe lyned with flannell' and 'v [five] quiltes of holland clothe filled with wolle'.[4]

The second important source of evidence is found in surviving imported quilts that have a firm provenance indicating their use in Britain before the eighteenth century. A notable example is a late-sixteenth-century quilt preserved at Hardwick Hall in Derbyshire. With a ground of cotton embroidered with coloured silk thread and wadding of cotton waste, it was made in Bengal in eastern India, as a type of furnishing destined originally for the Portuguese market. Two 'Quilt[s] of India stuff embroidered with beasts' were listed in the inventory at Hardwick in 1601, and while the surviving quilt cannot be proved to be one of these, we know that such 'Bengala quilts' were available, at a price, in the London market in the early seventeenth century, imported by the East India Company.[5]

A third and rare type of evidence for the physical nature of early quilts is provided when they survive in an adapted form that can be accurately dated. There is a suit of doublet and breeches in the V&A's collection that is datable by its style to the late 1630s. The two parts are made from ivory-coloured silk satin quilted in running stitch. The seams within the quilting, and the varying directions of the quilt design, suggest that the satin was not quilted specifically for the suit, which appears to have been adapted from one or possibly two bedcovers that were earlier in date. No such cover survives in its original form, but the harmonious patterns created by the quilting stitches, and the lustrous quality of the silk satin, combine to suggest how fine it would have looked (pl.1).

There are many written references to quilts and quilting before 1700, but interpreting what they mean is made complicated by inconsistent terminology. A succinct definition was given by Randle Holme in *The Academy of Armoury* published in 1688: 'Quilting, is to put Cotton Wool of an equal thickness between two Silks, or a Callicoe or other Cloth undermost, and a Silk above, which is wrought in scrolls, flowers, &c. to keep the Cotton from shifting its place.' Quilts made in Britain were more often filled with wool, and could also use flock (wool waste from shearing) and down (the soft underplumage of birds). So there was some overlap with feather beds, flock beds, bed ticks, eiderdowns and other forms of soft bedding. Samuel Pepys noted in his diary, when retreating from the Great Fire of London on 3 September 1666: 'at night, lay down a little upon a quilt of W Hewer in the office (all my own things being packed up or gone)'. This may have been the type of bedding that was sometimes mentioned as an underquilt. For example, in the Drayton House inventory of 1710, there was 'in the Bedchamber ... One white Sattain under quilt'.[6] This reference helps to explain why there can be multiple quilts made of different fabrics listed for one bed. In particular, it was not always clear how a quilt was distinguished from an eiderdown. That type of bedding used plumage from the breast of the eider duck, sometimes mis-transcribed as 'otters down' or, as in the Ham

House inventory of 1679, 'a blew sticht silke quilt with adders downe in it'.[7]

Flock was the most inferior filling for quilts, but cheap. The Worshipful Company of Upholders (Upholsterers) of the City of London, which was supplying quilts and trying to keep up standards, ordered against its use in 1686:

> Whereas the using of Sheer fflocks in Quilts and other Wares belonging to the Upholders Trade is a great cheat and abuse to his Ma[jes]ties Subjects This Court taking notice of the same have Ordered that no sheer fflocks shall be put into any silk Quilts, Holland Quilts, Calico Quilts or Quilted Cushons.[8]

Quilting as an upholsterers' technique gave rise to a further interpretation of the word. Used to secure padding into position in furniture, quilting was a logical variation on the practice of enclosing a soft filling between two outer layers and stitching it in place. 'Quilt' was the term given, for example, to the cushions used with cane-seated chairs, which were increasingly popular in the later seventeenth century.

Early and mid-eighteenth-century quilts

In early eighteenth-century Britain quilts could be bought ready-made, worked at home or made with a combination of both approaches, adapting professionally made quilting for a specific domestic use. This was a period when skill in needlework was to a woman's credit at almost all levels in society; even if she did not need to earn her living by it, she was expected to be active in contributing to the furnishing of her home. Embroidered or stitched textiles played a major part in the comfort and decoration of homes in Britain. This was in large part because they could be made in a domestic setting, and girls learnt needlework as an essential part of their education (pl.2).

A wide variety of textiles was available as the material from which quilts could be made. The fibres were linen, cotton, silk and wool, sometimes in combination, in varying qualities and colours, and the fabrics were plain or decorated by a range of types of weave, by printing and painting, by embroidery and other needle skills. Textiles on sale in Britain were available both through home manufacture and in the form of goods imported from Europe and Asia, although the availability of imports was affected by trade legislation at various periods in the eighteenth century. They might be obtained by the quilt-maker as unused yardage, as ribbons and braids or as recycled objects and salvaged fragments (pl.3, pl.4). While constantly increasing international trade and the concurrent development of British textile manufacture led to the availability of a wider range of textiles, they did not necessarily decrease in perceived value. The incorporation of fragments of silver-thread-embroidered silk, cut down from some larger piece, into

3 Bedcover (back). Printed cotton and fustian. English, mid-18th century. V&A: T.19–1987 (cat. no.13)

OPPOSITE:
4 Bedcover. Silk patchwork, quilted. English, mid-18th century. V&A: T.117–1973

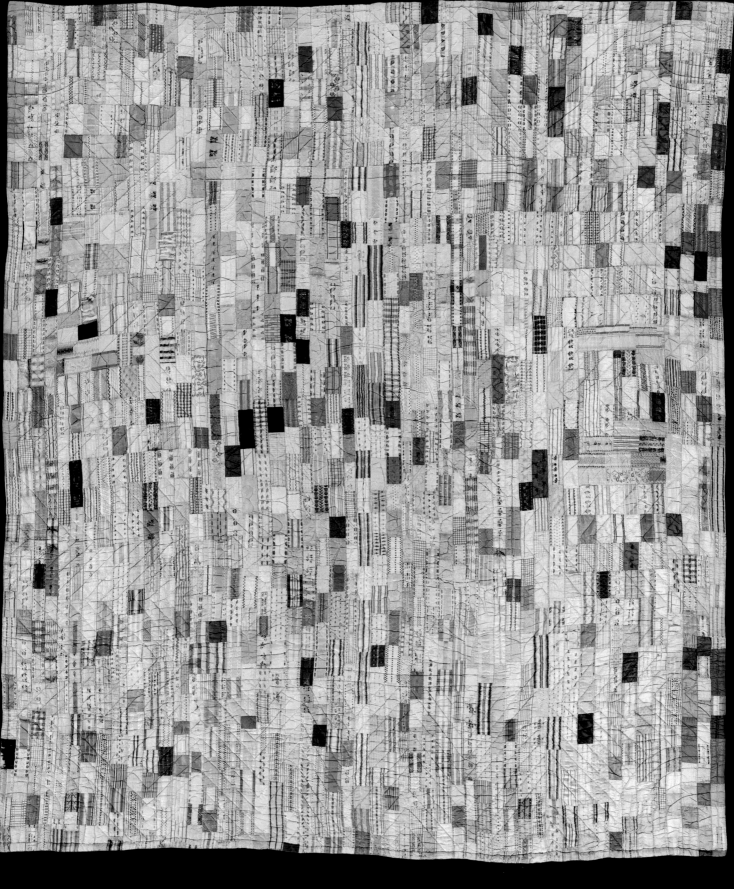

5 Bedcover. Painted and resist-dyed cotton, quilted. Indian, Coromandel Coast, early 18th century. Rijksmuseum, Amsterdam: inv. no.BK-NM-10619

the appliqué wall hangings and upholstery of a magnificent suite of furnishings now at Penshurst Place in Kent shows the recycling of textiles at the top of the social scale. It prompts the question of whether the development of patchwork in the eighteenth century was inspired by the desire or need to salvage and reuse valuable textiles, or was more a celebration of small quantities of a specific fabric, such as the panel of fine woven silk at the centre of the 'Deal quilt' (cat. no.2), or the bed hangings and quilt incorporating patches of Indian chintz at Levens Hall in Cumbria.

Indian textiles were particularly influential in the development of quilt styles. Although it had been a long-established technique in Britain, the use of quilting in the late seventeenth and early eighteenth centuries seems to have been stimulated by imported Indian quilt-

ing. Such quilting remained desirable long after it was first available. At Blenheim Palace in 1740 there was 'a bed of Indian Quilting bordered with very fine Indian Callico which I bought of my Lady Pembroke & paid for it my self & is mine', according to a note written by Sarah, Duchess of Marlborough.[9] And chintz quilts – bedcovers decorated with hand-drawn and painted designs in clear, bright colours – were imported in quantities from the Coromandel coast of India, either already wadded with cotton waste or suitable for quilting with woollen filling and linings by professional quilt-makers in Britain. The quilt illustrated in pl.5 is a fine example of the complexity of colour combination and design that such Indian textiles brought into British bedrooms. Legislation in the early eighteenth century – encouraged by pressure from the British silk and wool manufacturing trades, which

6 Bed curtain. Patchwork, mostly of printed cottons. English, 1730–50. V&A: 242–1908 (cat. no.1)

suffered from their competition – banned the import of Indian cottons. In further more drastic measures, their use in Britain at all was banned, along with that of the British-produced printed cottons that were trying to compete with them in the marketplace. But loopholes in the law, as well as their great desirability for both clothing and furnishings, kept chintzes in circulation and made possible the accumulation of Indian painted cottons that contribute to the great variety of patterns in the V&A's set of patchwork hangings illustrated in pl.6.

Quilts were also imported into Britain from France in the early eighteenth century, worked in the stuffed or cord technique on fine white cotton. There had been a significant industry around Marseilles from the seventeenth century, where quilts were produced in large quantities in professional workshops and extensively exported. The workshops were allowed to use imported Indian cotton, despite its general prohibition in France. They retained their French identity in the British market, and were advertised and described with variations on the name Marseilles, such as the 'one white stitch't Marsela Quilt' recorded at Houghton Hall in 1745.[10]

Alongside imported Indian and French quilts and quilting, professional quilters supplied British products, working in the techniques of wadded, stuffed, cord and flat quilting. A description of quilt-making, given in 1747 in the context of advice to young people choosing a trade or profession, suggests that it was not a lucrative one:

> [quilted petticoats] are made mostly by Women and some Men, who are employed by the Shops and earn but little. They quilt likewise Quilts for Beds for the Upholder. This they make more of than the petticoats, but not very considerable, nothing to get rich by, unless they are able to purchase the Materials and sell them finished to the Shops, which few of them do. They rarely take Apprentices, and the Women they employ to help them, earn Three or Four Shillings a Week and their Diet.[11]

Eighteenth-century insurance records support this evidence that remuneration was modest, by demonstrating that quilt-making often needed to be combined with another trade. Joseph Long, quilt-maker and draper in the Parish of St Giles in London, was successful enough to insure his property for the substantial sum of £1,000 in 1724.[12] In the same parish 40 years later, Thomas Leach, with goods valued more modestly at £200, combined a curious pair of professions in quilting and dentistry ('Operator for the Teeth and Quilter, next the Four Coffins, King Street').[13]

A series of letters written over two months in 1735 provides a vivid view of how the demand and supply of professional quilting for beds worked in practice, and of customer/supplier relationships. They were written by a widowed landowner, Elizabeth Purefoy, and her son Henry, living at a distance from the capital, to a mercer in Covent Garden, London:

> (11 JANUARY) I desire you will send mee ... some patterns of Quilting you mention together wth the lowest prices of each pattern ... if I like the Quilting & the price I will let you know the exact quantity.
>
> (1 FEBRUARY) My mother would have one of the new fashioned low beds with 4 posts to them & a quilt to the same ... she shall be unwilling to give above 10s[hillings] a yard for the Quilting ... I have returned your 4 patterns of quilting ... there are none of the Quiltings will do but that whereon H Purefoy is wrote on the Edge. That will not do neither unless the same holds like ye pattern both in cloath & work ... if it was finer stitched & as good a cloath I should like it better.
>
> (10 FEBRUARY) Since you warrant ye quilting as good as the pattern ... my mother will have five & forty yards of it at ten shillings & sixpence a yard. But if it is not so good you must expect to have it returned for she would not have any of the others if she might have it for nothing. Therefore see that the two cloaths of each side the Quilting be as good as the pattern & the work as good ...
>
> (10 MARCH) Have recd ye Quilting ... The Quilting was very bare measure.

7 Unknown artist, *Margaret ('Peg') Woffington*. Oil on canvas, c.1758. National Portrait Gallery: NPG 650

8 William Hogarth, *Gerard Anne Edwards in his cradle*. Oil on canvas, 1733. The National Trust, Bearsted Collection, Upton House

This transaction shows that the mercer must have had access to quantities of quilting in various designs and qualities already made up for sale, for although it would have been possible to have quilted 45 yards in such a short time using a number of workers, this seems an unlikely course, to cater for one of many customers. The necessity for several different workers to be involved in this quantity of quilting explains Elizabeth Purefoy's concern for the consistency of its quality.[14]

Professional quilters made quilts for beds using silk, linen and wool for the upper layers, as well as quilting fillings and linings onto Indian chintzes when legislation did not ban such imports. The evidence of trade cards also shows them imitating the fabric as well as the technique of Marseilles quilts, with wholesale supplies of 'French quilting cotton, Cotton wool for Quilting' on offer to the London trade.[15] Silk was the most luxurious fabric, and a simple wadded quilt of white silk satin can be seen among the actress Peg Woffington's bedclothes; this is a rare illustration for the eighteenth century of a bed in respectable use, to which she was confined by illness (pl.7). Similar silk quilting was used for cradle sets for privileged children, such as the baby Gerard Anne Edwards in his portrait by William Hogarth (pl.8); a comparable set is described in

9 Cot cover. Quilted linen. English, early 18th century. V&A: T.167–1978

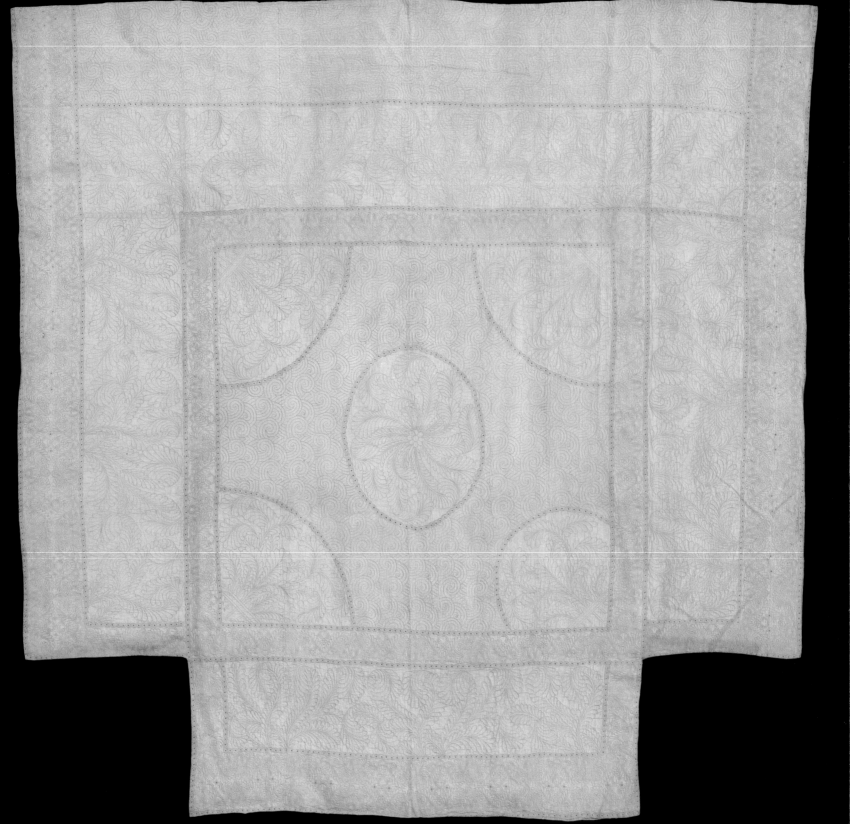

10 Bedcover and curtain. Quilted linen. English, mid-18th century. V&A: T.386&a–1970 (cat. no.9)

cat. no.8. Cord quilting between layers of linen was a more practical alternative for use with babies and children, being more readily washable, and the small scale of cot quilts allowed for exquisite detailed decoration (pl.9). Flat quilting could provide a restful repeating pattern, often executed in one or more shades of yellow silk (a popular style during much of the first half of the eighteenth century, which may have derived originally from imported Indian embroidery) and very suitable for the matching hangings and quilt of a bed (pl.10). It might also provide the restrained background effect to bedcovers embroidered with spectacular designs and extravagant materials, like the one in pl.11, part of a set with matching valances, bolster and pillows.

Quilt-making was also carried out domestically, for personal use, by women who either had the resources (in time and money for materials) to undertake such a project, or who could not afford to own a quilt by other means. Those that have survived mostly owe their preservation to fine workmanship, and their status as inherited possessions, and so represent the best of amateur skills, sometimes incorporating the maker's initials and date as a record (pl.12). If the domestic quilt-maker was a skilled needlewoman, but not accomplished in drawing, she could pay for the pattern, buying it from a tradesman like the Haberdasher and Pattern Drawer Spilsbury in London's Covent Garden, who advertised on his trade card 'Patterns for Ladies-Work', including 'French Quilting'; another offered 'Neatest and Genteelest Patterns for Stiching, French Quilting'.[16] Outside the cities, with less access to professional pattern-drawers, women might commission a pattern for their quilt from a local artist. A schoolmaster in Sussex recorded in his diary various commissions for artwork from the local community; among the maps, church decorations and tombstones he was asked to design, he drew embroidery patterns for the local squire's family, including handkerchiefs, shoes, waistcoats and a quilt – 26 December 1750: 'I began to draw the quilt belonging to Mr Godman'; 30 December: 'I finished the bed-quilt after five days' close application. It gave satisfaction and I received 10s. 6d. for the drawing.'[17] Spending such a length of time on the drawing suggests a design of great complexity, and that

11 Bedcover. Linen embroidered in coloured silks and metal thread, and quilted. V&A: T.48–1967

the ladies of the Godman family were skilled (or at least ambitious) in their undertaking.

The development of patchwork

Among different types of quilt-making in early eighteenth-century Britain, patchwork seems to be the only technique that was predominantly a domestic, rather than professional, production. There is a shortage of written and visual evidence for patchwork, which makes all conclusions drawn about it in this period speculative, and only two examples are known that incorporate a date (convincingly the date of their making) from the first 30 years of the eighteenth century. The first is in the collection of the Quilters' Guild of the British Isles, dated 1718 (pl.13), and the second in the McCord Museum of Canadian History, dated 1726 (pl.14).

12 Bedcover. Quilted and embroidered linen. English, with initials ES, dated 1703. V&A: 1564–1902 (cat. no.5)

13 Bedcover. Silk patchwork. English, with initials EH, dated 1718. Quilters' Guild of the British Isles

The use of the word 'patchwork' to indicate an assembly of pieces of different textiles can be found at the end of the seventeenth century – for example, in the inventory of a wealthy Londoner's house in 1695, where there was 'in the Widdows Chamber, 1 bedsted mohair bed lined with florence sarsnett & quilt; 1 feather bed 1 Bolster 3 Blanketts 1 Rugg; 1 patchwork Counterpain & 2 stooles of ye same'.[18] The terminology is, however, once again problematic. If this patchwork was also used to cover stools, it may have been a type of appliqué, like

14 Bedcover. Silk patchwork. English, with initials IN, dated 1726. McCord Museum of Canadian History, Montreal: M972.3.1

15 Bedcover. Silk patchwork. English,
early to mid-18th century.
V&A: 1475–1902 (cat. no.15)

16 Bedcover. Silk patchwork, quilted.
English, mid-18th century.
V&A: T.19–1987 (cat. no.13)

that on the suite of furnishings at Penshurst noted above, rather than the technique of piecing (usually over papers) that is often considered typical of early British patchwork. Another reference in an inventory to patchwork, from the 1730s, describes 'A walnutttree Couch 2 squabs 4 pillows covered with patchwork & blew mohair & printed linen cases to d[itt]o'. It may also suggest a type of appliqué more suitable for upholstery than pieced patchwork would be.[19] Whatever the nature of the patchwork in that case, it was considered precious enough to merit linen loose covers to protect it when not in use.

No biographical details are known about the makers of the 1718 and 1726 patchworks, beyond their initials, but the quilts are close in date to two literary references that may give some social context for their making. In their joining of small, multicoloured fabric pieces, the patchworks suggest the type of object referred to by the writers Jonathan Swift and Jane Barker. Swift's words are often quoted as evidence that patchwork was a familiar pastime in England by the time of the publication of *Gulliver's Travels* in 1726. Describing the attempts of the tiny Lilliputians to house and clothe the giant Gulliver, Swift wrote:

> Two hundred sempstresses were employed to make me shirts, and linen for my bed and table, all of the strongest and coarsest kind they could get; which, however, they were forced to quilt together in several folds, for the thickest was some degrees finer than lawn ... Three hundred tailors were employed to make me clothes ... When my clothes were finished ... they looked like the patchwork made by the ladies in England, only that mine were all of a colour.

Jane Barker's references to patchwork are less well known. In her preface to *A Patch-Work Screen for the Ladies*, published in 1723, she uses the analogy of the needlework skill of 'Patch-Work' to explain the form of her narrative, and implies that it is a newly fashionable pastime:

Indeed, I am not much of an Historian; but in the little I have read, I do not remember any thing recorded relating to Patch-Work, since the Patriarch Joseph (whose garment was of sundry colours) by which means it has not been common in all Ages; and 'tis certain, the Uncommonness of any Fashion, renders it acceptable to the Ladies. And I do not know but this may have been the chief Reason why our Ladies, in this latter Age, have pleas'd themselves with this sort of Entertainment; for, whenever one sees a Set of Ladies together, their sentiments are as differently mix'd as the Patches in their work.

Two patchworks in the V&A's collection, although undated, have a relationship with the 1718 and 1726 quilts in the layout of their pieced designs and the range of types of textile incorporated, predominantly silks (pl.15, pl.16), A patchwork bed set of curtains and valances also in the Museum's collection is in strong visual contrast to these, but nevertheless shares their discipline of geometry and balance imposed on a miscellany of colours and textures (pl.6). The range of textiles incorporated into the four curtains and four valances is astonishingly wide, including dress and furnishing fabrics made of cotton, linen, fustian (mixed linen and cotton) and silk, decorated with block-printing, painting, resist-dyeing, stencilling and embroidery: in all, more than 6,400 patches. A number of the textiles are Indian. The clamshell-shaped patches, which are awkward because of their curved shape to cut accurately and sew in consistent lines, have linen rather than paper templates, and the bed set seems likely to be the production of a professional workshop. The types of textile incorporated, and the absence of any plate-printed linens or cottons amongst all the other techniques, suggests that they may have been made in the 1730s or '40s. By this period the supply of patchwork may well have been added to the professional embroiderer's or quilt-maker's range of skills on offer.

Changes in the making and use of quilts through the eighteenth century

As the century progressed, quilted and patchwork bed-covers changed their nature and the circumstances of their use. This was partly due to developments in textile technology and in manufacturing legislation during the period, which influenced clothing fashions through what they made available and affordable, particularly with the increasing production of printed textiles. Although printing on all-cotton cloth had not been allowed for the home market between 1720 and the lifting of the ban in 1774, printing on mixed fabrics of linen and cotton was legal, and printed cottons could also be exported. The industry therefore had an incentive to develop its production methods and designs. By the mid-century, woodblock-printing on cotton and linen textiles had reached a high standard, and the dyeing techniques used to produce the strong, fast colours on imported Indian chintzes had been mastered. So women were able to choose British-made 'chints ... [that] can imitate the richest silk brocades, with a great variety of beautiful colours'[20] for their clothes, and these fabrics started to find their way in increasing quantities into patchwork.

Changes inevitably took place in the choice of house-hold furnishings too, although they had a slower turnover in use and replacement. The practical benefits of washable linen and cotton for bedding would have been a clear part of their attraction over silk and wool. Woven substitutes for hand-quilting were realized to be a desirable commodity, and the development of their manufacture was encouraged, with prizes offered by the Society for the Encouragement of Arts, Manufactures and Commerce. In 1760 John Bolland submitted a 'specimen sent of English wove Quilting in Imitation of the French', and this new textile was being widely advertised by the late 1760s as 'wove Cotton Quiltings'. It was available in wider and longer pieces than hand-quilting, and was more washable and durable. This development of quilting on the loom was taking place alongside a decline in the popularity of quilting in clothing, as women's fashions moved on towards slimmer silhouettes and more easily drapeable fabrics like the new soft cottons. Business for professional quilt-makers gradually fell away, and the wadded quilts now being made were more often a domestic production, being more practical and utilitarian than the luxury silk quilts earlier in the century.

A further new source of decorated textiles suitable for bed furnishings, including quilts, came with the introduction of plate-printing. From the late 1750s the technology was mastered to print fine designs on a large scale onto linens and fustians using engraved copper plates. These were particularly suitable for beds – their long, repeating patterns with pictorial subjects being seen to full advantage in bed curtains and coverlets. The cover shown in pl.17 is wadded with wool and quilted simply in running stitch; it may have been used on a bed with matching hangings. While its front uses a fine length of high-quality plate-printed fustian, the back comprises a number of recycled fragments of plain white linen joined together. This gesture towards utility represents one of two clear trends in quilt-making in the later eighteenth century. Written references, in sources ranging from inventories through crime reports to literature, show quilts being used in an increasingly wide range of households, many of them modest in their income. Such purely practical quilts do not survive intact; typically making use of already-worn textile remnants, their functional nature would have kept them in use to the point of disintegration.

Those patchworks that do survive from this period have been preserved for their decorative qualities and workmanship. Predominantly pieced from printed cottons, they incorporate fabrics that are datable to within a much shorter time period than their silk predecessors, which in most cases appear to have been accumulated over several decades. There is plenty of evidence that by now the pastime of patchwork required the purchase of new fabrics – albeit sometimes remnants – to supply it. The Reverend James Woodforde, for example, bought '1 yrd of different kinds of Cotton for patch-work for my Niece' (Nancy Woodforde) in 1789, and on another occasion '1 yard and half of Patches for Nancy', from a salesman who

17 Bedcover (part). Quilted fustian, plate-printed, after an engraved drawing by Angelica Kauffman. English, late 18th century. V&A: T.204–1958

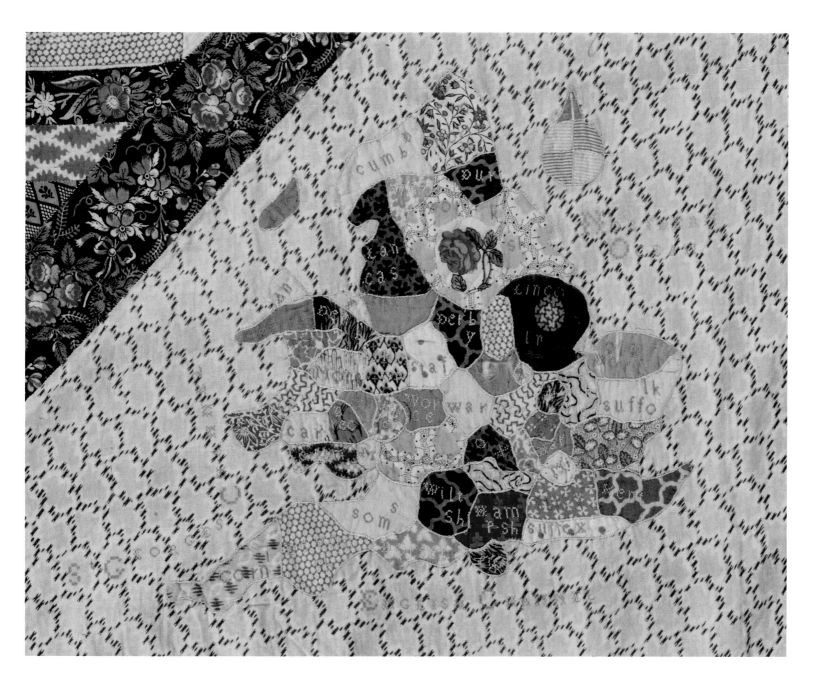

18 and **19** Bedcover (details). Cotton patchwork. English, with initials MCB, dated 1797. V&A: T.102–1938 (cat. no.16)

called at the Parsonage in Norfolk 'with various kinds of Goods in the Linen Drapery way'.[21] He noted later that 'Miss Woodforde's new Patch-Work [was] very much admired', and the demonstration of taste and skill on display in such a project must have been as significant a motivation for many quilt-makers as domestic economy and the provision of decorative furnishings. A large part of the impact made by the patchwork in pl.18 lies in the quantity and quality of skilled labour that must have been invested in it, and by the expenditure of time that it represents.[22] The block-printed cottons are mostly modest in themselves, but by this period the individual textiles played a lesser role than the overall decorative scheme of the patchwork.

No 16516

Male C

Xtned Charles

11 Febry 1767

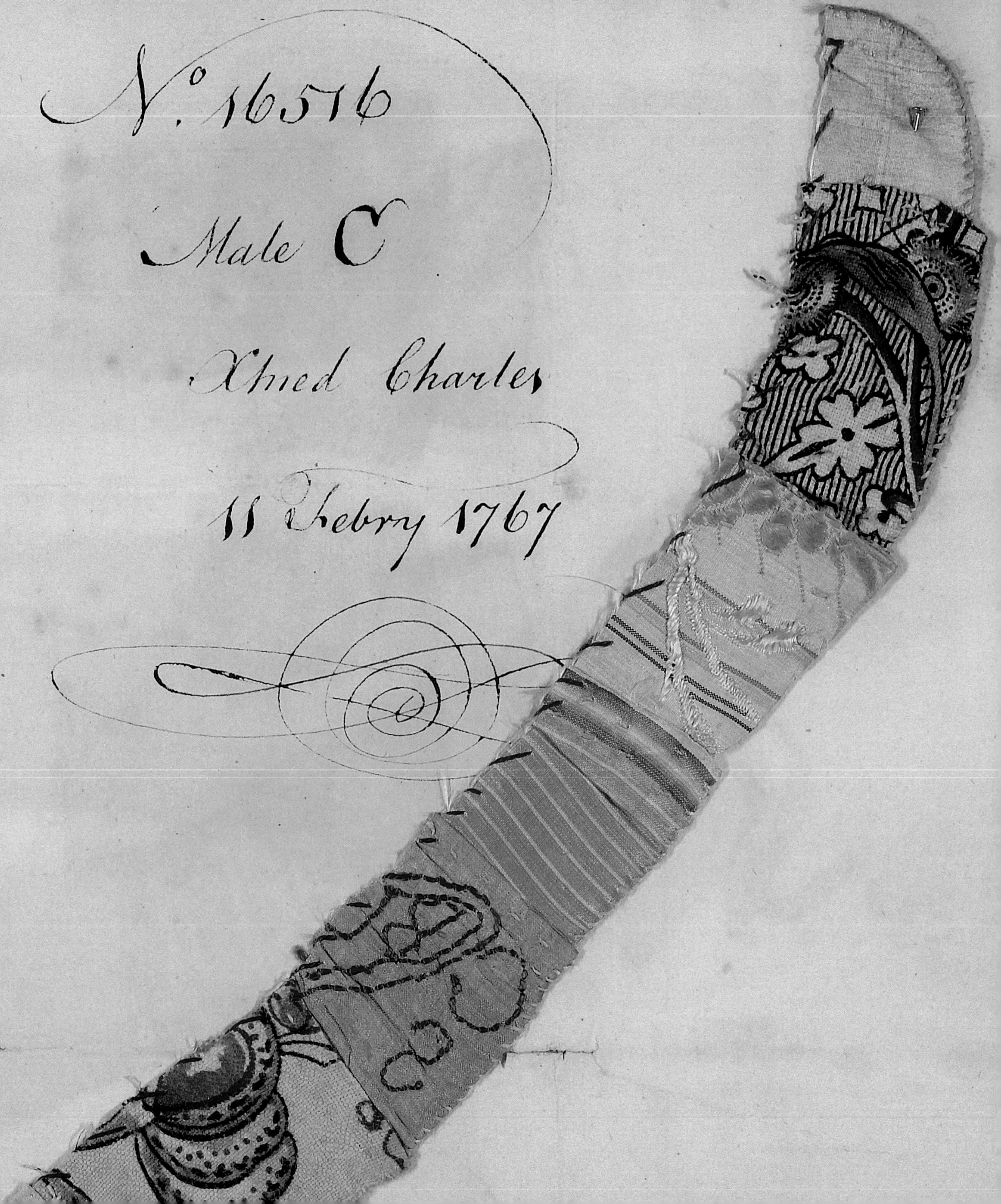

Patchwork on the page

John Styles

Very little British patchwork survives from before the start of the eighteenth century. Intriguingly, the same is true of the word 'patchwork' in print. Rare before 1700, it proliferates thereafter, although seldom being used to describe actual textile patchwork. It was as a negative metaphor that the word enjoyed its wide currency in the eighteenth century. Again and again 'patchwork' was employed to highlight incoherence and disharmony, whether in poems, plays, designs, laws, governments, medicines or education.

References to actual patchwork were fewer, although they can be found from the very start of the century. In Thomas Baker's 1703 play, *Tunbridge-Walks*, an effeminate fop, the appropriately named *Mr Maiden*, boasts about ingratiating himself with the ladies by helping them make their patchwork. Already, at this early date, patchwork was being identified in plays and novels as a distinctively female practice, one that in the hands of women had few, if any, negative connotations. It was also identified as new and fashionable among wealthy women. In the prologue to his 1706 play *Hampstead Heath*, Baker insisted that 'Patchwork is the Fashion of this Age'.[1] Jonathan Swift, too, stressed the novelty of patchwork in his *Directions to Servants*, published after his death in 1745, but written earlier. He noted the 'Custom got among Ladies' of making their old clothes 'into Patch-work for Skreens, Stools, Cushions and the like'.[2]

After 1750, actual patchwork appears more frequently in print, but in a different guise. No longer is it treated just as a new, distinctively female activity. It becomes a sign of morally uplifting female domestic economy in households rich and poor, representing an ideal for the virtuous woman. In the anonymous novel *The Wedding Ring; or, History of Miss Sidney* (1779) 'the neat patch-work quilt' in a farm labourer's cottage is described as 'the emblem of industry', providing 'a most exact pattern of rural economy' (pl.1).[3] While home-made patchwork served as a sign of admirable industriousness among the female poor, it did not automatically excite approval when undertaken by their wealthier cousins. Sarah Trimmer, in her *Oeconomy of Charity* (1802), recommended the charitable example of a young lady who clothed Sunday-school girls in linen patchwork gowns: 'Materials for these gowns were easily procured in the usual way for Patchwork, by the contributions of friends.' This new kind of charitable patchwork, Mrs Trimmer insisted, was superior to the ornamental variety, which she damned with faint praise.

> I would by no means condemn the taste which had led Ladies of late years to the composition of patch-work, for various ornamental uses; great leisure justifies the practice. Performances of this kind I have viewed with admiration; and it always gives me pleasure to see the needle made subservient to the purpose of amusement, for those hands cannot have been employed in dealing and shuffling cards, which have by patient perseverance in joining inch to inch, produced the bed or the window curtains.[4]

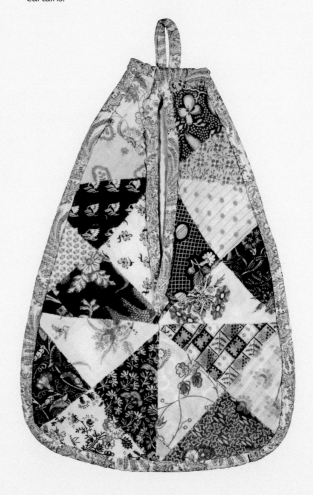

1 A strip of patchwork made from pieces of woven silk and printed cotton or linen, embroidered with a heart and cut in half. Foundling Hospital Billet Book, 1764–7, London Metropolitan Archives A/FH/A/9/1/179.
Patchwork left as an identifying token with a baby boy at the London Foundling Hospital on 11 February 1767, by a mother who was almost certainly poor.

2 A woman's tie-on pocket. Front made from a patchwork of printed cotton pieces, *c*.1800. National Museums of Scotland: 1964.1473

1 Baker (1706), Prologue
2 Swift (1745), p.81
3 Anon., *The Wedding Ring* (1779), p.165
4 Trimmer (1802), vol.1, pp.238–9

3 Francis Wheatley, *The Sailor's Return*. Oil on canvas, 1786. National Maritime Museum: BHC1076. In a miserable garret lodging, a rudimentary bed is furnished with a woollen blanket or rug, the cheapest bed covering.

4 A white, cotton counterpane (detail). Woven in an elaborate decorative pattern at Bolton, Lancashire, 1809. V&A: T.12–1935

There is one other kind of printed text where patchwork regularly appears during the eighteenth century: the published transcripts of evidence given in criminal trials at the Old Bailey in London. Here we encounter patchwork not as a signifier of femininity or morality, but as an everyday material presence in the metropolis, stolen from lodging rooms and houses. Almost all this stolen patchwork was in the form of bedcovers – most of them quilts, but also counterpanes and coverlets – many of them owned by working people, such as weavers, shoe-makers and watch-makers. The one exception was a pair of tie-on pockets stolen from a Bloomsbury publican's wife in 1794 (pl.2). They were made from patchwork of her 'own doing'.[5] Not all were so industrious. Others bought their patchwork bedcovers ready-made.

Very few patchwork bedcovers were stolen before 1780, and the only patchwork materials mentioned before that date were silks and woollens. After 1780, patchwork thefts increased rapidly. Materials were exclusively linens and cottons. Stolen patchwork was sometimes made from pieces collected from friends, but materials were also available commercially. Drapers sold short lengths of printed cotton for patchwork, while cotton remnants were sold 'in all the markets' for this purpose. One thief pointed out in her defence that 'you can buy pieces of calico in Rag-fair, of three yards for sixpence'.[6]

Evidently patchwork flourished as the Industrial Revolution progressed, and colourful, affordable cotton dress fabrics replaced other, duller materials in women's wardrobes. Patchwork offered an attractive alternative to the woollen blankets and rugs that had long served as bedcovers in cheaper lodgings (pl.3). We should not exaggerate, however. Cotton patchwork was only one of the decorative alternatives spawned by the Industrial Revolution. The burgeoning cotton industry also generated the crisp white cotton counterpane, woven at Bolton, Lancashire, in distinctive tufted patterns (pl.4). By the end of the century these counterpanes far outnumbered both quilts and patchwork in cases at the Old Bailey.

5 *Old Bailey Proceedings Online*, December 1794, Elizabeth Harrison and Mary Quinlan (t17941208-22)

6 *Old Bailey Proceedings Online*, September 1807, James Adamson (t18070916-67); April 1804, Eleanor Flaherty and Mary Langford (t18040411-40)

Claire Smith

The governor's daughter

My daughter Judeth Redding fell into the brooke *&*
swame under two bridges *&* then by hir gowne hanging
at a bridge was preserved from drowning: January 21:
1703/4 which great mercy I desire always to remember
with thankfulness to almighty god.

Priscilla Redding, *Her Booke April 24 1678*[1]

As AN EVOCATIVE SYMBOL of childhood, this quilt (cat. no.2)
offers a glimpse of 1690s' familial life (pl.1). The maker of this
quilt was probably Priscilla Redding (1654–1723), who was born
at Deal Castle, Kent (pl.2). Priscilla was the daughter of Captain
Samuel Tavenor and his wife Anna. Tavenor, the governor of
Deal Castle and a Baptist preacher, suffered religious persecution
during the Restoration of 1660. Accused of plotting to bring
about a Dutch invasion, he left his family and fled to London.
On his return, the family established a church and grocery shop
in Dover, where Priscilla settled after her marriage in 1691.

Priscilla records this time of upheaval in a spiritual diary,
which she inscribed 'Priscilla Tavenor, Her Booke April 24 1678'

(pl.3). Documenting the turmoil of her father's arrest in 1682,
the remainder of her narrative is grounded in the family. Her
writings reveal steadfast support for her father, and piety
expressed through scripture and the celebration of lifecycle
events. She follows in the footsteps of diarists such as Alice
Thornton (1626–1707), who recorded the safe arrival and
keeping of family members 'from the wombe, until the grave
bury them in silence'.[2] Alice left behind more than 800 pages
of autobiographical writings commemorating her father and
mother, and describing in detail her relations to her husband
and her children, as well as the 'dangerous perils' of childbirth.
Priscilla's diary similarly omits many of the day-to-day tasks of
domestic life, instead meticulously chronicling births, marriages
and deaths, mapping out the intricate web of familial relations
that helped to underpin her social connections.

The diary also contains a hidden history. Several pages are
written in shorthand, while further passages have been neatly
censored. In the seventeenth century, shorthand became a
fashionable accomplishment, recommended for the purpose of

1 Small quilted patchwork cover
created from a variety of silks and
velvets. Made by Prisicilla Redding,
probably in the 1690s. V&A:
T.615–1996

2 An early drawing of Deal Castle,
the home of the Tavenor family at
the time of Priscilla's birth

1 Redding (1678–1723), entry for 21
January 1703/4
2 Menderson (1985), p.187

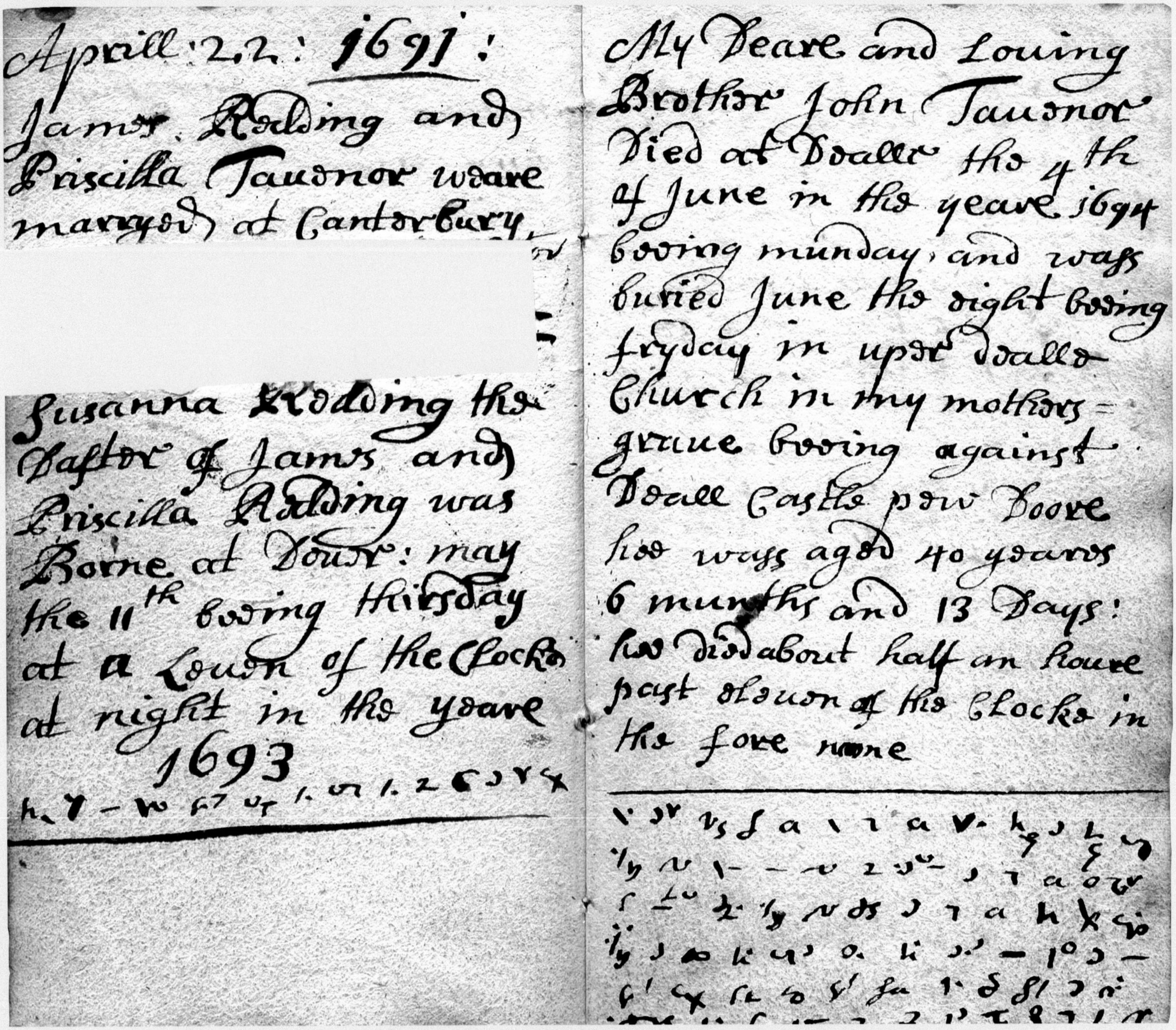

Aprill :22: 1691:
James Redding and
Priscilla Tauenor weare
marryed at Cantorbury

Susanna Redding the
Dafter of James and
Priscilla Redding was
Borne at Douer: may
the 11th being Thursday
at a Louen of the Clocke
at night in the yeare
1693

My Deare and Louing
Brother John Tauenor
Died at Doalle the 4th
of June in the yeare 1694
being munday, and waß
buried June the eight being
fryday in upper doalle
Church in my mothers =
graue being against
Doalle Castle pow Doore
hee waß aged 40 yeares
6 munths and 13 Days!
hee died about half an houre
past eleuon of the Clocke in
the fore none

recording sermons, but also as a means of 'secrete' writing.[3] Elizabeth Bury (1644–1720) took active steps to conceal her writing by use of her own variant, to the frustration of her family: 'her accounts … cannot be recovered … because of many peculiar characters and Abbreviations of her own'.[4] As the daughter of a Baptist preacher, Priscilla's use of a shorthand variant might signal her role in transcribing the weekly sermon in the family church, or perhaps a desire for a more personal, private space.

The quilt itself highlights the wider significance of textiles as a

3 Priscilla Redding's *Her Booke*. Private Collection

4 Wholecloth quilt gifted to Priscilla's daughter, Susanna, and inscribed in cross-stitch in red wool. *c.*1709. V&A: T.616–1996

currency for love, friendship and sociability. Textiles were used as one of the major forms of property and memory bequeathed down the generations. This small patchwork quilt, created for a child's bed, can be read in relation to a second, wholecloth quilt from the same family. Inscribed 'SR 1709', it was made either by or for Priscilla's first-born daughter, Susanna (1693–1731) while she was still a member of the Redding household. A small cross-stitch panel to one side (pl.4) states that it was gifted to Susanna on the birth of her first child, James Pierce, in 1713. Gifting at this time could be public or private, and the gifts were frequently selected from objects that were already valued possessions. Their presentation was deeply symbolic and part of regular social exchanges.[5] The quilt, with all its associations of warmth and comfort, could be gifted in a domestic setting to promote familial cohesion.

The later inscription acknowledges the power of the object as a personal keepsake, nurturing the emotional bond between mother and daughter. While 'SR 1709' evokes Susanna's time in the Redding household, the panel speaks of her new role as wife and mother. As Priscilla's diary testifies, the birth and survival of a new baby, as well as the survival of the mother, were important and poignant events. It would have been celebrated in a special, enclosed space in which the newborn could be presented to visitors. This second quilt conveys the emotional warmth surrounding the new family, recognizing the safe delivery of both mother and child.

Both quilts were passed to Susanna, who took up the mantle of family chronicler in 1723. At a later date, possibly in the mid-nineteenth century, the diary and the quilts were separated. As the diary passed down the male line of the family, the quilts established a female lineage in which the women became the proprietors of their oral and textile history. Reinforcing familial affection, both quilts document the importance of the maternal role and the preservation of associated memories via their entwined narratives.

3 Henderson (2008), p.4
4 Menderson (1985), p.184
5. Lambert (2004), p.24

2

Complexity and context: nineteenth-century British quilts

Linda Parry

NINETEENTH-CENTURY BRITISH QUILTS provide unique historical, aesthetic and social links with the past. Through the silks and cottons used, it is possible to follow the astonishing technological changes of the age, surviving evidence of one of Britain's greatest industries: textiles. But this is not all, for a study of the circumstances under which they were made provides important social history, an intimate insight into how people lived during a period when Britain's foremost position as an industrial nation changed every aspect of life – not just at the grass roots, but also throughout its complex, multi-layered social strata.

Until the late eighteenth century British quilting and patchwork tended to be carried out by professionals, generally those already involved in making clothes or furnishings, or by wealthy women with practical skills who were keen to occupy their time by providing fashionable furnishings for their home (see chapter one). This continued into the first decade of the nineteenth century, but soon great changes developed – due, almost entirely, to the effects of domestic upheaval throughout Britain brought about as a result of the Industrial Revolution some 30 years before. Regional developments in quilt-making testify to the extraordinary shift of labour around Britain, which in the space of a few years changed from an agrarian to an industrial-based society.

However, movement was not all from the countryside to the town, as new businesses were set up throughout Britain and the invention of machinery that made processing and manufacture more efficient not only encouraged new enterprises, but also revived old industries. With the reopening of tin, slate, copper, lead, gypsum and coal mines, for instance, workers and their families moved from one part of the countryside to another in search of work. The farmer became the miner, and the quilts made within such communities show a wide range of earlier traditions gathered from all over Britain, but melded into a range of styles controlled by the makers' new lives and environment. Limited to the use of locally available and affordable textiles, the patterns and methods of quilt production were determined by the needs and preferences of particular individuals or small groups, rather than by any predetermined national trend, as had occurred in the past. Patchwork and quilting were no longer the fashionable choice for decorating the bedrooms of wealthy homes. Instead, the making of quilts took on a new pragmatic character, becoming the craft of the people in the widest general sense. Production increased and widened in scope. Neither before nor since have so many people become involved in manufacture, nor so many quilts been produced.

Despite a huge revival of interest in patchwork and quilting throughout the twentieth century, knowledge of the history of the craft in Britain remains limited and, with a few notable exceptions,[1] historical research has concentrated on regional patterns and variations rather than on national trends.[2] Textile historians have also viewed quilts as a unique and extensive source of patterned textiles, without giving much consideration as to how quilt patterns have evolved or to the more soc-iological aspects of the subject – for instance, the lives of makers and how they fitted into the community as a whole. However, producing a comprehensive history of the craft, taking all these factors into consideration and examining quilt-making within the industrial and polit-ical context of the times, is difficult because the vast amount of surviving information on Victorian work is fragmentary. As a skill practised and used in the home, it has not been the habit of makers (apart from a few who dated and signed their work) to leave detailed doc-umentation about quilt-making. This sets it apart from other domestic products, such as furniture and pottery, which were generally manufactured commercially, and for which records survive. As a consequence, the his-tory of quilt-making has relied to a greater extent on reminiscences and anecdotes handed down through the family. Although a valuable source of familial history, these accounts have, through time, often become dis-torted and inaccurate. It is also tempting to accept that the traditions followed by individuals or groups repre-sent the entire national production, and this has led to misconceptions about the nature and development of the craft in the nineteenth century. As a result, its sta-tus as a significant art form within the decorative arts has often been ignored.

Despite a great deal of published evidence to the contrary, many still believe that Victorian quilts in par-ticular were made by the poor out of a necessity to keep warm. This was not the case. From the early years of the nineteenth century Britain witnessed a shift in the levels of wealth and poverty not experienced since the Middle Ages. The poor flocked to cities in search of work, where many found only basic subsistence. They owned little clothing or furnishings (their homes and beds were shared) and had neither the time nor the means to sit and sew, even if patching and darning became a necessity (pl.1). Quilt-makers came from a higher level of society: a new industrial middle class in which social identity was created around a set of values separating them from the aristocracy above and the working classes below. Respectability, hard work and

domesticity became the new moral code, and women played the central role in this as model wives, mothers and daughters. The home – whether manor house or cottage, town house or terrace – became an important icon of the age, providing stability and protection from the ravages of change.

Quilts were part of the same ethos, symbolizing comfort and warmth during a period of uncertainty. Generally, quilt-makers were members of families with at least one wage earner; or, in the case of mining wid-ows, the craft provided a means of maintaining family cohesion.[3] Men were not completely excluded. Some helped by drawing out designs, cutting templates and even sewing (pl.2),[4] whereas a number of tailors, sol-diers and sailors produced their own spectacular quilts. Like their female counterparts, few men relied on this work for their livelihood – quilts were more a vehicle to show off their skills or even to promote a particular message. John Monro, a Paisley tailor, took 15 years to finish his quilt, which he called 'The Royal Clothograph' (see cat. no.45). Working for three hours every evening and for five days a week, the quilt provided him with a platform from which he was able to show what perse-verance, hard work and abstinence could achieve.[5]

A few professional nineteenth-century quilters and patchworkers are known by name,[6] but the number was small compared with the previous century. Whereas insurance records for the seventeenth and eighteenth centuries list a range of individuals and shops involved in the sewing and selling of quilts and bedcovers, *Kelly's London Directory* for 1854 lists just two businesses. These are 'Quilting Warehouses',[7] which were proba-bly retail outlets for machine-woven counterpanes and covers rather than hand-sewn pieces. Design registra-tions and patent applications held by the National Archive endorse the view that the few advertised com-panies associated with quilt-making were industrial, for they include a patent for a counterpane loom[8] and records of quilting factories in industrial towns.[9] By the mid-nineteenth century the term 'quilt' had taken on a quite different commercial meaning.

A further misconception about quilt-making is that it

1 William Henry Midwood, *The Patchwork Quilt*. Oil on canvas. English, 19th century. Private collection. Midwood lived and worked in London. His idealized domestic scenes celebrate family life.

2 Walter Langley, *The Old Quilt*. Oil on canvas. English, late 19th/early 20th century. Private Collection. Langley was the first major artist to settle in Newlyn and was noted for his realistic paintings of Cornish fishermen and their families.

was a rural craft, developed in isolation by individuals living in the countryside, rather than one popular also with town and city dwellers. Elizabeth Hake, in her 1937 publication *English Quilting Old and New*, insisted that English quilting persisted as a home industry in Durham, Northumberland and Wales, but 'Elsewhere has developed a desire to emulate.' Whereas she was referring specifically to quilting, and the regions that she cited excelled in this work, this was not true of the hundreds of examples of quilted patchworks that were made in urban areas of Britain throughout the nineteenth century and have little or no visible comparison with work produced in the North-East and Wales. An obituary for the 90-year-old Londoner Catherine Hutton in *The Gentleman's Magazine* for 1846 cited her own

list of achievements with the needle, including: 'I have made furniture for beds with window curtains ... I have quilted counterpanes ... I have made patchwork beyond calculation.'[10] The catalogue of the Great Exhibition of 1851 also hints at the widespread popularity of patchwork and quilting, with exhibits by makers living in such diverse locations as Hull and Margate.

Wherever they were made, hand-sewn quilts never became an extensive or lucrative industry in the nineteenth century and, as a consequence, few economic or social historians have studied the subject. This is a pity, as it remains a largely untapped source of information on both domestic life and the demographics of a constantly changing society. It is possible to trace quite major movements of families around Britain through the history of one quilt or maker. In the 1930s a patchwork bed-cover dated to around 1840 was given to Rachel Kay-Shuttleworth of Gawthorpe Hall in Padiham near Burnley.[11] Its only recorded history is that its maker was 'Grace Slater of Skelda'. Why a bedcover made by a Shet-lander should find its way to Lancashire is intriguing. Research has uncovered that Grace Slater was born in 1803 and died in Bracewell near Burley in 1872. Her father, John, was a local man, but her mother, Margaret, died in Skelda on the Shetland Islands in 1855 at the age of 92 years. This suggests that Grace, who never married, also lived there and looked after her mother in old age, and this is why she became associated with the islands. The large number of fashionable, highly coloured printed cottons used in the bedcover suggests that it was made in Lancashire; or, alternatively, that the cottons were such valuable possessions that they moved with Grace. Did the family relocate to Shetland after the father's death in 1819, or did they go there earlier to find work? This goes against known population drifts for the time, when the move was away from isolated rural areas with little means of employment towards the industrial mainland. At some point Grace came back to her father's place of birth, as she, her father, mother and brother Richard are all buried in Slaidburn in the Forest of Bowland.

The occupation of wage earners became a signifi-cant factor in determining where families lived and contributed to the tradition of quilt-making, for example in most of the mining areas of Britain, including Devon and Cornwall, south Wales, north Lancashire, Cumbria, Durham and Northumberland. The villages that grew up around pits and quarries provided little opportunity for women to find employment outside the home. With their priorities centred on caring for their families, the design and sewing of quilts developed into a very popu-lar home occupation for many women, providing an important means of self-expression. The quilts – often made to celebrate important family occasions, wed-dings and births in particular – became treasured possessions. On a more practical level, patchwork and quilting could be fitted around domestic timetables, with frames being tucked away when the family returned home in the evening and brought out again the next morning. Not surprisingly, fewer quilts were made in the newly developed cotton, silk and woollen manufacturing towns of Lancashire, Cheshire and York-shire, where women were an important part of the factory workforce[12] and were absent from the home for many hours of the day and six days of the week. Ironi-cally, their time was spent manufacturing the fabrics for quilt-makers to use.

The use of printed cottons

From the late eighteenth century the British cotton industry developed into the most successful in the world, with technological advances in all aspects of production: spinning, weaving, printing and finishing. However, it was the beauty of the British designs and the quality of their printing that enabled manufacturers of furnishing textiles, in particular, to challenge the French – the acknowledged leaders – for supremacy. Woven silks had been the dominant fabric used for quilts and coverlets in the eighteenth century. They retained their appeal with the aristocracy, but by the early years of the nine-teenth century printed cottons became the preferred choice of furnishing for fashionable middle-class homes. Contemporary quilts show just how important it was to use up-to-date patterns and, because they were expen-sive to buy, that they should be used to best advantage. Consequently *broderie perse* became a popular tech-nique, as it showed the most fashionable details exactly as they had been printed.

A coverlet in the V&A's collection (pl.3, cat. no.19) shows a framed design of applied cottons with fashion-able Chinese-influenced buildings, people, flowers and birds, all produced between 1804 and 1811. The cotton used for the border of the coverlet is a red and black neo-classical design. The printing of this pattern can be precisely dated to August 1804, as identified by V&A cura-tor Barbara Morris from studying pattern books from the Bannister Hall Print Works near Preston in Lancashire, in preparation for an exhibition in 1960.[13] She also iden-tified another cotton used in the coverlet, an example of which is in the collection of the Whitworth Art Gallery,

3 Bedcover. *Broderie perse* on cotton ground. English, 1804–11. V&A: T.382–1960

4 Block-printed cotton. English, c.1810. Whitworth Art Gallery

Manchester (pl.4). From the Bannister Hall records, the textile printers and dyers Stead McAlpin (the present owners)[14] were able to identify two London shops that sold the cottons.[15] These were Anstey & Co. and Richard Ovey, the most sought-after decorator of the time, who was active between 1790 and 1831. Ovey supplied textiles to the Prince of Wales (later Prince Regent and eventually George IV) and other members of the royal family.[16] Trading from 22 Tavistock Street in London, Ovey was listed in directories as a linen draper, although he styled himself a 'Furniture Printer' – despite the fact that the prints were made elsewhere. His was just one of a large number of shops trading in textiles at the time, and of the 21 listed premises in Tavistock Street there were 14, including four linen drapers, two haberdashers, a lace warehouseman, a mercer, a woollen draper and an embroiderer, as well as a hosier and milliner. Despite the need to patronize these shops, for it was not until later that ready-made women's clothes and furnishings became available, the draper was not always the most favoured of tradesmen, as can be seen in C. Williams' 1818 satire *The Haberdasher Dandy* (pl.5).

THE HABERDASHER DANDY.

5 C. Williams, *The Haberdasher Dandy*.
Etching, published by Thomas Tegg.
English, *c.*1818. Guildhall Library

The need for cottons in the furnishing of bedrooms increased during the first half of the century, when the correct dressing of beds required a great deal of fabric. A hand-written note accompanying a set of patchwork hangings made between October 1801 and March 1816 lists 11 separate curtains and valances for the bed, with six for the windows.[17] They were made from hexagons of small-scale dress fabrics, some identified as having been printed at the Peel Works in Church, Lancashire, and the unknown maker has recorded the number of patches used in each curtain. The overall total is 102,148. The

fashion for complex sets of bed hangings, which dated from the sixteenth century, prevailed until the mid-century, although the tradition continued in stately homes. In *The Workwoman's Guide*, written by 'A Lady' and published in Birmingham in 1838 (reprinted London, 1840), a similar number of curtains to those listed above are recommended for a four-poster bed. They include 'a top, a back, two head curtains, two foot curtains, one top outer and one top inner valance, one bottom valance, and sometimes extra drapery laid on the back of the bed'; and apart from curtains or quilts, the book advises

6 Illustration of beds from *The Workwoman's Guide* (London, 1840)

that each bed should have three mattresses (one straw, one wool or hair and one feather), a bolster, two or three pillows, blankets and a watch pocket.[18]

The book lists 11 different types of beds, and recommends the covers and hangings for each type. The least grand of these are 'stump beds' (pl.6), which can be recognized as the type used in most homes today; these are singled out as being most commonly found in cottages, and it is for these alone that patchwork and quilted covers are recommended. This suggests that by 1838 hand-made quilts were considered practical and economic choices rather than being fashionable. The central part played by education in teaching the crafts is also made clear:

> Those [quilts] used by cottagers are often of patchwork made by them at school, or in their leisure moments … sometimes made of a succession of hexagons and six-sided pieces of print, at others, birds, figures and other devises … These quilts are durable when lined, and may be good work for school-children, though they certainly take up a good deal of time in the making.[19]

Education did not become the responsibility of the state, and therefore the right of every child, until the Education Act of 1870, although the Church and some voluntary organizations had run schools since the late eighteenth century. Dame schools, referred to by Charles Dickens in *Great Expectations* and a particular phenomenon of the nineteenth century, were held in the homes of philanthropic elderly women (pl.7). Almost all schools charged a small fee and schooling was random, with no nationally approved curriculum, so it is impossible to discover exactly what was taught beyond the basics of reading, writing and arithmetic. What is apparent, from the large amounts of surviving plain sewing samples, is that practical needlework was taught to most girls, whether they attended classes or had lessons at home, because it was seen as an important part of a young girl's preparation for future life, whether in the service of others or running a household and family. Evi-

dence suggests that quilt-making and patchwork, in particular, were also taught in some classrooms. Most of the quilts associated with young girls were made from dress fabrics – their small repeating patterns worked more successfully when cut into diamonds or hexagons, the simplest and most popular of template shapes. Dress fabrics were also more plentiful and cheaper to buy than furnishing textiles, and were more likely to be found in general drapers' shops in local towns or to be bought from itinerant traders.

It is possible to identify a few school quilts, although it is likely that many more surviving examples were sewn in the classroom. One – an unfinished, early nineteenth-century patchwork – can be singled out by the paper templates, which are written in a child's hand. The script, in brown ink, is of a single sentence repeated, as if part of an exercise. Only one small part of the patchwork measuring approximately 153 x 177cm has been completed, but the remaining unused rosettes, hexagons and cotton scraps, which were kept together for more than 150 years until presented to the V&A,[20] stand as a lasting memory of the diligence of the young maker. Another similar example, made in the 1830s, is now in the Powerhouse Museum in Melbourne, Australia.[21] Pages from exercise books with hand-written numbers, as well as geography and history lessons, have been used as templates alongside printed religious texts. It is puzzling why neither of the quilts mentioned above was finished, as most of the laborious preparation had been completed.

The idea that patchworks were made from scraps of cotton left over from dress-making or collected over a period of time has credence, but most quilts contain such large amounts of the same fabric that it is likely they were specially purchased. In 1811 Jane Austen wrote to her sister Cassandra, 'Have you remembered to collect pieces for the patchwork – we are now at a standstill?'[22] This suggests that the cottons they used came from different sources. The coverlet in question[23] contains 64 different fashionable cottons, many of which would have been purchased at the time. Most patchworks use fabrics from different periods, and one example, signed by Ann Randoll from Somerset (pl.8, cat. no.20 and pp.56–7), covers

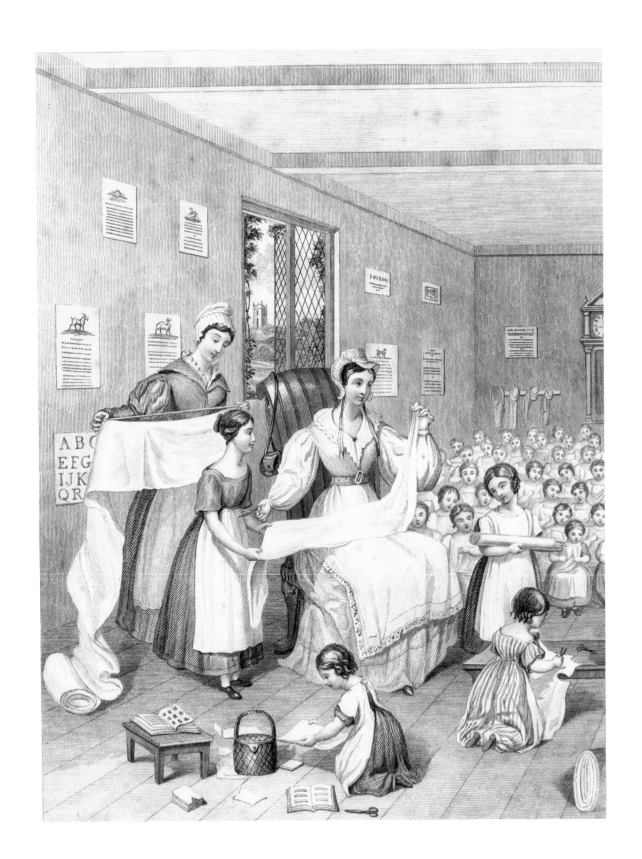

7 Frontispiece for *The Workwoman's Guide*, illustrating a dame school

8 Bedcover (detail). Patchwork, printed cotton and linen. English, signed and dated Ann Randoll, 27 October 1802. V&A: T.32–2007

a wider-than-normal span of 40 years. Despite being dated 'October 27 1802' (which may refer to the maker's date of birth or the time she started the coverlet), the block-, copperplate- and roller-printed cottons are of French, Indian and British origin and range in date from the 1780s to the 1820s. The quilt represents years of work, and as well as a complex design of triangles, hexagons and overlapping clam shapes, it also includes appliqué patches of hand-embroidered floral sprigs.

Quilts were often made for special occasions, and it is likely that most amateur makers produced only one or two in their lifetimes. Girls produced quilts for their own weddings, probably made as part of their dowry, before a suitable husband had even been found. Elisabeth

welcome ⚓ sweet ⚓ babe

hush my dear lie still and slumber
holy angels gard thy head
heavenly blessings without number
gentley falling on thy head 1834

the making of wedding quilts became group activities, and popular patterns to use in the North Country included hearts and baskets with quilted lovers' knots, and cable designs were used to signify a long life.[24]

Though dress fabrics were used for most rural quilts, there were exceptions. In parts of south Wales, Durham and Northumberland, where quilting became more important than patchwork, furnishing textiles with large pattern repeats provided a much better background for intricate quilting patterns. A bedcover in the V&A (pl.11, cat. no.28) is patched in large triangles and squares, with a wide border of plain fabric where the characteristic geometric patterns associated with Welsh quilting can clearly be seen.[25] The quilt, which can be dated to the 1840s from the most recent cotton used (a rosebud print on a black ground),[26] has a framed medallion design of furnishing textiles that was fashionable 20 years earlier. These cottons may well originally have been used as curtains because they show some wear, with evidence that they were originally glazed.

Professional and amateur sources of inspiration

Quilting is one of the oldest forms of decorative needle-work and, because of the high levels of skill required, it was a field in which professionals were most actively engaged in the nineteenth century. A number of these individuals are known by name, including Joe Hedley (known as 'Joe the Quilter'), one of the earliest recorded. Originally trained as a tailor, he worked as an itinerant quilter in the area around his home near Hexham in Northumberland, but became widely known through accounts of his murder in 1826.[27] Surviving quilts thought to have been sewn by Hedley are traditional wholecloths, in which quilting provides the only decoration on plain woollen, linen or cotton grounds. Later nineteenth-century professionals continued this tradition, but also developed attractive two-coloured pieced grounds for their quilting. This type flourished in America, particularly in Mennonite and Amish communities. Red and white bedcovers became a speciality in parts of Lancashire, Cumbria and areas of western Scotland, possibly because of the ready supplies of turkey-red cottons made

Chapman married in 1829 and added the date of the wedding, her new name and that of her husband John to an existing inscription (cat. no.21). Only Nancy Horsfall is identified in the appliqué cotton quilt that she made for her wedding in 1833. Her first year of marriage was a busy one, for in 1834 she produced another quilt for the cot of her first child (pl.9, pl.10). In some areas

11 Bedcover. Patchwork, printed cotton, quilted. Welsh, 1800–50. V&A: T.124–1937

12 Bedcover. Patchwork, flannel and silk. Welsh, c.1860. Private Collection

in Stockley near Manchester and in the Vale of Leven in Dunbartonshire, with striped grounds (or 'strippies') being popular with both amateur and itinerant professionals in the North Country and Wales (pl.12, cat. no.34). In the second half of the nineteenth century, framed star designs became a distinguishing feature of the work of shop owner George Gardiner and his pupil Elizabeth Sanderson, both professional quilt-makers working in Allenheads, Northumberland (see p.114 and cat.no.49).[28]

Inspiration for patchwork quilts came from many sources, and amateur quilt-makers lacked neither imagination nor confidence. One Lancashire example[29] represents a fertile and exuberant summer garden. Dated 1812 with the initials 'E.I.', the coverlet's central medallion is part of an early eighteenth-century bedcover embroidered in silk with floral sprigs (pl.13). This provides the theme for the entire quilt, with a profusion of garden plants and butterflies represented by the printed quilt centre and borders, two *broderie perse* flower vases and also hexagons and radiating patches. The outer frame is filled with hoverflies, all pointing towards the floral centre. Apart from the three 'parterres' from outer to inner garden, the design is naively conceived, but is all the more attractive for this. It is made entirely of dress cotton, one of which is printed with the address 37 Oxford Street. Whereas it is impossible to know to which town or city this refers, John Richards & Co., linen draper, occupied these premises in London at the time.[30]

Printed centres made specifically for use in quilts were manufactured throughout the first quarter of the nineteenth century and were so highly cherished that some were kept and used later on.[31] The two panels used in the 1812 garden coverlet can also be seen in another bedcover (cat. no.29) originally thought to have been made some time during the first half of the nineteenth century, although it can now be more precisely dated to between 1810 and 1845. Floral bouquets proved popular,[32] and were often inscribed to celebrate specific events. Royal occasions were prominent. The earliest datable quilt centres are those commemorating George III's Golden Jubilee in 1810 (cat. no.24). The V&A also has two identical versions[33] of one block-printed design made to celebrate the marriage of Princess Charlotte to Prince Leopold of Saxe-Coburg in 1816 (pl.15).[34] One of these has an excise stamp for 1816 and is inscribed 'John Lowe & Co. Furniture Printers, Shepley Hall', providing the name of the only identifiable manufacturer of these centres – although there are likely to have been others. John Lowe was a well-known firm of calico printers with large cotton factories and extensive bleaching grounds close to the River Tame near Ashton-under-Lyne in Lancashire.

13 Bedcover. Pieced cotton appliqué on linen. English, with initials EI and dated 1812. Rachel Kay-Shuttleworth Collection, Gawthorpe Hall, Padiham, Lancashire

Celebration and commemoration

Celebration took many forms, and nineteenth-century quilts tend to follow patriotic themes rather than reflect popular opinion. Occasionally both come together. Public admiration for Horatio Nelson became a cult in the early years of the century, and a range of decorative items, made commercially and by amateurs, was produced in homage. These included printed textiles and at least one bedcover. Made by an admirer, for Nelson's use at sea, the bedcover is of printed cotton appliqué on linen (pl.14, cat. no.43). Displayed in the 'Historic and Relic' section of the *Naval, Shipping and Fisheries Exhibition* held in 1905, it was accompanied by a handwritten note stating, 'Nelson's quilt, was on Nelson's bed on board the *Victory* at Trafalgar'. Although it is impossible to know if the cover was actually used by Nelson, the cottons and the style of applied work closely follow the fashions for the period when he was in command of HMS *Victory* between 1803 and his death in 1805. It is also of unusual dimensions, and would have fitted a ship's swinging cot or fixed bunk as either a bedcover or as a valance hung above it.[35]

In the aftermath of republican revolution throughout Europe, a continuing preoccupation by the British with royal celebration suggests a general satisfaction with the status quo. However, dissenting views can sometimes be found. A cotton patchwork quilt in the National Museum of Wales at St Fagans uses, as its centre, a printed portrait of Caroline of Brunswick, the much-maligned wife of the unpopular George IV (pl.17, cat. no.27). This is a surprising choice as Caroline – who became known as 'The Immoral Queen' – became the subject of much public derision. The portrait is a finely engraved, plate-printed sepia handkerchief,[36] which identifies its subject as 'Her Most Gracious Majesty', so it can be dated between 29 January 1820 (when she became Queen Consort) and 7 August 1821 (the date of her death). This romanticized image of Caroline shows her as she was in portraits 25 years earlier. Contemporary cartoons of her were much less kind.

Public respect for the Crown did not return until the 1850s, when Queen Victoria finally proved a popular monarch. However, two surviving patchworks that depict her coronation in 1838 show that printers continued to view royal events as lucrative subjects for textiles. The roller-printed cotton used as the centre for both bedcovers shows the scene in Westminster at the moment that Victoria was crowned (cat. no.26). The design is loosely based on an original engraving by the lithographic artist G.E. Maddeley, although this is a poor version, with the image distorted and simplified to suit the printing process. The reduction in the quality of both design and printing suggests that it was made primarily for export, so it is interesting to note that the second quilt is in America, part of the collections at the Munson-Williams-Proctor Arts Institute in Utica, New York State.

The popularity of printed cottons with pictorial designs was already waning when this print was manufactured. It is a far cry from the finely blocked and engraved copperplate-printed centres produced in the early part of the century, and marks a departure in the way quiltmakers celebrated people and events.

The use of wool and silk

British patchwork quilts made during the second half of the nineteenth century tend to be more colourful and flamboyant that those from the late Georgian and early Victorian periods. Inexpensive roller-printed cottons dominated the market, providing greater choice for a wider audience than ever before. Considering this, it is

14 Valance. Printed cotton appliqué on linen. English, 1770–99. Displayed in the 'Historical and Relic' section of the *Naval, Shipping and Fisheries Exhibition*, 1905, to commemorate the Battle of Trafalgar.
V&A: T.312–1977

strange to note that silks and woollen fabrics provide the most original patchworks of the period. Often these were made specially as exhibition pieces, or as aids in conveying a particular message, like John Monro's 'Royal Clothograph' mentioned earlier. Men took to the craft with enthusiasm. Examples made by soldiers and sailors in service (cat. no.47, and see pp.84–7) show intricate and beautifully conceived geometric designs made from pieces of felted, woollen uniform fabric. The cloth is thick, and the use of inlaid or mosaic technique difficult, requiring tough fingers and some training. Tailors who were used to handling such fabrics also produced spectacular mosaic panels. James Williams of Wrexham took 10 years to finish his cover. The design mixes the old

world with the new, and tradition with science, showing Old Testament Bible stories alongside Thomas Telford's Menai suspension bridge and the Cefn Viaduct near Ruabon (cat. no.44), both of which were local to the tailor. Another cover now in the V&A has more wide-ranging subject matter, providing – alongside the Apostles and parables – a miscellany of portraits (pl.18, cat. no.46). Made in about 1856, its 61 separate panels depict the maker's idiosyncratic choice of characters. These include characters from Shakespeare, as well as European rulers past and present; other near-contemporaries include Jenny Lind, the Swedish singer; Edmund Kean, the actor; and British military heroes of the Napoleonic Wars (1803–15), Afghan Wars (1839–42) and Crimean

15 Panel. Block-printed cotton commemorating Princess Charlotte of Wales' marriage to Leopold, Prince of Saxe-Coburg. English, 1816.
V&A: T.293–1913.

16 Panel. Block-printed
cotton. English, *c.*1815.
V&A: Circ.606–1956

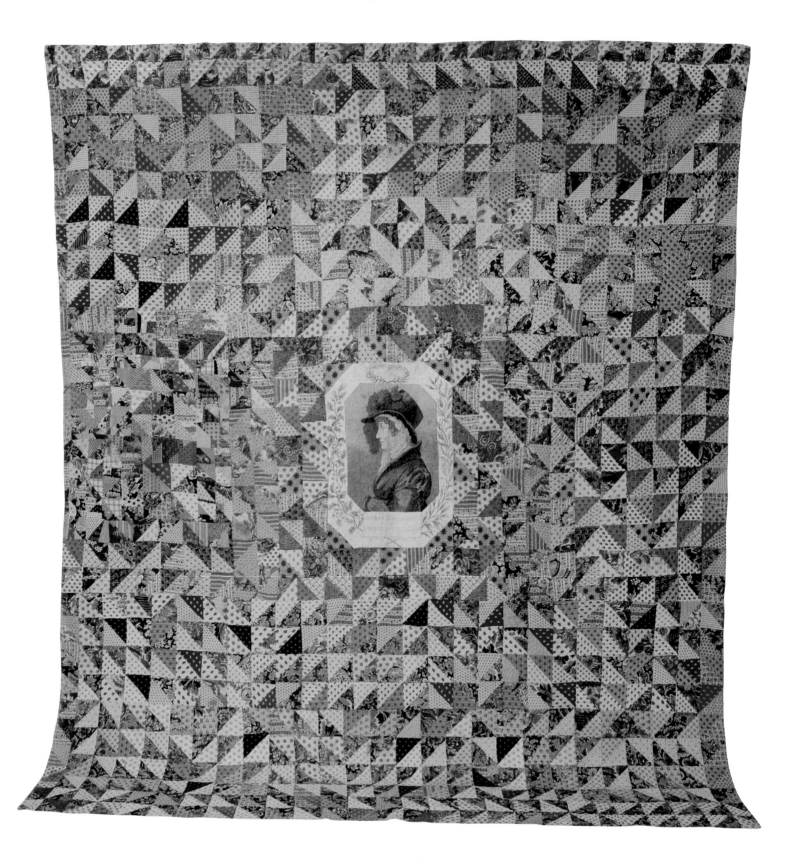

18 Cover (detail). Wool intarsia with wool and silk appliqué and silk embroidered details. British, 1856–69.
V&A: Circ.114–1962

War (1853–6). These luminaries were joined by historical figures and ordinary people: a servant, a dustman and, incongruously, an executioner, who was probably one of the most popular figures of all.

By the 1860s fashion journals either ignored cotton patchwork altogether or declared it unsuitable for modern homes. Instead, urban middle-class women turned to using silks and velvets for furnishings throughout the house, encouraged by a new exciting range of colours that had recently become available. Chemical aniline dyes, first discovered in 1856, proved particularly suc-cessful when used on the weighted silks [37] of the period. Britain led the field in dye technology, and brighter colours and new shades were soon developed (pl.19). At first patchworks used plain silks and velvets in simple diamond and hexagon patterns, which showed the new colours to perfection, but by the late 1860s a new technique – called crazy or Japanese patchwork[38] – took over as the most widely practised form of domestic needlework, and hundreds of examples have survived. As a technique requiring patience, yet limited sewing skills, it proved perfect for the socially active. It also provided an

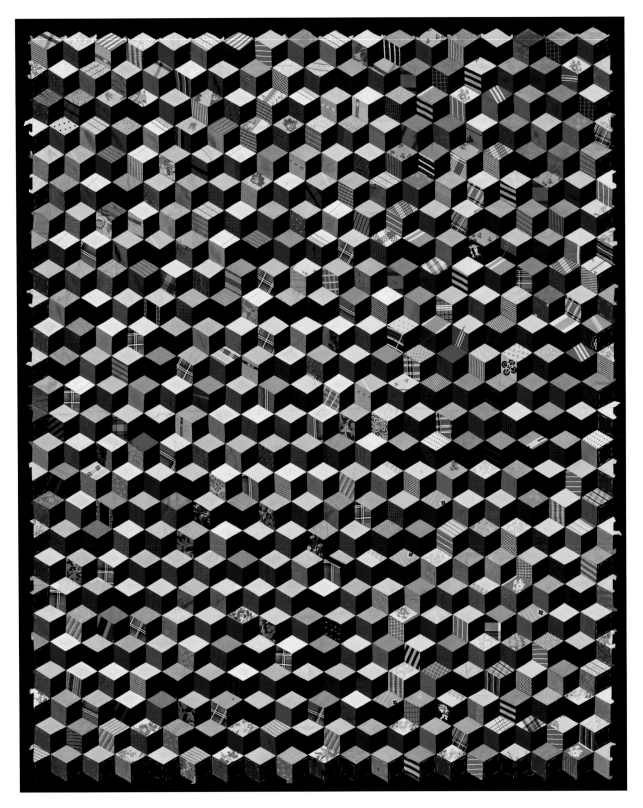

19 Coverlet. Unfinished patchwork of silks. British, c.1860–70.
V&A: T.427–1980

20 Water Langley, *Day Dreams.*
Oil on canvas. English, 1914. Bristol
City Museum and Art Gallery.

excuse for the most extraordinary application of *objets trouvés*, with the silk and velvet grounds being covered with a range of applied embroidery, buttons, bows, braids, laces and beads, to name but a few of the items used (cat. no.38). Japanese patchwork became the perfect furnishing accessory for the cluttered Victorian home.

The nineteenth century proved a watershed for quilt-making in Britain. Rural and urban traditions were secured, and new patterns and techniques established. Quilts from the time illustrate all aspects of life, from the new age of technology and fashionable retailing to the enduring rituals of family life. They record public events and celebrations in what was then the most powerful nation in the world; but they also provide a unique insight into the lives of ordinary people (pl.20) and it is here, at the grass roots, that the craft is at its most powerful and enduring.

Christopher Breward

Sewing soldiers

IN THE POPULAR IMAGINATION, nineteenth-century patchwork has generally been associated with domestic contexts and feminine pursuits, and while the subjects chosen for figurative works have often engaged with robust religious, historical and political issues, the gentler themes of sisterly devotion and pastoral escapism have tended to dominate our understanding of the language of this branch of the textile arts. The lesser-known genre of the military quilt offers a bracing corrective to such received wisdom (pl.2). These extraordinary artefacts, produced between c.1850

and 1910 (from the Crimean War to the more widespread introduction of khaki), reveal a thriving culture of masculine creativity that extended beyond the world of the home to embrace the spaces of Empire and the professional skills associated with both the menswear trades and soldiery.

The V&A owns a superb example of one such quilt (pl.1, cat. no.47). Measuring about 238 x 238cm square and backed with patched green silk damask, it is a complex geometrical design of concentric lozenges around a central star – broad

1 Cover (detail). Pieced wool. Indian, c.1863–77. Believed to have been made by Francis Brayley, Private, 1st/11th Foot. V&A: T.58–2007

2 Thomas Wood, *Portrait of Private Thomas Walker*. English, 1856. Royal College of Surgeons: RCSSC/P 228. Walker was injured at the Battle of Inkerman and was visited by Queen Victoria.

enough to have lain over a bed. The individual components are regular hexagonal pieces, cut from the sort of Melton wool employed in the manufacture of military dress, in complementary shades of black, white, red, green and yellow. Though family and regimental traditions often imbue military quilts with romantic but questionable histories involving the use of fallen comrades' uniforms, it would be a mistake to assume that all were either made by soldiers or from scraps derived from their clothes. The textiles are certainly of the same type, but as various historians have pointed out, the sources of these could have ranged from specialist manufacturers to rag dealers. Whether produced in the provinces of the British Isles, the battlefields of the Black Sea or the outposts of Empire, military quilts also display a weight, precision and rigidity of design that suggest not only the sense of control associated with the parade ground, but also the trained hand and eye of the tailor. What is beyond question, however, is the degree to which these objects were celebrated at the time of their making. More than 30 examples were exhibited at the Great Exhibition of 1851, and they enjoyed regular exposure at succeeding industrial and charitable displays, including those sponsored by military agencies to showcase regimental prowess (pl.3).

Constructed by a member of the Devonshire Regiment of the British Army, 1st/11th Foot – possibly Private Francis Brayley – this V&A quilt is likely to have been produced during the regiment's 13-year-tour of Bengal, India, in 1864–77. Such postings were stressful and monotonous in equal degree. Extreme heat, combined with unfamiliar and often threatening surroundings, gave rise to a variety of physical and psychological complaints. Indeed, in 1875–6 Brayley was hospitalized with 'Rifle Drill Fatigue', a precursor perhaps to his death from tuberculosis three years after his return to England in 1880. It is possible, given that an engagement with craft processes was acknowledged as a powerful aid to healing in military/medical circles, that the quilt was pieced together during Brayley's convalescence. Whatever its precise provenance, his quilt displays all the characteristics of an item produced under the aegis of the Raj. Its relatively bright mosaic of colour contrasts with the more subdued palette of Crimean quilts and with the figurative content of home-produced regimental quilts, and its complexity and neat finish suggest that the labour of skilled Indian artisans may have been employed in its execution.

3 Samuel Attwood with his patchwork quilt, made in India, 1850–60. The Quilters' Guild

Francis Brayley's descendants cherished a more personal history through the handing down of the quilt from father to son in a family that retained military connections to the 'Bloody Eleventh'. For them it embodied memories of patriotism, sacrifice and adventure in foreign lands, and in this respect its rigid order has much in common with the sort of quilts that might have been produced by the wives and daughters of nineteenth-century soldiers, farmers, doctors and lawyers (pl.4). Whether produced by men or women, the glory of a well-made quilt lies in the resonances achieved between the emotional context of its making and the beauty of its finish.

4 Private Roberts and his patchwork quilt. Published in *The British Workman*, March 1873, p.152

'Remember Me': Ann West's coverlet

Jenny Lister

THIS WOOL COVERLET (cat. no.35), made by Ann West in 1820, is at once a feat of technical ingenuity and a window onto a vibrant view of daily life in early nineteenth-century rural England (pl.1).

Many other British inlaid patchworks of this type were made by men (usually tailors) and were intended for public display, often depicting political events and military heroes. For Ann West, the Bible was her inspiration, and her appliquéd and embroidered coverlet shows all of creation, with the Garden of Eden at the centre of 14 other biblical scenes. Above and below, 54 smaller patches show contemporary characters and occupations. Her materials were offcuts from fine blue-black cloth for tailored coats, scarlet for army uniforms and other

woollen fabrics for ordinary garments and blankets, all products of the cloth-weaving industry that was vital to the prosperity of south-west England. Ann West signed her coverlet twice, with the embroidered caption 'Ann West's work, 1820'. She intended her work to survive as a personal memento and incorporated the phrases 'Forget me not' and 'Remember Me'.

The coverlet is traditionally associated with the town of Warminster in Wiltshire, a family story suggesting that Ann West worked at Longleat (the Marquess of Bath's country estate), four miles away. No records survive to confirm this. Ann West was a common name, but a milliner called Ann West, listed at High Street, Chippenham, in Pigot & Co.'s *National and Commercial Directory* of 1829, may have been the coverlet's

1 Ann West, coverlet or hanging. Wool patchwork and embroidered appliqué, 1820. V&A: T.23–2007. Purchased with the support of the Contributing and Life Members of the Friends of the V&A

2 Ann West, coverlet, 'A Wedding' (detail)

maker. Census records from 1841 show that this Ann West's nephew, a tailor, lived with her. One of the most intriguing panels shows a marriage ceremony, with two women wearing matching plumed bonnets and elegant pelisses that were typical of fashion plates at the time (pl.2). Ann West embroidered her initials on the pages of the minister's book of service, which reads 'I will A W [all ways] love her', but it has not been possible to find records that indicate whether this marriage was Ann West's own or that of a family member.

Other appliqué panels show a country play and agricultural workers. The smaller squares contain the social mix of a country town: shepherds, milkmaids, an auctioneer, as well as cavalry officers and two duelling soldiers. A well-dressed 'Mother, Child, and a Nurse' and a 'Sportsman' are among those representing the leisured classes. Other figures entitled 'A Distressed Widow' and 'Pray help a poor sailor' depict individuals left to fend for themselves in a world in flux. Industrialization had brought a slump in the wool trade as it moved north to the mills of Manchester, and the end of the Napoleonic Wars in 1815 increased unemployment, as soldiers and sailors returned home.

Some figures on the coverlet appear to be portraits of real local characters, while others could be based on illustrations from prints and song-sheets, or popular pottery figure groups. The panel labelled 'Caffres' (see bottom row, third from left) shows an African man and woman, an image that may have been copied from anti-slavery pamphlets. Its position next to a square worked with a 'Negro servant and Master' highlights the fact that existing slaves were not set free, and the trade was not banned in the British Empire until 1833. South Africa was known as 'Caffraria', and 'caffres' was a generic name, rather than the racist term it later became.

Ann West's handwriting shows that she was a well-educated woman. As such, she was able to gain access to a range of reference material to use as sources for her figures and the diverse animals and birds that she depicts from all continents. Embroiderers had used Bible stories as subject matter for their work for centuries, and Ann West used several compositions from illustrated bibles as the basis for her depictions of Cain and Abel, Moses and other Old Testament patriarchs. These figures

3 Mrs Trimmer, 'Our Saviour conversing with the Woman of Sameria' [*sic*], Plate XVI from *A Series of Prints from the New Testament* (London, 1825). NAL: 60.T.83

4 Ann West, coverlet, 'Christ and a Woman of Samaria' (detail)

are united by their common theme as 'forerunners' of Christ, who is represented talking with the woman of Samaria (pl.4) in a depiction of a parable used to reveal Christ's mission as the Messiah, and the gospel of everlasting life (John 4:1–30). This panel is similar to a plate from Mrs Trimmer's *A Series of Prints from the New Testament* (pl.3), which was designed to be displayed in schoolrooms and nurseries. Sarah Trimmer (1741–1810) was instrumental in setting up the Charity School Movement and published many books for children, which were widely circulated by the Society for the Promotion of Christian Knowledge (SPCK). The print shows both figures in the robes of biblical times. Ann West, however, updates the scene, dressing the Samaritan woman in a cheap printed short gown and woollen skirt – the clothes of poor women in 1820. The choice of this particular parable adds weight to the idea that Ann West intended her 'coverlet' to be a hanging, perhaps for a Sunday school.

Although the identity of Ann West remains elusive, 200 years later her work still has the power to educate and entertain, with the evangelical message that Christ came to save all of humanity, regardless of racial origin or place in society.

Creativity and confinement

Sue Prichard

> Formerly, patchwork occupied much of the time of the women confined to Newgate, as it still does that of the female convicts on the voyage to New South Wales. It is an exceptional mode of employing the women, if no other work can be procured for them, and is useful as a means of teaching them the art of sewing.
>
> Elizabeth Fry, *Observations on the Visiting, Superintending, and Government of Female Prisoners*, 1827

THE NINETEENTH-CENTURY prison reformer, Elizabeth Fry, became one of the leading exponents of the importance of rehabilitation for prisoners. Her small bands of like-minded women worked directly with incarcerated women and children, supplying much-needed food and clothing, but also teaching and providing spiritual guidance. The British Ladies' Society for the Reformation of Female Prisoners (formed in 1821) supplied the sewing materials required to create the 'Rajah quilt' (pl.1, cat. no.61), the only known transportation quilt in a public collection, stitched by some of the 180 women on board HMS *Rajah*, which set sail from Woolwich for Van Diemen's Land in 1841.

For centuries, the relationship between creativity and confinement has been narrated and documented. The Lady of Shalott, imprisoned in her castle, weaved her mirror-image of Camelot. Mary, Queen of Scots vented her frustration during her 19-year imprisonment in England in a series of embroideries celebrating courage in adversity. Stitching performs an important function, occupying the hand during the long, tedious hours spent locked in either room or cell. Perhaps more importantly, the rhythmic coordination of hand and eye can also act as a form of meditation, a refocusing of the mind, offering an

1 'The Rajah Quilt, 1841'. Unlined coverlet, cotton sheeting and chintz appliqué, silk thread embroidery. National Gallery of Australia, Canberra: 89.2285. 325 x 337cm. Each female convict was given tape, 10 yards of fabric, four balls of white cotton sewing thread, a ball each of black, red and blue thread, black wool, 24 hangs of colour thread, a thimble, 100 needles, threads, pins, scissors and two pounds of patchwork pieces.

2 Jerry Barrett, *Elizabeth Fry Reading to the Prisoners at Newgate*. 1860. Private Collection. Fry's interest in prison conditions began after visiting Newgate Prison in 1813 and witnessing the living conditions of the women and children there.

opportunity to create something of worth in the most abject of circumstances.

HMP Wandsworth is the biggest prison in London, one of the two largest in Europe. Built in 1851, the same year as the opening of the Great Exhibition, its residential areas remain in the original Victorian building. Fine Cell Work, a registered charity founded by Lady Anne Tree, teaches needlework to inmates. Tree, like Fry, recognized the importance of keeping both the hand and the mind occupied during long periods of confinement and isolation (pl.2). With the help of the Royal School of Needlework, she launched the initiative that now employs inmates in 22 prisons in England and Scotland. The resulting cushions, tapestries and quilts are produced to the highest standards, maintaining a quality control that has become the hallmark of Fine Cell Work. This level of expertise, the commitment of the many (mostly female) volunteers who work closely with the prisoners, and the ethos of the charity's philanthropic work formed the basis of a collaboration between the inmates of HMP Wandsworth, Fine Cell Work and the V&A.

The commission set out to articulate the reality and experience of incarceration through stitch, culminating in a vivid and highly personalized account of both individual and collective experiences of twenty-first-century prison life. Each single hexagon was produced in the grittiest and most desolate of environments: as the title of the charity makes clear, stitching takes place within the confines of the cell. The volunteers who teach are not sentimental about their work; indeed, they are adept at demanding, and getting, the very best out of their male 'stitchers' – only the finest work would be selected for the finished quilt. The journey from conception to completion was intensely challenging: offering the disenfranchised the opportunity to design and create something unique, with a strong personal narrative, was risk-taking at its most extreme. Yet, as the men worked on the commission, they had the chance to explore the realities of captivity – and the complexities of the design process.

The footprint of the design of the quilt is based on the panopticon floor plan of the prison, whereby all cells are visible from the central well around which they are arranged. Navigating through the imagery, it is easy to spot recurring themes. Alongside these, however, are motifs that seem more enigmatic, demanding a greater level of insight into the world behind bars.

Inmates were asked to contribute to the selection process, and were adamant about which motifs should be included. The hexagon that featured three pairs of trainer-clad feet – a rare mark of individuality in a deliberately depersonalized institution – was in. Oscar Wilde's verse 'I never saw a man who looked/With such a wistful eye/Upon that little tent of blue/Which prisoners call the sky' was out. The importance of the erosion of the individual, defined by an anonymous numbering system, appears in the guise of a bunch of flowers, an ironic twist on the 'Welcome to your new home' tradition (pl.3). The desolation of a prison cell is juxtaposed with the exuberant anticipation of freedom. All inmates were in agreement that the difficulties facing former members of the armed services who were serving time should be highlighted (pl.4).

The seeds of the idea of the Fine Cell collaboration were planted by research into the origins of Elizabeth Fry's prison reform movement. Separated by more than 150 years, the *Rajah* and HMP Wandsworth quilts are united in documenting creativity in confinement.

3 Embroidered Hexagon. Coloured wool thread and cotton patches on white cotton ground, 2008. Fine Cell Work.

4 Embroidered Hexagon. Coloured wool thread and cotton patches on white cotton ground, 2008. Fine Cell Work.

IRAQ N.IRELAND
ROYAL AIR FORCE
ROYAL NAVY
FALKLANDS
BOSNIA ARMY
KOSOVO
AFGHANISTAN
A NEW HOME FOR HERO'S
HEARSAY EVIDENCE CONVICTS ANYONE
SERVE YOUR COUNTRY AND DO TIME

3

Maintaining the craft:
British quilt-making 1900–45

Dorothy Osler

THERE IS NO BETTER METAPHOR for the social and cultural shifts, both in British quilt-making and in women's lives in the early twentieth century, than the image of two urbane, middle-class ladies driving their motor car through the mining villages of Durham and south Wales in 1934 in search of quilters. Dynamic, influential and metropolitan, Muriel Rose and Mavis FitzRandolph embodied the increasing freedoms and professional opportunities of the inter-war years for educated and affluent women. The purpose of their travels was commercial; they represented an organizational body – the Rural Industries Bureau – one as an employee, the other as a contracted marketing agent. As such, they were the lynchpins of a successful quilting scheme established in the 1920s under government aegis to relieve depression in mining areas, and were monitoring the quilters already employed, as well as looking for new recruits.

In a pocket-book diary, Rose recorded her daily observations and impressions of the women they visited and their domestic circumstances. In the clipped notes and personal shorthand of this singular document, she captured a world where women's opportunities were constrained, by lack of financial resource and education as well as by culture and lower social status. Thankfully for history, Rose's diary survives to sketch the old-world lifestyles in which quilt-making had thrived in nineteenth-century regional cultures, and where quilt-makers' skills were honed by the designs and technical expertise passed down through the generations.[1]

The intervention of Rose and FitzRandolph, and of the organization they represented, was timely. By the 1920s regional quilt-making cultures were in decline. Never the darling of the burgeoning popular media of women's magazines and needlecraft books, in the new world of mass communication patchwork and quilting were refined and confined to a middle-class domestic ideal of paper-pieced patchwork and 'dainty' quilting. Despite their background, Rose and FitzRandolph did not share this ideal and worked instead within two organizational

1 Group of students at an NFWI 'School for Quilting Judges', London, April 1936. National Federation of Women's Institutes Archive

2 Miss Hamilton of Rye, Sussex, working on an embroidered and quilted handkerchief for presentation to Princess Margaret at the NFWI 'Handicrafts' exhibition, 1938. National Federation of Women's Institutes Archive, Box 212 (5/FWI/E/4/2/5)

forces that would situate quilts in a new and powerful arena: national exhibition space. The first, the Women's Institute movement, was begun by women themselves; the second, the Rural Industries Bureau, was government-funded. Both had remits to encourage and sustain traditional rural crafts, but, despite their operational focus, their respective hierarchies included energetic metropolitan women like Rose and FitzRandolph, whose connections provided opportunities to develop new craft enterprises. In the years that followed the First World War, quilt-making was reawakened by these new organizational initiatives.

The Women's Institute movement

From its earliest years, textile crafts were at the heart of the Women's Institute (WI) movement. Initially, commercially focused ventures were set up by the newly formed National Federation of Women's Institutes (NFWI) immediately after the First World War to generate local and national funds. Centralizing these 'cottage industries' was not, however, a success, and the flagship enterprise – the Women's Institute Toy Society – collapsed in bankruptcy after only two years. As a result, this unhappy and (for some) uncomfortable engagement with trade was replaced by a more conservative policy that repositioned rural crafts within women's role as home-maker and emphasized the creative and domestic pleasures to be gained from craft skills. In the 1920s the NFWI's craft activities focused on expanding the newly established Guild of Learners, whereby members could progress by examination from basic proficiency to qualification as a WI teacher, demonstrator and judge (pl.1). Though patchwork and quilting were never among the WI's high-profile crafts, they were incorporated into the scheme, but as separate crafts.

Keen to showcase members' work and fund-raise for central funds, the NFWI embarked on a series of national 'Handicrafts' exhibitions at prestigious venues, mainly in London. These included the Victoria and Albert Museum (V&A) in 1921 and 1922. Finding space was difficult, and frequent changes of venue were required for subsequent exhibitions in the 1920s and '30s (pl.2). It was to be 30

years before the WI's national exhibition again returned to the V&A, though the Museum itself staged an exhibition of British and American quilts in 1937.

When quilts and patchwork coverlets featured in WI exhibitions from the mid-1920s onwards, the exhibition reports in the WI's *Home and Country* magazine reveal a singular level of praise for these textiles, especially for the wholecloth quilts from Northumberland, Durham and Wales:

> The quilts were the most beautiful of the embroidery exhibits [January 1925, p.26].
>
> Here are quilts not designed by superior people but straightforward old-time patterns [November 1927, p.472].
>
> I feel sure that the north country workers would have been amazed had they heard the admiration expressed in the remarks of visitors to the exhibition [November 1927, p.473].
>
> Quilting caused a traffic block. This is one of the few needlecrafts which showed originality in design [January 1933, p.11].
>
> Here are two quilts … possessing such nobility and sweeping grace of design (based on the traditional Durham units) that one is grateful to have looked on them [December 1938, p.500].

The interest generated in the regional quilt-making traditions surprised everyone, not least the quilters themselves. By placing quilts in an exhibition space, what had previously been regarded as domestic products of low status were now seen as designs of real aesthetic quality: 'Queer how much store the folks down here set on our quilts. We think them just ordinary' was the reaction of one North Country visitor to the 1932 exhibition.[2] But looking at the softly sculptured and sensuous appeal of the quilt in pl.3, crafted by a WI exhibitor in the mid-1930s, it is not hard to understand how these provincial 'discoveries' created such a sensation.

The painter George Marston was 'judging advisor' to the Handicrafts Committee of the NFWI and Handicraft Advisor to the RIB. Like others, he admired the 'quilted

3 Silk cot quilt made by WI member Mrs Hird, of Sherburn, County Durham, and presented by the Durham Federation of Women's Institutes to the Bowes Museum, Barnard Castle, in 1933. Bowes Museum, Barnard Castle 1964.548.Q.3

quilts' but, with keen artistic judgement, recognized how much their design quality owed to the vibrancy of a living cultural tradition, and he believed that the prescriptive nature of the WI's testing scheme could dilute its vernacular strength. As early as 1926 he emphasized that the aesthetic side of craftwork was more important than technical dexterity; in his opinion, over-emphasis on technique led to 'the narrowing of one's outlook and to the loss of spontaneity'.[3] More than a decade later, he was giving the same warnings following the NFWI's 1938 exhibition.

But the aesthetic judgements of the WI hierarchy were too strongly rooted in notions of class and taste, and in their enthusiasm for the testing scheme they failed to appreciate the negative impact of a craft philosophy narrowly weighted in favour of technical ability. Moreover, in Miss Alice Armes, the National Handicrafts Advisor appointed in 1925, the WI had someone who believed in, and could forcibly express, the hegemony's views on patchwork and quilting. In the December 1931 issue of *Home and Country* she wrote: 'It is entirely against the principles of patchwork to buy new materials … and to cut it up … Scraps of material, new and old … should be used.' Such views were also enshrined in the WI's patchwork handbooks, which concentrated on that style of piecing so long beloved of the urbane middle classes: mosaic patchwork pieced over paper templates, normally constructed using the ubiquitous hexagon. The cultural wealth of both British and American nineteenth-century designs was largely ignored; even the Victorian fancy-work style of crazy patchwork was 'not acceptable' for exhibition. The strictures on quilting were no less stringent and, referencing back to a rural idyll and cosy fireside stitching, hand-sewing was deemed the only appropriate form of surface stitching.

Though the aim of the Handicrafts Committee had been to raise standards, the over-prescriptive nature of the process constrained patchwork and quilting in a top-down straitjacket. The structures and strictures that were imposed maintained the artificial gulf between the two crafts and restricted innovation. For patchwork, the perception that it was purely a scrap craft took even firmer hold, as did equating patchwork quilts with hand-sewn mosaic coverlets. When bedcovers were made by county federations for the beds of the WI's newly established residential college, Denman College in Oxfordshire, which opened in 1948, the quilts produced reflected this craft division (pl.4). Durham Federation

members made traditional wholecloth quilts; the counties that pieced patchwork coverlets restrained their designs to hexagon mosaics.

Judged from a twenty-first-century perspective, WI perceptions of patchwork and quilting seem narrow and socially confined, but they did no more than echo the early twentieth-century media portrayals of these crafts. The real achievement of the NFWI, in embracing an exhibition culture that undoubtedly raised the profile and cultural value of Britain's vernacular quilting traditions, has to be set against the limitations of the overall crafts scheme.

The Rural Industries Bureau

It was the success of the WI exhibitions, and the exposure of the quilting traditions of north-east England and Wales, that led directly to the second formal intervention in British quilt-making. The Ministry of Agriculture's Rural Industries Bureau (RIB) included a Women's Advisory Committee, which – seeing the wholecloth quilts in the WI's 1927 exhibition – recognized an opportunity to promote a women's craft that was rooted in what were then called 'distressed areas'. In the inter-war Depression years, these areas were of particular concern to the RIB and, if quilting could be revived and promoted as a commercial venture, this might bring much-needed income to households that were struggling to survive.

To this end, in 1928 FitzRandolph was sent to Durham and south Wales to carry out preliminary investigations. Following her encouraging report, two quilting exhibitions were held in London in the same year, one at the RIB's own commercial outlet, Country Industries, and the other at Rose's privately owned Little Gallery, just off Sloane Square. Both exhibitions were immediately successful and, by the end of 1928, the RIB had recruited 70 women quilters and placed £800 worth of orders. A year later the number of registered quilters had increased to 170. The immediate impact of the scheme is recorded in the minutes of the WI Handicraft Committee for Durham County, with which FitzRandolph had liaised in order to find suitable quilters. By March 1929 nearly £2,000 had been paid from the RIB to Durham quilters, and 'as far as possible those in most need received most orders'.[4] By November 1930, RIB committee minutes reveal that the sale of items from Wales and Durham had grossed more than £7,000, of which £3,600 had been paid to quilters.[5]

The commercial success of the RIB quilting scheme was due in no small part to the tireless efforts of FitzRandolph, who continued to coordinate the operation, and to Rose, whose Little Gallery outlet became the commercial hub. Rose was a key figure in the fledgling crafts movement of the inter-war years, and promoted the work of potter Bernard Leach and many other high-profile figures of the early twentieth-century crafts movement. Described as 'a remarkable woman, with an immediate eye for separating the genuine from the spurious',[6] she quickly recognized the inherent qualities of the vernacular quilting tradition and its commercial application and appeal. The personal friendship and professional synergy forged with FitzRandolph enabled them to identify the high-end market to which luxury quilted products could be geared. By careful quality control, constant monitoring and supplying only high-quality materials to their chosen quilters, they harnessed the skills of Welsh and Durham women to products whose design quality would meet market expectations. The quilters received payment according to the size of product and type of fabric, with silk commanding a premium. Alongside bed quilts in silk, cotton sateen or poplin, all filled with soft lamb's wool (see pl.5, cat. no.55), other bedroom accoutrements were produced: cushions, bed-jackets, dressing gowns and the ever-popular nursery quilts. The dramatic evening cape in pl.6, however, represents an apparent departure from this boudoir 'stock in trade'.

Using their influential social and commercial networks, FitzRandolph and Rose set up further exhibitions. The Earl and Countess of Strafford, Sir Philip Sassoon and Lord Howard of Walden all hosted exhibitions in their homes – an indication of the appeal of these products to Britain's fashionable elite. There was, of course, a strong philanthropic motive in a period of Depression, but such high-end patronage cannot be explained by philanthropy alone. The two key protagonists had developed products and designs that resonated with stylish Art Deco interiors and with a new fashion for quilted textiles, both domestic and personal. Orders were received from royalty, with a quilt being made especially for the Queen of Spain, possibly after her exile to England in 1931. The RIB itself attributed the aesthetic quality of the designs as being a key factor in the success of the scheme; its *Report* for 1929–36 records that sales in the first three years totalled £10,000 and comments: 'that these were by no means compassionate sales is shown by the continuance of sales at the high yearly average of £3750'.[7]

4 Members of Hayling Island WI making patchwork quilts for Denman College, Oxfordshire, 1949–50. National Federation of Women's Institutes Archive, Box 118 (5/FWI/B/2/2/11)

Support also came from more overtly political quarters. Ramsey MacDonald, Britain's first Labour Prime Minister, is believed to have owned a Durham RIB quilt. His Minister of Labour, Margaret Bondfield, Britain's first woman Cabinet minister, opened an exhibition of RIB quilts in the summer of 1930 at the Dorchester Hotel in London. Her opening address revealed a developing philosophy of the inter-war years – a reaction to, and rejection of, the growing mechanization of consumer goods and a belief in the value of hand-crafted work for leisure and pleasure:

It is not merely a question of economic necessity that makes these women do the work … I want to stress the importance of maintaining this original craft for its own sake. In these times when nearly everything we wear and use must be turned out in millions by machines, it is a

refreshing glimpse of beauty to see the work that these women are able to do with their fingers and their native genius. I am convinced that in the future if our people are to remain balanced, they must develop in crafts and creative work.

Her speech also made telling reference to the change in cultural and aesthetic value now being given to these 'cottage' quilts:

I am glad that you have been able to save, among the Durham and Welsh women, those roots of pride in the old designs which have been handed down for generations, and which you are now bringing to London for the benefit of benighted Londoners who have never known anything of the artistic powers and the quality of work found in the cottage life of this country.[8]

The minister's comments may reflect the first stirrings of a reconstruction of the aesthetic of the quilt beyond the familial.

Another of London's top hotels, Claridge's, placed a substantial and prestigious order in 1932, requesting quilts and pillow slips for all the bedrooms in the new Art Deco wing designed by Oswald Milne (pl.7, cat. no.54). In each room, two colours were chosen to tone with the colour schemes, 'using one side of the quilt for day and the reverse side for artificial light'. The quilters worked hard to complete the order on schedule, sometimes in pairs, but reward came with glowing praise for the quilts at the opening of the new wing (pl.8). In an article of 11 June 1932 describing the new rooms, *Country Life* magazine reported that 'The beds are all provided with the lovely quilts made by the Welsh miners' wives ... The traditional designs employed are exquisite, and perfectly match the general character of modern work.' Amy Thomas of Aberdare later wrote:

To my delight I gazed upon a few specimens of our own handiwork, little had I dreamed that our quilts would ever occupy such a place. What

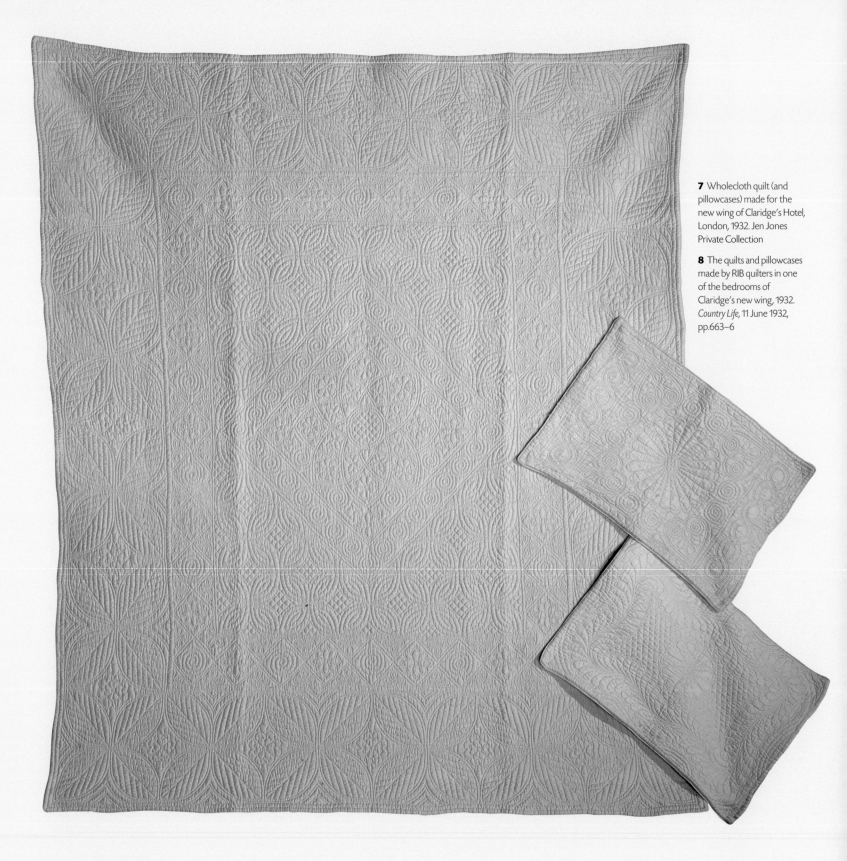

7 Wholecloth quilt (and pillowcases) made for the new wing of Claridge's Hotel, London, 1932. Jen Jones Private Collection

8 The quilts and pillowcases made by RIB quilters in one of the bedrooms of Claridge's new wing, 1932. *Country Life*, 11 June 1932, pp.663–6

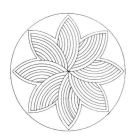

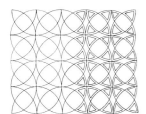

pleased me most was to discover the wonderful blending in design and colour of the quilts with the tone of the decorations of the rooms.[9]

In terms of product sales, the RIB quilting scheme was an undoubted success, and indeed the Bureau regarded it as its most successful venture in the period leading up to the Second World War. In Wales, where the RIB had found it necessary to introduce quilting classes in order to train sufficient skilled quilters, the scheme certainly revived a marginalized craft (pl.9) and developed a skills base among the generation of girls and young women who benefited from a 16-week training course in design and technique (pl.10). Such a formal teaching programme was less necessary in Durham because those recruited were, for the most part, technically competent, though sometimes limited in design ability.

Did the RIB scheme succeed in its key goal of relieving hardship? Records certainly confirm that a quilter's income from the RIB scheme was the only income coming into some households during the 1930s Depression. But the claims of relief from destitution in the RIB's formal reports need to be read alongside the sometimes poignant, but always insightful, entries in Rose's diaries from her 1934 trips to Durham and south Wales with FitzRandolph, and from two later trips to Wales. Of the nearly 60 quilters whom they visited to check on quality of work, domestic status and ability to deliver on time, by no means all were suffering hardship and, sadly, those in the most difficult circumstances were sometimes least able to achieve the standard of work required. Rose's notes on one Durham quilter in Esh Winning record this 60-year-old as being 'very needy' with a husband out of work for four years, but she also notes that her work was 'very coarse'. By contrast, one of the favoured quilters was a regular exhibition demonstrator who did 'fine sewing' and 'good dressing gowns', but was 'not very needy'.[10]

A similar picture emerges from south Wales. Rose's diary records two women with the same name, but contrasting fortunes: Miss M. Edwards of Sennybridge kept a loss-making store and needed additional income, but her namesake of Nantgeridig was 'quite comfortably off'. Oral testimonies from the 1980s, taken from surviving members of the group in Abertridw, suggest that income need was not the prime motivation, at least for the young girls who joined; it was a convivial occupation between school and setting up home. Though this group had begun with 20 members, numbers dwindled throughout the 1930s – not through lack of orders, but through marriage. When war broke out in 1939, the group was left with just two members.[11]

Professional quilters

Though it took the organizational power of the RIB and the WI to bring Britain's vernacular tradition to national attention, quilt-making had been a domestic practice of long standing that had gone unremarked and largely unrecorded for decades. Alongside those who made quilts for their own use, there were small groups of professional quilters – itinerant and village quilters, 'club' quilters and quilt designers – for whom quilting and its associated activities were commercial ventures, though whether they would have afforded themselves the status of 'professionals' is open to doubt.

In Wales, women who worked as itinerant and village quilters had been part of the quilting landscape for generations. Itinerant quilters moved from farm to farm, making whatever quilts were required in return for bed and board. The financial rewards were undoubtedly low, but the itinerant had a social role in spreading news, views and maintaining community contact. Village quilters continued to ply their trade after the itinerants' peripatetic life had ceased, working in their own homes and making quilts to order for a local customer base (pl.11). Commonplace in Wales and also in the North of England, they survived through the inter-war years.

In the North-East, how miners' widows and other women bereft of income formed quilt 'clubs' to raise money for their families is now a legendary and well-documented narrative, but a no less compelling and poignant one for all that. Mrs M.E. Shepherd of Amble, Northumberland. was one such quilter, with a story typical of those who operated quilt 'clubs' in mining villages throughout the Northumberland and Durham coalfield (see also pp.96–7 and pl.12, cat. no.52). The eloquent testimony of her daughter Belle, recorded in the 1980s, graphically evokes memories of that difficult time:

> … my father was injured in the mines and he was denied compensation … But he never worked again after the accident, the roof of the pit fell in on him and he was brought home battered and bruised from head to foot … he lay untreated for at least a year … And so my mother stuck in to quilting to help us out with the housekeeping. I had to go out and knock on people's doors and ask them if they wanted to join our club … we would stop collecting customers when we reached twenty … it took my mother a fortnight to make a quilt, she would sit down to quilt at about 9 o'clock … and would carry on until at least eight o'clock at night. And I helped with the housework and the quilt as soon as I was able to sit down.
>
> My mother had many patterns, just at her finger tips. She was able to draw them quite easily … I collected the money every week, a shilling a week and took it straight to the Co-op … A full sized quilt was three pounds ten [£3.50] … As far as I can remember the profit on a quilt would be a pound to thirty shillings [£1.50] … I always thought it would be more profitable to scrub floors.[12]

In articulating her recollections, Belle Shepherd described characteristics that were common to most of the North-East's quilt 'clubs'. They operated with a small customer base, each customer paying a regular weekly sum in order to provide the capital required to purchase fabrics, usually from the local co-operative stores. Quilters worked long hours in small cottage homes where the quilt frame dominated the family's living space, yet they produced quilts at the rate of one every two or three weeks, perhaps with family help. Some were roughly made and of limited design content, but others were skil-

11 Village quilters at Solva, Pembrokeshire, 1928. St Fagans: National History Museum

12 Peach wholecloth quilt made by Mrs M.E. Shepherd of Amble, Northumberland, from cotton sateens bought from her local Co-op, with a corner design based on a bentwood chair seat, 1935 (see also pp.96–7). Beamish Museum, County Durham: 1980-744

13 'Sanderson Star' quilt in cotton sateens. Designed by Elizabeth Sanderson, quilt 'stamper' of Allenheads, Northumberland, *c.*1910–20. V&A: T.255–1979

14 Elizabeth Sanderson (far right) and two apprentices outside her home in Allenheads, Northumberland, *c.*1910. Beamish Museum, County Durham

fully crafted wholecloth and 'strippy' quilts of uncompromisingly high-quality designs that belied the circumstances in which they were made. Begun in the latter part of the nineteenth century, quilt clubs were a lifeline for the women who ran them. It was, however, the altruism of close-knit communities – especially the mining communities – that was crucial to their survival, particularly after the First World War when quilts and patchwork coverlets had declined in popularity. In northeast England it was a system based on social rather than functional need, but, as a general practice, it also extended to other regions, including Northern Ireland.

An apparently unique quilting business that evolved in Britain was the trade of quilt designing, or 'quilt stamping' as it was colloquially known. It flourished as a mail-order operation from a remote part of northern England – the North Pennine Dales. A small group of trained individuals drew quilting designs onto fabric tops for customers, who either ordered a top from the designers' stock or sent their own quilt top for marking. The majority of the tops produced were wholecloth ones, but they also marked out designs onto strippy quilt tops and some patchwork tops. The quilting designs were drawn by hand with a blue pencil using a combination of templates and freehand drawing; the customer had only to add a quilt back and filling and then stitch along the marked lines to produce a characterful and stylistically unique quilt.

Oral testimonies indicate that this trade was begun by George Gardiner, a draper of Allenheads in Northumberland. He took young apprentices, one of whom was Elizabeth Sanderson, also from Allenheads. Perhaps the most notable of the quilt designers, she was the creator and maker of the much-copied and eponymously named design of the quilt in pl.13 (cat. no.49). Miss Sanderson in turn took apprentices (pl.14) who would board weekly with her for sometimes up to six years. In later years a niece remembered 'Aunt Lizzie' as being 'quiet spoken, prim and proper, quick to work, but very exact', and always with a pile of quilt tops waiting to be marked on the large circular table that stood in the farmhouse parlour.[13]

These workrooms were in operation in Allenheads from the late nineteenth century until the early 1930s,
mailing out marked quilt tops to customers at the rate of one or sometimes two a day. It flourished because planning and marking out a quilt design are demanding skills, and leisure quilters were only too keen to purchase a high-quality design, which they could then enjoy stitching. By the end of the 1930s, when trade was interrupted by the outbreak of war, the quilt designers of Allendale and Weardale had marked out thousands of quilt tops. Many survive and are easily identified by the fluid and confident lines of the characteristic patterns pencilled into unique design combinations.

The professional quilters all operated within a domestic space. They did not advertise, but relied on the tacit knowledge of cultural and community practices and on word-of-mouth advocacy to broadcast their trades. Only one of the quilt designers is known to have produced even a trade card. So knowledge of those who sought to earn a living from the craft was, like the craft itself, woven into the domestic and gender cultures of the communities in which they operated. When a major survey of rural crafts was undertaken by a department of Oxford University in 1920–23, quilting was not recorded in Wales and received only brief mention in the North of England.[14] Yet, as FitzRandolph observed, 'at the time the survey was made there were certainly dozens of village quilters at work … and perhaps hundreds of quilt clubs in profitable action'.[15]

As well as commenting on the 'invisibility' of quiltmaking, FitzRandolph did not conceal her views on the value placed on quilters' skills: 'Even considering the lower cost of living some fifty years or more ago, and the simple way of life in the villages, one wonders how the labour of the professional quilters really provided them with a *living*: live they did, however, many of them to a ripe old age.'[16] In recording quilters' earnings from 1890 to the early 1950s, she remarked that the notoriously poor wages of agricultural labourers 'look like wealth besides the quilters' earnings'.[17] It seems likely that what FitzRandolph encountered in the North of England and Wales in her 1920s survey for the RIB influenced the favourable rates of pay that quilters employed by the Bureau subsequently enjoyed.

15 Patchwork quilt of Welsh flannels, possibly mill offcuts, incorporating the American 'cake stand' block design. Mid-Wales, early 1900s. Ceredigion Museum Aberystwyth: 1999/83/2

Fabrics and resources

Quilt-makers past and present have used both bought and found fabrics. For quilts that required large areas of a single fabric, dedicated purchases were necessary, perhaps for large borders and certainly for wholecloth quilts. But using fabrics from the scrap bag and from other freely available or inexpensive sources has always appealed to the thrifty quilter.

At certain times and in specific places, specialized fabric resources were on hand. In the first half of the twentieth century, textile production thrived in certain regions of Britain. Where active quilt-making and textile production coincided, quilt-makers were not slow to utilize the available resource of factory waste. In Wales, offcuts from woollen factories found their way into innumerable quilts, such as the multi-coloured patchwork in pl.15, with its arresting 'basket' blocks of red flannel. The quilt in pl.16 has a different history. It was made by Matilda Clish of Anfield Plain, a mining town in Durham, who had privileged access at the local co-operative store to the cotton sateens from which the quilt is made, and which most 'Co-ops' stocked for wholecloth quilts. In their pieced designs, however, both quilts reference another influence. They incorporate block units of characteristic American form, the likely result of dramatically increased movement and cultural exchange between Britain and North America from the second half of the nineteenth century onwards – the point at which sailing ships gave way to faster and cheaper steamship crossings.[18]

Like Wales, Northern Ireland had a thriving textile industry in the first half of the twentieth century. As well as its famous linens, the province also produced specialized cotton goods. Derry, for example, was a major centre of shirt manufacture, with a peak of production in the 1920s and '30s (pl.17), and factory workers such as Matilda Tadley's husband could purchase bags of cotton waste for a small sum. Matilda's quilt pieced from shirt remnants and illustrated in pl.18, together with the quilt in pl.19 (cat. no.56) pieced from striped pyjama fabrics supplied by the maker's sister, are examples of the many Irish bedcovers produced from such recycled materials. In a 2001 exhibition of these quilts in the collections of the Ulster Folk and Transport Museum, the catalogue succinctly commented, 'The history of the local textile industries in Northern Ireland can be traced through the fragments of underwear, aprons, handkerchiefs, blouse [sic] and shirts pieced in these utility quilts.'[19] Though created with notions of thrift and inventive recycling, their disordered construction resonates with a modernist aesthetic.

The two world wars that Britain endured in the first half of the twentieth century had mixed effects on quilt-making. In the First World War, manufacturing uniform

16 Patchwork quilt. Pieced by Matilda Clish of Anfield Plain, County Durham, in the American 'orange peel' block design, using cotton sateens sourced at her local Co-op, c.1910. Beamish Museum, County Durham: 1981-365.1

17 Factory worker in the City Factory, Derry, sewing in a shirt collar, 1949. Harbour Museum, Derry

fabrics was important to the Welsh woollen trade, with the result that pieces of army khaki and navy blue often found their way into Welsh 'flannel quilts'. The specialized cloths that were manufactured during the Second World War, such as parachute silk and blackout cloth, were also recycled in quilts. But, taken overall, the social and economic changes forced on the country when war broke out in 1939 had a negative effect on quilt-making. The RIB scheme ended, and the activities of the other professional quilters dwindled, because changes in textile production and rationing made suitable fabrics very difficult to obtain, even for some years after war ended. So at the point when the styles, skills and 'native genius' of Britain's quilt-makers were being set alongside high-status contemporary craft, were reaching a social elite and were impacting on cultural values, force of circumstance brought an abrupt halt to the changes in perception that had been made. The momentum lost was not regained in the aftermath of war; quilt-making became increasingly marginalized and the characteristic 'Britishness' of this particular textile tradition was largely forgotten.

18 Patchwork coverlet. Machine-pieced by Matilda Tadley of Derry, from remnants of shirting cottons, mid-1920s. Ulster Folk & Transport Museum, Cultra, Northern Ireland

19 Patchwork coverlet. Machine-pieced by Annie O'Hare of Strabane from remnants of pyjama fabrics, 1940. Loan from Ulster Folk & Transport Museum, Cultra, Northern Ireland

Joanne Hackett

Beneath the layers: conserving the 'Pomegranate coverlet'

THE 'POMEGRANATE COVERLET' (cat. no.15) was acquired by the V&A in 1902. Purchased from a local antique dealer, the patchwork had no known provenance. The velvets, brocade and embroidered silks mainly dated from the early eighteenth century and were described as 'much damaged and repaired'. Preparation for the V&A's 2010 quilt exhibition offered an opportunity to re-examine the coverlet, using new technology. The conservation process also revealed the variety of plain and recycled printed papers used as templates. While the papers cannot help to trace the maker, the printed text can assist in dating the making and the repairs.

Special considerations have to be made when a textile has been in a museum collection for more than 100 years.

1 Detail of embroidered silk and velvet patchwork, with a typical area of damage. English, 1700–20. V&A: 1475–1902

2 Infrared image of a patent-medicine handbill used as a paper template, c.1700. V&A: 1475–1902

It is important to determine which repairs were done while the coverlet was in use, and may therefore be worth retaining, versus repairs done by restorers and conservators in the past, which may need to be removed or redone. Examination of the front of the coverlet revealed much damage to the patchwork, especially the black velvet patches, which were very worn with little remaining pile. Many of these patches had been repaired in the past, but it was unclear when or how (pl.1).

The keystone of good conservation practice is record-keeping and documentation. Unfortunately, in this case, the only record of repair within the Museum was a small paper label sewn to the lining of the coverlet, stating: 'March 1968. Lining previously too tight shrank further with washing. Extra strips added.' The fact that the lining had previously been removed enabled its removal a second time, so that a more detailed examination could be undertaken. Conservators plan their treatment mindful of the dual concept of minimal intervention and reversibility; if possible, nothing should be done to a textile that cannot be totally reversed without damaging the original material. As no original threads would be cut or removed in order to take off the lining, it would be safe to do so. The lining – a heavy unbleached linen – was also probably a later addition: the original lining was likely to have been silk.

Examination of the back of the coverlet after the linen was removed revealed at least four types of previous repair, done with two types of adhesive and with sewn replacement patches. The oldest of these repairs involved the complete replacement of damaged patchwork. The original silk-velvet patches had been cut out, and a new patch neatly sewn into its place using the same method employed when the coverlet was originally made. Black velvet was folded around a paper template and basted in place, and then sewn into the coverlet using whip-stitches (overcast stitches). Tellingly, the paper used for the template was a nineteenth-century printed paper made from chemically processed wood pulp. This paper has a characteristic brittleness and brown discoloration, but its identity can be confirmed using transmitted light microscopy to examine the paper fibres (pl.2). These repairs may have been made while the coverlet was still in use.

3 Detail of the back of a 19th-century patch. V&A: 1475–1902

3/1
6, and 6/
6, 5/6 to 8
6/6 and
, N, and
d and $\frac{1}{2}$d per y
3$\frac{1}{2}$d and   per ya
4$\frac{1}{2}$d a   per ya
d, and   per ya
2/6, 3/6 6, and
3d, 3$\frac{1}{2}$d, 4   and
6d 8$\frac{1}{2}$d nd
8$\frac{1}{2}$d a d
6$\frac{1}{2}$d per

4 Patch with mismatched repair before conservation treatment. V&A: 1475–1902

5 The same patch after conservation treatment. V&A: 1475–1902

Further repairs, probably dating from the 1960s when the lining was last removed, had been made using adhesives to attach new materials to damaged original patches. By reading conservation manuals and consulting with colleagues who were familiar with past practice, it was determined that the adhesives were probably a polyvinyl acetate (PVA) adhesive coated onto nylon net and then applied to the coverlet with a small travel iron, and sodium carboxymethylcellulose (SCMC), a carbohydrate-based adhesive applied directly to the fabric and then to the coverlet.[1] The PVA and nylon-net patches, though stiff, were still well adhered to the coverlet and were offering support to the damaged original textiles. However, the SCMC patches were failing and were coming away from the coverlet in numerous areas.

Removal of the linen lining also gave access to the original seventeenth-century and early eighteenth-century paper templates on the reverse, and to important information about how the silk patchwork had been assembled. One of the templates appeared to be a printed advertising handbill for a patent medicine, popular in the late seventeenth century.

Unfortunately, the printed side of the paper was facing the back of the coverlet. The paper template was photographed using infrared photography, which intensified the appearance of the carbon-based printing ink and enabled the handbill to be read from the reverse (pl.3).

Conservation treatment for the coverlet in 2009 was considerably more conservative than past restoration. The nineteenth-century patches and those with PVA and nylon-net repairs were left in place; the patches with SCMC adhesive were removed, as were any with mismatched support fabric. Silk habutae (a lightweight, plain-weave silk, sometimes called 'China' silk) and nylon bobbin net were dyed, using Lanaset pre-metalized dyes to match the original materials in the coverlet. The silk was laid underneath holes, the nylon net was placed over the damage and the layers were then sewn together using very fine polyester thread (pl.4, pl.5). The whole coverlet was given a support lining of fine silk to help keep the patches together. Unfortunately the 'Pomegranate coverlet' is now too frail to hang under its own weight or to be draped on a bed, so it was sewn to a padded, fabric-covered board for display.

1 Landi (1992), pp.121–30, 188–90; and Hillyer (2002)

WELLINGTON

VITTORIA

John   September 19
And   O luck husband blest of heav'n 1829   Thrice haPPy mortal envied Lot
Elisabeth To thee the Priv lege is given   What a rare treasure thou hast
ChaPm & much lov'd wife at home to Keep   Who to a woman can lay claim &
an Caress touch talk to — even sleeP   Who s temPer s ev ry day the sam

The Chapman coverlet: texts, myths and mysteries

*Angela McShane,
Ann Christie,
Abigail Turner*

THE UNFINISHED, 1829 'Chapman coverlet' (pl.1, cat. no.21) is surrounded by texts: words form part of its decoration, letters document its accession, and a range of papers play an intrinsic role in its structure (pl.2). Strangely, this myriad of texts has served only to create myths and intensify the mystery of the coverlet's making. At first glance, the coverlet seems to commemorate a marriage: a verse commends his perfect wife to the lucky husband; the Wellington panel perhaps being explained by the husband's occupation or interests. We can imagine the maker lovingly gathering fabrics, imbued with memories of family life, to create her patchwork coverlet. But, perhaps due to the untimely death of husband or wife, the project was abandoned, becoming both a sad reminder and an heirloom. How far does a 'close reading' of the coverlet substantiate this romantic tale?

The coverlet consists of nearly 250 square blocks, a printed centrepiece and a panel with a stitched text. Each block comprises eight pieces of printed cotton fabric, totalling nearly 2,000 individual pieces. None of the fabrics is used very frequently – the most frequent appears about 40 times, representing a piece of fabric little more than 30cm square. The fabrics seem not to be recycled, and relate closely to each other in colour and style of print, suggesting that they were mostly bought in as pieces for the project, rather than being collected over time from family scraps. Moreover, the coverlet was worked outwards from the centre, with the distribution,

1 Bedcover. Patchwork of printed cottons with a block-printed commemorative panel. English, inscribed 'John and Elisabeth Chapman', 1829. V&A: T.428–1985. The Chapman bedcover is decorated with a strange combination of texts and images: the names of a couple and a date, an image celebrating Wellington's victory 16 years earlier and an 18th-century epitaph.

2 Detail showing the reverse of the 'Chapman coverlet'. The papers left inside quilts gave additional warmth to the original users and some clue as to their identities.

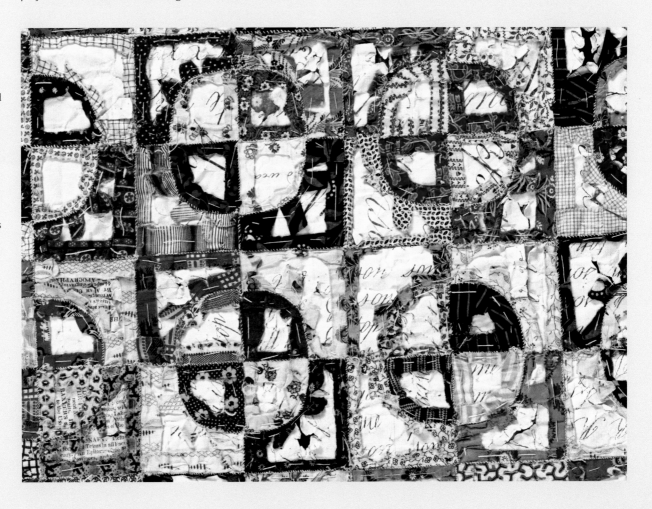

combination and balance of colours being inspired by the centre panel celebrating the Duke of Wellington's victory at Vittoria in Spain in 1813 – an event preceding the embroidered date underneath by 16 years (see p.75 on commemorative panels).

The stitched poem panel is an unusual touch, but is combined with the names 'John and Elisabeth Chapman' and the date 1829. At first glance a love poem, this verse has been traced to a collection of epitaphs, a popular literary genre of the period. The epitaph was first written in 1775 for an eccentric inventor, Martin Van Butchell, who had his first wife Mary embalmed after her death and placed in a glass case. The coverlet-maker may not have known this story, but linking symbols of death and marriage was not unusual, though how they relate to a commemorative battle panel remains intriguing.

According to letters in the Museum's accession documents, these mysteries may be unravelled if we turn to the back of the unfinished coverlet, where the 'pieced-in' papers are exposed to view (pl.2). Forming a key element in the coverlet's myth, the family tradition has it that the Chapmans' love letters were used for 'piecing in' the patches. This appealing story draws upon an assumption that a fastidious maker would remove such papers before backing – unless, as here, they had significance of their own. However, a comparison with three other 'papers-in' patchwork in the V&A's collection, from the same period, leads us to quite different conclusions.

Papers used for 'piecing in' the 'Chapman' and other similar coverlets fall into four main categories (pl.3). Most numerous are children's copy-books: written in several hands, on both sides of the paper, they repeat lists of numbers, grammatical sentences, historical fact, and so on. Second are personal papers, including correspondence (one scrap in the Chapman quilt uses the word 'dear'), ledger accounts and bills. Third are printed papers, including pamphlets, newspapers, announcements and invitations. Least numerous are blank papers. Paper was hand-made until the mid-nineteenth century and was both expensive and extremely useful. Waste-paper was a valuable household commodity and was kept over a long period. In addition to sewing, it was used to cover pots, light fires and, ultimately, in the lavatory. The information gleaned from these scraps of household paper is both limited and problematic. Nevertheless, some Chapman papers document purchases from a Rochester wine merchant and fabrics from the Scotch and Manchester

Warehouse, and several relate to Rochester town-council events. This seems to place the coverlet firmly in Rochester, and its owners amongst the upper-middling class of people in the town.

The romance of the Chapman coverlet seems to reside in its making and use over many years, rather than in the materials of which it was made. But why were the papers left in the coverlet? This cannot be answered with certainty, but another coverlet in the V&A's collection may offer a clue (pl.4). This coverlet not only retains its original papers, but, during a revamp later in its lifecycle, a further layer of newspaper was added, underneath a new backing. Should we conclude that 'piecing-in' papers were not considered disposable, but formed part of a quilt's layering, adding both insulation and, incidentally, some contextual clues for historians? Perhaps many historical patchwork coverlets have lost their piecing-in papers, due to later washing rather than deliberate removal?

3 The loose hexagonal templates for this unfinished bedcover clearly show the variety of hands and topics found on paper templates. V&A: T.169–1978

4 Detail showing the reverse of a quilt. V&A: T.75–1937. This bedcover was revamped and updated, front and back, at some point in the 19th century. Age damage to the poorer-quality patches added at that time has revealed how a whole sheet of newspaper was used as a backing sheet, adding strength and warmth to the original quilt.

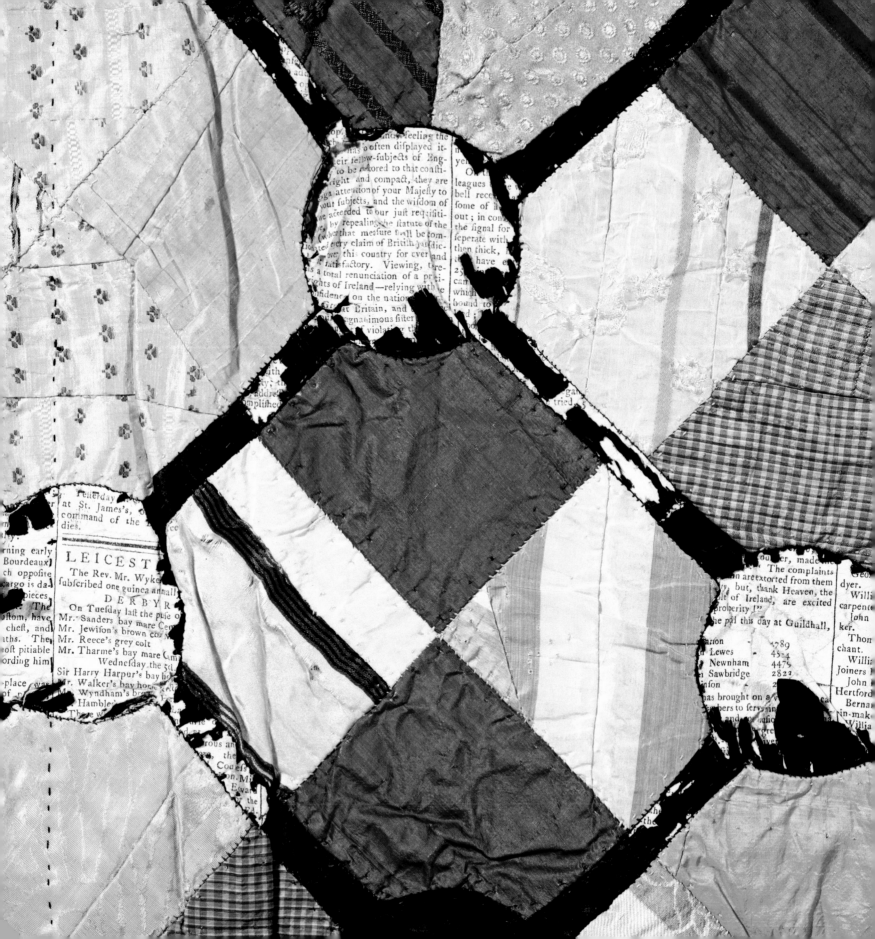

feeling the
has so often displayed it-
their fellow-subjects of Eng-
to be restored to that consti-
right and compact, they are
attention of your Majesty to
your subjects, and the wisdom of
acceded to our just requisiti-
by repealing the statute of the
(where that measure shall be com-
every claim of British jurisdic-
over this country for ever and
satisfactory. Viewing, there-
is a total renunciation of a pre-
rights of Ireland —relying with
confidence on the nation
Great Britain, and
magnanimous sister
violation of th

Of
leagues
bell rece
some of
out; in con
the signal for
seperate with
then thick,
have e
25,
cam
which
bound to

tried

Yesterday
at St. James's,
command of the
dies.

LEICEST
The Rev. Mr. Wyke
subscribed one guinea annual

DERBY
On Tuesday last the pu
Mr. Sanders bay mare Cen
Mr. Jewison's brown co
Mr. Reece's grey colt
Mr. Tharme's bay mare Cam
Wednesday the 5
Sir Harry Harpur's bay ho
Mr. Walker's bay hor
Mr. Wyndham's br
Hamble

morning early
Bourdeaux
opposite
cargo is da
pieces
The
ostom, have
chest, and
aths. The
oft pitiable
ording him

place was
of

ourier, made
The complaints
are extorted from them
but, thank Heaven, the
ole of Ireland, are excited
prosperity!"
he po this day at Guildhall,

ation   1789
Lewes   45 4
Newnham   4479
Sawbridge 2822

has brought on a
bers to serv
and

dyer.
Willi
carpente
John
ker.
Thom
chant.
Willia
Joiners
John
Hertford
Berna
in-mak
Willia

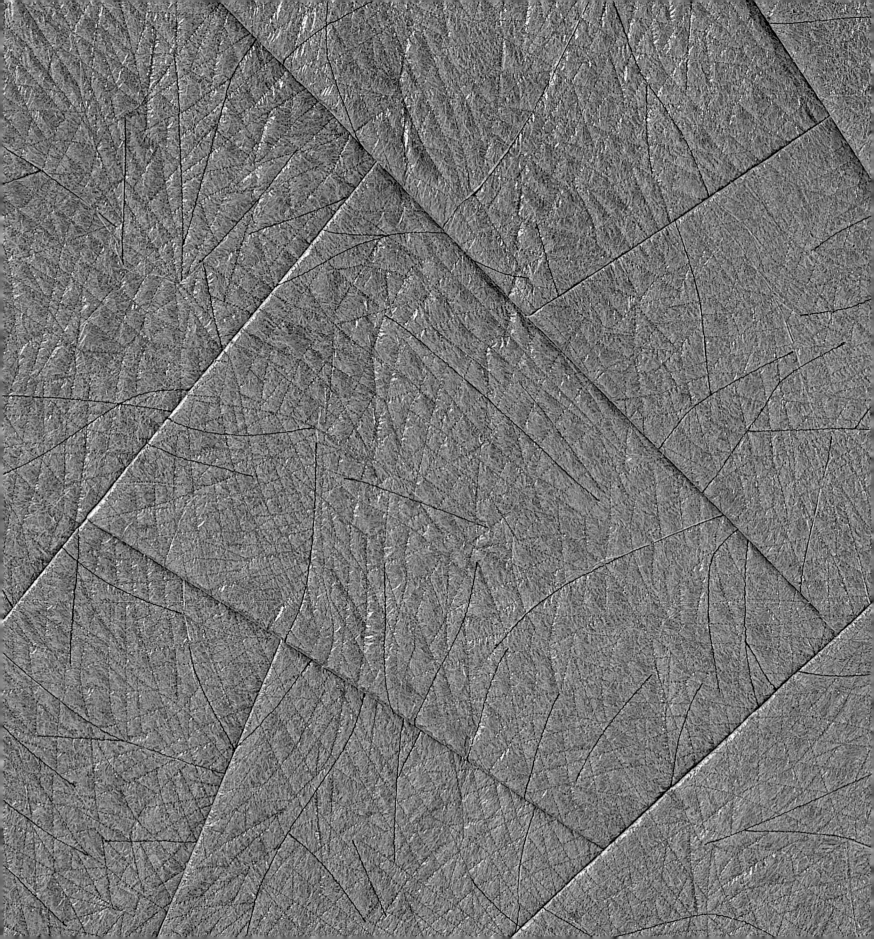

Negotiating space: fabric and the feminine 1945–2010

Sue Prichard

IN 2007 THE FEMINIST WRITER and journalist Germaine Greer reviewed a retrospective exhibition of patchwork by the artist Edrica Huws.[1] Greer's controversial column raised the question: 'Why any women would set about to make a portable artwork, a picture, out of bits of old fabric?'[2] Greer's apparent incredulity regarding the value of stitched work elicited much criticism within the textile community. Yet her apparent offhand dismissal of Huws' artistic practice has perhaps been misinterpreted. Greer's review in the national press guaranteed an unprecedented degree of publicity for what has long been regarded as little more than 'women's work'. Indeed, her article highlighted the continuing tension over issues of domestic and professional production, which have been at the forefront of passion-ate debate and artistic practice throughout the twentieth century and continue into the twenty-first (pl.1).

Patchwork and quilt-making are among the most accessible of all domestic crafts, appreciated for their visually stunning designs, patterns and technique, but also multi-layered with references to the home, the bed, warmth, security and the body. Although there are male artists who draw on the tradition, most notably Clyde Oliver in Britain and Michael James in the US, quilt-making is most often linked with the female experience. Despite Greer's mixed opinions, when read from a feminist perspective, her article actually seeks to validate Huws' practice, citing her work within the context of generations of women who have consciously subverted the gendered hierarchies and prejudices of the fine-art

1 Edrica Huws, 'The Greenhouse'. Cotton patchwork, 1959. 134 x 83cm. Huws made her first patchwork while living in Llanrwst, Wales; it took almost a year to complete.

2 Screenprint on paper from *Guerrilla Girls Talk Back*, 1985–90, Tate: P78793 Guerrilla Girls was established in 1985 by a group of women artists. Their mission statement is to expose sexism, racism and corruption in politics, art, film and popular culture. Maintaining their anonymity through the use of guerrilla masks, the Guerrilla Girls combine humour and provocative text with a serious message.

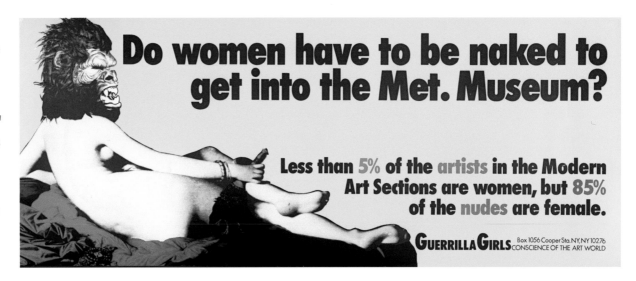

world. By rendering her personal narrative into her art, Huws continued the dialogue, focusing on domesticity and femininity, which were explored by second-wave feminists in the 1960s and '70s. Yet Huws also acknowledged the limitations of her practice, declaring 'That which restricts a woman's creative efforts more than either lack of time or lack of money is lack of space.'[3]

Huws' comment was focused on the availability of space within the home, yet the issue of space relates not only to the creative environment. It is an uncomfortable truth that, for many women artists, the opportunities to display and exhibit their work are limited. As Catherine de Zegher's exhibition *Inside the Invisible* made clear, the art of women and their role as 'active agents of culture have too often been minimized'.[4] Despite groundbreaking initiatives, such as *Womanhouse* (1972) in the US, *Postal Event: Portrait of the Artist as Housewife* (1976 and 1977) and *Women Artists and Textiles: Their Lives and Their Work* (1983) in the UK, Maureen Paley, founder of Interim Art, believes that 'All the battles that were fought in the 1970s and early 1980s led many people to feel that there is no longer a barrier to women being shown … There is still an enormous amount of ground to cover' (pl.2).[5] Research by Alicia Foster supports Paley's assertion: 'In the 103 years between the opening of the first Tate Gallery and the publication of the biennial report in 2000, only around 10% of individual exhibitions have been given to women artists.'[6]

Tracey Emin took control of her own exhibition space by creating 'The Tracey Emin Museum' (1995–7). Unhappy with the installation of *Everyone I Have Ever Slept With, 1963–1995* in *Brillant! New Art from London* at the Walker Art Center, Minneapolis, in 1995, Emin's 'museum' doubled as both studio and exhibition space, enabling the artist to interact with visitors to discuss her work. Despite her increasing success, and the mass-media attention directed at Emin, few reviews or column inches are actually devoted to her stitched work. Foster, who has written extensively on the work of women artists, suggests this is because Emin's appliquéd blankets represent 'the most subversive aspect of her practice'[7] – yet the memories evoked by Emin's use of

3 Tracey Emin made patchwork curtains to transform her garden shed for the alternative *The Other Flower Show* held at the V&A in 2004.

4 Tracey Emin, 'Hotel International'. Appliquéd blanket, 1993. Rachel and Jean-Pierre Lehmann Collection. 260 x 240cm. Described as a 'CV-on-a-blanket', 'Hotel International' references Emin's and her twin brother's date of birth, her school, friends and family.

old and stained textiles, each with its visible trace of a life lived, are perhaps one of the most evocative aspects of her work.

Emin – loud, proud and celebratory of her working-class roots – appears to have broken down the ideological barriers of the established art world with her overt references to the female experience. Yet she has never won the controversial Turner Prize and, of the 19 works acquired by Tate, only one is an appliquéd blanket.[8] Emin's love of stitching, and her comments relating to the process of making with her grandmother (her adored 'Plum') and her mother, perhaps offer a clue to the continuing marginalization of women artists, and by extension any practice connected with the feminine. Foster believes it is the very domesticity of this work that negates its inclusion in theoretical debates surrounding

Emin's practice (pl.3).[9] In many of her stitched works, Emin follows in the 'make-do-and-mend' tradition: including patches from her old clothes, even material cut from the family sofa, which appeared in her first appliquéd blanket, 'Hotel International' (1993). When it was exhibited at the New York Gramercy International Art Fair, held in the Gramercy Park Hotel, Emin appeared in bed covered by 'Hotel International', reclaiming both the origin and the function of the work, but also toying with the tension between private and public space (pl.4). Early reviews were uncomfortable with the sentimentality expressed in this work, yet Emin continues to draw on the medium, acknowledging the importance to her of domestic space. While studying at Medway College of Design in Rochester in 1982, she was unable to travel from her home in Margate:

> Because of the rail strike I had been doing all my things at home. We did a textiles project at Medway and instead of doing what you would normally do I painted on pieces of calico and sewed on top of them. It was completely different from what you'd do in class. When I was at home I was much more experimental. I got good marks. I did well when I went out on a wing.[10]

Artistic involvement with the domestic interior has had a long and well-documented past (pl.5), and yet the dichotomy between domesticity and artistic production is summed up by Barbara Rose's pithy comment, 'If a woman paints while watching soap opera it's hobby art.'[11] Greer made a similar comment, distinguishing between 'consumer craftwork' – the variously packaged patterns, kits, magazines, materials and books – and the professional practice reflected in Huws' work. Love her or loathe her, Emin's heady (and sometimes uncomfortable) mix of intimate biographical details and explicit sexual confessions has often taken second place to accusations of her 'faux' amateurism, as epitomized by her misspelt words, bad drawings and crudely stitched blankets. Indeed, the craft theorist and curator Glenn Adamson makes the point that the 'workmanship in her art has

noticeably improved' with the outsourcing to skilled assistants.[12] Yet as vehicles for personal narrative, Emin's appliquéd blankets resonate with historical precedents, marking life events and documenting her female lineage.

'I used to feel the lack of qualifications was a drawback in the quilting world':
SARA IMPEY, 2009

Patchwork and quilt-making provide a visual and contextual language for artists interested in exploring a range of personal, social and economic issues via the more tactile qualities of fabric. However, Emin's adoption of 'sloppy craft' is anathema to professional quilters, many of whom earn their living through teaching (most notably via the City and Guilds Patchwork and Quilting courses), lecturing and selling quilts. The domestic sphere is one in which they are able to embrace creativity through a process of making that functions outside the professional art world. Regional and national quilt competitions, with clear definitions and structures of rules for entry, provide an opportunity for exhibiting within a system that is both understandable and accessible. The fact that, in the majority of cases, entries will never receive the recognition or status awarded by major cultural institutions such as Tate or the Metropolitan Museum of Art is, on the whole, irrelevant as each quilt is displayed, admired and validated by the maker's own peer group. The rules and regulations that bind quilt competitions provide the framework in which individuals are able to recognize and appreciate the technical achievements of someone who has expert knowledge of that process.

Sara Impey, winner of the 'Excellence in Quilt Making Today' (2006) competition at the annual Festival of Quilts held in Birmingham, believes that 'Exhibiting is important – the end process in the life-cycle of making. The work is not complete until it has been presented to an audience.'[13] Impey, who trained as a journalist, working for *The Times*, joined a local quilt-making group in the 1980s, eventually joining the Quilters' Guild of the British Isles. She started exhibiting in the 1990s and is open about her lack of formal training:

5 Sonia Delaunay, 'Couverture'. Appliqué, 1911. Musée National d'Art Moderne, Paris. 109 x 81cm. Delaunay worked across a variety of media, including painting, furniture and textile design, book covers and posters. She made 'Couverture' for her son Charles' cradle, insisting that she put the career of her husband, Robert Delaunay, first: 'From the day we started living together, I played second fiddle and I never put myself first until the 1950s.'

7 Sara Impey, 'Punctuation'. Machine-stitched silk, 2009. Impey based the text for 'Punctuation' on a letter written to her mother, which included the words 'never did like punctuation / see you suddenly one day'. V&A

6 Creating your sewing room. Photo from *Practical Home Dressmaking Illustrated*, 1948

I haven't even got City and Guilds patchwork and quilting, let alone any art qualification, and my only training in quilt-making was in workshops I took many years ago, notably with Siripan Kidd and Lynne Edwards. I used to feel this lack of qualifications to be a drawback in the quilting world, but I am now quite proud that people are taking me seriously, when my quilt-making grew out of a hobby and is still produced in the home on a domestic sewing machine – in fact, on my dining table (pl.6, pl.7).[14]

'One of the great indigenous American art forms': *New York Magazine*, 1971

Textile art and the domestic crafts have in general been less marginalized in America than in the UK, the mythology of the 'age of homespun' continuing well into the twentieth century.[15] This accounts for the global recognition and acknowledgement of the tradition of the American quilt. However, while the American women's movement was perhaps more successful in celebrating and reclaiming traditional materials and processes, during the 1960s women artists were still underrepresented in the exhibition programmes of most major cultural institutions. In 1970 a demonstration against the exhibition policy of the Whitney Museum of American Art demanded equality for women artists. The African-American artist and feminist Faith Ringgold and the activist, curator and supporter of feminist art Lucy Lippard led the 'sit-in'. Ringgold recalls 'Lucy Lippard and I began to blow our whistles … The people gathered around us and we formed a big circle sitting on the floor. Then we got up and started chanting, "Fifty percent women, fifty percent women".'[16] As the debate regarding women's art gained momentum, Faith Ringgold, Judy Chicago and Miriam Schapiro continued to explore and exalt the female condition, overtly appropriating female sexual imagery and domestic craft materials, most famously via Chicago's *The Dinner Party* (1974–9), Schapiro's *Femmages* and the site-specific installation *Womanhouse* (pl.8, pl.9).

SEE · YOU · SUDDENLY · ONE · DAY
AT
THE · GAP · BETWEEN · THOUGHTS
OR · IN
THE · COLOUR · OF · SPEECH
OR · ALONG
THE · DASH · OF · THE · STITCH
OR · AROUND
THE · CURVE · OF · THE · QUESTION
OR · BEYOND
THE · PINPOINT · OF · FOCUS
OR · ON
THE · BRINK · OF · OMISSION
OR · UNDER
THE · IMPRINT · OF · FOOTNOTES
OR · THROUGH
THE · TEXTURE · OF · SCRIPT
OR · ABOVE
THE · SHOUT · OF · THE · SURFACE
OR · INSIDE
THE · WEB · OF · CROSS-REFERENCE
OR · BEFORE
THE · LILT · OF · THE · COMMA
OR · AFTER
THE · FINAL · FULL · STOP

NEVER · DID · LIKE
PUNCTUATION
SEE · YOU · SUDDENLY · ONE · DAY

8 Miriam Schapiro, *Collaboration: Mary Cassatt and Me*. Collage, 1976. Private Collection. Schapiro's series of collaborations with dead women artists, celebrated their artistic legacy in paint and fabric. Cassatt produced a series of paintings on the theme of women caring for children, based on meticulous observation, rather than idealization. In *Mary Cassatt and Me* Schapiro uses a reproduction of Cassatt's *The Child's Bath* (1893), paying homage both to Cassatt as an artist and to the domestic sphere that she portrays.

9 Faith Ringgold, 'Mother's Quilt'. Acrylic painted, appliquéd and embroidered fabric with sequins, 1983. Artist's Collection. Ringgold made her first quilt in collaboration with her mother. They also worked together on a range of doll kits entitled the 'International Ringgold Doll Collection'. When her mother died, Ringgold discovered a stash of pre-cut doll's dresses ready to be made up into kits. She paid homage to her mother by incorporating the dresses into *Mother's Quilt*.

By 1971 America faced increasing social and political unrest. Preparations for the country's bicentennial celebrations were juxtaposed with increasingly violent demonstrations against the Vietnam War, while tensions arising from both the women's movement and the civil-rights movement were fracturing communities and threatening the fabric of society. A year after the demonstrations by Ringgold et al., the Whitney Museum of American Art took the decision to host an exhibition that celebrated perhaps the most humble of all the domestic crafts: the ubiquitous quilt. Private collector Jonathan Holstein had originally approached the Guggenheim Museum for advice regarding a quilt exhibition and was advised by Diana Waldman, the museum's deputy director, to approach the Whitney, 'because of their long-standing interest in American Folk Art'.[17] Holstein and his partner Gail van der Hoof had specifically assembled their collection around the notions of abstraction inherent in the quilts' designs, and they were adamant that the exhibition should serve to re-evaluate quilts as art rather than folk craft. The Whitney accepted Holstein's proposal and *Abstract Design in American Quilts* was scheduled to run throughout what was traditionally seen as the quiet summer season.[18]

The enthusiastic reviews that followed the opening of the exhibition were unprecedented, and yet – consciously or unconsciously – missed the dichotomy inherent in an exhibition that set out to celebrate the innate artistry of nineteenth-century 'anonymous' quilt-makers at a time when feminist artists were critiquing the inequalities of the fine-art system. Linda Nochlin's essay 'Why Have There Been No Great Women Artists' appeared the same year as the Whitney exhibition, an apt commentary on the continuing exclusion of women practitioners within the fine-art arena. Despite the lack of an overt female presence within *Abstract Design in American Quilts*, the *New York* magazine enthusiastically declared that quilts were 'one of the great indigenous American art forms'.[19]

The intense media interest and proliferation of articles, publications, lectures and events created by the exhibition have since been rivalled only by the phenomenal success of *The Quilts of Gee's Bend* exhibition (2002–6).[20] This appropriation of historical and, more recently, marginalized quilters by collectors has been debated by feminists and critics. Both *Abstract Design in American Quilts* and, latterly, the *Gee's Bend* exhibitions captured the art world's attention in a way in which the feminist artist could not. Yet each exhibition either successfully effaced women from the context of production or, more controversially, attempted to create artists from women who, in the opinion of Anna Chave (Professor of Contemporary Art and Theory at the City University of New York), 'had to sew to survive'.[21] Feminist art historians Rozsika Parker and Griselda Pollock critiqued this appropriation as being within that practice of misinterpreting and misrepresenting female production.[22] While not denying the aesthetic qualities of the quilts presented in both exhibitions, Parker, Pollock and Chave believe that the misrepresentation of the makers denies the complexity surrounding their production. Alicia Foster concurs, referencing the findings of a UNESCO-commissioned paper entitled 'Women and Cultural Politics', in which 'there is evidence to suggest that aesthetics in society remain almost exclusively controlled by male "gatekeepers"'.[23]

The mythology surrounding the inherent qualities of the American quilt can be identified as having its roots firmly fixed within the context of the development of a strong national identity. The success of this strategy is revealed in the visual and textual imagery of America's mass media,[24] where the quilt acts as signifier for hearth and home, strong familial ties and, inherently, the female experience. In 1971 the title of *Abstract Design in American Quilts*, and its inaugural opening at the Whitney Museum of American Art, immediately provoked associations with the American abstract expressionist movement and the ideology of artistic freedom promoted during the height of the Cold War. Just as American abstract expressionism emphasized the use of form, colour and line to create new meanings, so the emphasis on the aesthetic qualities of historical quilts provided a new perspective on the origins of European abstraction. Indeed, the unconscious artistic process by which the 'unknown' makers created such seminal work could only have been facilitated by a different kind of space – one that tolerated and celebrated religious and political freedom. The success of the exhibition, the subsequent national and international tours and associated publicity, together with the approaching bicentennial celebrations, precipitated a nationwide quilting revival. As both interest and demand grew, the revival was constantly fuelled by an explosion of magazines, publications, festivals and competitions. Holstein's influence in the promotion of a distinct American design aesthetic in quilt-making has reverberated over the years, creating an almost continuous demand for American quilt exhibitions, generating both national and international media interest and critical attention.

10 Front cover of *American Pieced Quilts*, 1975, featuring the 'Carpenter's Wheel', 'Dutch Rose' or 'Broken Star', 1887. NAL: 607.AJ.0373

'The whole thing might indeed have been an American invention': JONATHAN HOLSTEIN, 1991

In Britain, attempts to revive traditional quilt-making were more or less abandoned after the Second World War. The relative emancipation of the war years was replaced by a retrenching of the dictum 'a woman's place is in the home'. Ideals of domesticity for the middle classes had, however, changed. Post-war reconstruction placed greater emphasis on efficiency within the home. The explosion of mass-produced, new consumer goods meant that many laborious tasks were mechanized; 'housework' gave way to 'household management'; and women were advised to shun superficial decoration and display, in favour of a more rational approach to the home. Within this new social, cultural and economic context, traditional crafts were seen as 'old-fashioned' and redundant. With dwindling demand, particularly from the more affluent urban centres, professional quilters had little incentive to practise or pass on their skills.

In Wales, efforts by the Welsh Folk Museum in 1951 to emulate the work of the Rural Industries Bureau in the 1930s and stimulate a revival generated some local interest, but this was largely confined to Adult Education classes. However, in areas such as Durham, attitudes towards more traditional models of domesticity, driven by both economic and social reasons, together with the success of Local Education Authority classes in the 1950s, paved the way for a new generation of grass-root quilters. The legacy of committed and energetic teachers such as Mary Lough, Florence Fletcher and Amy Emms ensured that the high level of craftsmanship that had been the hallmark of the previous century was maintained, albeit within a regional rather than a national context.

However, by the 1990s, the Shipley Art Gallery's ambitious programme of exhibitions, workshops and support for grass-roots quilters developed a regional, national and international audience.

Given the virtual invisibility of British quilt-making, it is hardly surprising that the bright and abstract designs and patterns of American quilts created excitement among British designers, artists and textile collectors. Recalling his trip to England in 1972, Jonathan Holstein discovered

so few English quilts that he believed 'the whole thing might indeed have been an American invention'.[25] Reviews of *Abstract Design in American Quilts* had been covered by the British press, and in 1974 the Christmas edition of the *Illustrated London News* ran a full-colour feature on Holstein's publication *The Pieced Quilt*. The following year 26 quilts (13 of them from the original exhibition) toured to England, to the City Art Gallery, Bristol, and the Whitworth Art Gallery, Manchester (pl.10).[26]

Graphic designer and artist Michele Walker had been introduced to North American quilt-making techniques during a prolonged trip to Canada, seeing her first American quilt exhibition at the Felicity Samuel Gallery in London's Savile Row in 1974. She also emphasizes the importance of Holstein's exhibition, particularly in terms of visual stimulus: 'We had never seen anything like it – it was so exciting. It was their strong graphic impact – the bold, simple, abstract designs and use of repeated blocks – which really attracted me.'[27] Walker, who was involved in the creation of the Quilters' Guild of the British Isles, also cites the importance of the collectors Jane Kasmin, Ron Simpson and Joen Zinnie Lask, whose gallery in Chelsea exhibited American Folk Art, including Amish quilts. The gallery and Lask's Camden Town shop (The Calico Cat and Patchwork Dog) became the focus for a core group of artists, collectors and quilters, including Walker, Simpson, Pauline Burbidge, Deirdre Amsden, Mary Fogg, Jenny and Alec Hutchinson. Walker, who went on to research traditional North Country and Welsh quilts, believes that Burbidge played a key role in forging links between contemporary British and American quilt designers, including Beth and Jeffrey Gutcheon, Michael James and Nancy Crow. Burbidge, who saw her first exhibition of quilts from the American Museum in Bath, held at the Commonwealth Institute in Kensington, London,[28] remembers Lask's shop as 'buzzing with anything to do with quilts, antique and contemporary – she also ran classes in the top room there, and invited us to run some classes and to meet more people'.[29]

The industrial and social unrest of the 1970s paved the way for a resurgence of interest in an idealized, pre-industrial past, epitomized by Laura Ashley's spriggy

11 Anne E. Michie, 'Bodies Quilt'. Photo-linen sewn by hand onto cotton sheeting, with white lace edging and ribbon, 1987. 243.8 x 243.8cm. Michie described her quilt as a symbol for women's 'anonymous craft work', equating anonymity with 'public death'.

prints and patchwork kits and by publication of Edith Holden's *The Country Diary of an Edwardian Lady* (1977). However, when interviewed for the book *Women and Craft* in 1987, Kate Walker stated her ambivalence towards such revivals:

I, like my mother, maintain some scepticism about the rediscovery of craftwork because for working-class women, any nostalgia about it is bogus. Exploited, unpaid work was the very thing that my grandmothers left North Yorkshire and County Mayo to escape. My mother and I are all too aware that although we respect the skills passed onto us, they stink of poverty. It is impossible to pretend that those objects are 'good works' or 'art'.[30]

Although traditional models of domesticity were increasingly rejected by the British feminist movement, throughout the 1980s and '90s a series of exhibitions sought to re-evaluate traditional skills as a valid form of artistic expression. June Freeman's exhibition *Quilting Patchwork, and Appliqué 1700–1982: Sewing as Women's Art* (1982) focused on the significance of sewing for women. *The Subversive Stitch* (1984) touring exhibition, curated by Pennina Barnett, featured a number of Goldsmiths College graduates who sought to articulate the debate surrounding women, textiles and femininity. Designed in response to Rozsika Parker's seminal 1984 publication, *The Subversive Stitch* was in fact two independent exhibitions: the first, *Embroidery in Women's Lives 1300–1900*, examined the changing social, cultural and economic role of women in relation to textile production; the second, *Women and Textiles Today*, explored the dichotomy between artists working within the textile field and the ongoing prejudice surrounding female artistic practice, particularly in relation to art, class and leisure (pl.11).

By the 1990s a number of British quilt exhibitions had toured the country, many focusing on social and economic issues, including *Quilts with Conviction* (1994), *Recycling, Forms for the Next Century* (1996) and *Revelation, Textile Artists Addressing Issues* (1997–8). *Take 4: New Perspectives on the British Art Quilt* (Whitworth Art Gallery, 1998) featured the work of Jo Budd, Pauline Burbidge, Dinah Prentice and Michele Walker. By the time of *Take 4*, Walker's inspiration had moved away from the graphic designs of the American tradition, since she had discovered North Country and Welsh quilts while researching her book *The Passionate Quilter*. Moreover, in *Take 4* Walker exhibited a new body of work, using plastics and other packaging material instead of cloth. Jennifer Harris, deputy director of the Whitworth, described how some visitors had been offended by 'No Home, No Hope' (1994), a cot-sized quilt constructed from plastic sacking and newspaper; they 'either missed or objected to the irony in its subversion of the quilt's associations with comfort, family and protection' (pl.12).[31]

Griselda Pollock believed that British artists were less competent than their American counterparts in taking their place within the cultural framework. Writing in 1988, she claimed that 'Women's education in general in Britain schools women to be silent, if not silent, quiet in direct contrast to the North American model where artists are frequently articulate speakers and educated writers.'[32] Dinah Prentice challenges Pollock's view. Politicized, articulate and extremely well read, in more than three decades she has explored, challenged and reclaimed 'an already discredited medium'.[33] Recently Prentice has abandoned the preoccupations with war and destruction in *Take 4*, to focus on the female body, but has never relinquished her concern for language. In her recent exhibition, *Fragments* (2008) at the Butter Market in Birmingham, Prentice included a scroll of images of earlier work with accompanying text – an amalgamation of thoughts, ideas and commentary on her practice and on the issues facing any woman artist: 'Why feminism? What has feminism to do with the human condition that drives the search for expression? This extraordinary desire to understand the relationship of our short human span … Women have to find out who they are and most importantly what they experience in their own estimation.'[34]

'Can I go home yet?': JOANNE HOLLOWS, 2006

Edrica Huws maintained that her choice of fabric over paint was both pragmatic and deliberate: oil paint was messy and smelly, whereas fabric, by its very nature, could be manipulated and treated differently to other media. Most importantly, patchwork could be absorbed within the busy family environment. As an artist who preferred to focus on the representational rather than the abstract, Huws rose to the challenge of exploring her world through the medium of fabric, collected over the years and stored in her 'rag bag'. This somewhat romanticized interpretation of Huws' practice belies the artist's ability to engage in both a changing urban and rural landscape. As she nurtured her growing brood of children, moving around the country in response to her husband's career path, she reflected not only her own

12 Michele Walker, 'No Home, No Hope'. Plastic sacking and newspaper, 1994. Hove Museum and Art Gallery

13 Dinah Prentice in her studio with 'Billowing Maenads' 2008. 'The manipulation of a woven limp surface which needs support, be it a wall or ceiling or armature, is incredibly human; a sort of witness to vulnerability.'

OPPOSITE:
14 Jo Budd in her studio with Male/Winter (vertical) and Female/Summer (horizontal)

interior space, but one in which she recorded her progressive journeys. It is an experience shared by Dinah Prentice: 'David [Prentice] and I come from a Fine Art background, so apart from bringing up four daughters, it was always an absolute priority that he should have a studio in the house from the start, and I followed when I could turn a room into my own studio' (pl.13).[35]

Jo Budd creates large-scale textile pieces, which need both access to natural light and space in order to assemble them. She dyes and distresses her own fabrics, exploring and exploiting their ability to capture colour, texture and pattern. Budd studied fine art at Newcastle University, abandoning paint to concentrate on layered and stitched compositions, which reflected initially Newcastle's industrial landscape and, later, the changing seasons of East Anglia's vast expanse of land, sea and sky. She has always chosen houses for their outlook and studio potential:

> My living space has always been of great importance to me. It needs to be nurturing and as harmonious as I can make it. My studio space is brilliant. It is my sacred space, dedicated only to one thing. Since I have had this space the work has poured out, more ideas than I have time to play with. What I have produced in it is both a celebration of my surroundings and an expression of liberation, which this space makes me feel (pl.14).[36]

Budd's painterly approach to her work is not at the expense of the inherent qualities of fabric; however, the layers of hand-dyed and stitched pieces also act as metaphors for the layers of memory and feelings that she has experienced. She remembers her mother's love of stitching, overlaid with an appreciation and acceptance of the importance of the well-made.

Sara Impey, who made her first quilt at the age of 17, also recalls her mother, a 'keen dressmaker' who 'kept a bag of fabric scraps dating back to the 1950s. I raided these to make [the] quilt. I still have this quilt. It is full of memories and associations: dresses my mother

wore, a nightdress I lost on holiday as a teenager, a party-frock I had as a child'.[37] These memories of 'making' resonate among many who were growing up in post-war Britain, still in the grip of rationing and the 'make-do-and-mend' mentality that had seen people through the harsh war years.

The powerful connection between memory and experience lies at the heart of Jane Whiteley's work. Born in Bromley, Whiteley moved to Australia in 1988, completing a second BA in visual arts (textiles) at Perth's Edith Cowan University. Like Budd, Whiteley dyes her own cloth, before stitching together layers of silk or cotton gauze. Indigo dyeing – in some societies practised only by women and inextricably linked with female fertility and reproduction – is both technically complex and unpredictable. Whiteley learnt the techniques of indigo dyeing from her teacher and mentor, Elsje van Keppel. She is also drawn to old utility cloth – the worn and stained bed sheets, tea towels, nappies and bandages that have strong associations with the domestic sphere. In the series *Sides to the Middle*, Whiteley explored and celebrated the utility tradition of prolonging the life of bed sheets by cutting the fabric down the middle and joining the outer sides together, leaving a seam down the centre; she remembers 'the comfort of lying in bed and following the line of stitch with her toe'.[38] She both acknowledges and chal-

15 The strip cartoon 'Mother Tells You How …' was published in *Girl*, a weekly magazine launched in 1951 as the companion to the more adventurous *Eagle* for boys. Each week Judy would turn to her mother for advice on those 'essential life skills for modern young women'.

16 Janey Forgan, 'Liberty Jack'. Machine-pieced and quilted printed cotton, 2008. Courtesy of Janey Forgan

lenges the expectations and traditions of quilt-making, hand-stitching the layers of gauze with a fine eye for detail, then breaking the rules by stitching a central seam. She at once sets out to validate the domestic experience, but within the framework of her own artistic practice: 'My works' concern has been to explore the humanity and power of cloth … to use cloth to explore the body's memory.'[39] The memories embedded in *Sides to the Middle* are both personal and collective. The lifecycle of the sheet, from marriage trousseau to metaphorical winding sheet, follows our own journey through life.

Australian lecturer and author Gail Jones has written of 'a woman labouring, in dim light, with scissors, cloth, pins and thread, the lift and fall of slow hand-sewing, its hypnotic repetition, its fastidious concentration … [it] is thus familiar and iconographic, but it is also the personalized glimpse … that millions of children everywhere carry'.[40] For many, the feminist backlash against domesticity in the 1970s, when stitching equalled oppression, has resulted not only in a dearth of skills and memories being handed down, but also in the breakdown of the mother–daughter relationship, whereby sewing became part of the female bonding relationship (pl.15). Generations of children have grown up without learning even the basic skills of sewing on buttons, since sewing has been all but eradicated from the National Curriculum. Teacher Fiona Howell, who runs after-school 'Stitchclub' classes, believes that women are simply too busy 'to sit down, pick up a basket of mending and show their child how to do the repairs. In today's throwaway society we just bin the offending item and buy a new one.'[41]

Artist Nikki Goldup has taught textile courses for 12 years. She is interested in how child-rearing, motherhood and female memory are expressed within contemporary British society. She recently completed a series of workshops at Romsey Mill, Cambridge, aimed at young mothers with little experience in 'making'. Starting with simple, personalized 'bags for life' with embroidered patches, the group moved on to larger pieces of work that reflected an individual's personal views of motherhood. The women all gained a Level 1 Creative Skills Development qualification from the National Open College Network. Goldup believes the experience went beyond the acquisition of a certificate; the group discussed feelings of solidarity, friendship and empathy as well as pride, the enjoyment of making a finished and functional object, and the quietness and calm that working with textiles gave.[42]

Joanne Hollows, co-editor of *Feminism in Popular Culture*, acknowledges that many feminist-influenced women in their thirties and forties harbour secret fantasies of 'giving up their careers in order to bake cakes, tend the garden, knit or do home improvements'.[43] Janey Forgan, winner of the Festival of Quilts' 'Quilt 2008' competition, concurs:

I had been working overseas in difficult places, doing a job that I ate, slept and breathed. When I decided to step away from that life I was looking for interests and activities that were creative, calming and fulfilling in a very different way from the high-pressure environment I was used to. The very domesticity of the craft was part of its appeal. The soft, careful, creative process of patchwork, which builds over time, seemed the perfect antidote. I had always liked fabric – the feel and beauty – and used to play with my mother's fabric drawer as a child, but was never that interested in making clothes. Patchwork, with its combination of colours and patterns, allows me to play with shapes and forms – and represent ideas in a tactile form (pl.16).[44]

Hollows suggests that the cultural significance of domesticity has largely been ignored in post-feminist writing. In reviewing Edrica Huws' exhibition, Germaine Greer reversed this trend. The question 'why any woman would set about to make … artwork … out of bits of old fabric' was rhetorical. Throughout the centuries women have documented their personal narratives via the medium of fabric and stitch. The fact that – despite continuing prejudice and lack of recognition – they should continue to do so validates both the medium and the maker (pl.17).

17 Rita Donagh, *Counterpane*. Oil on canvas, 1987–8. Tate: T05838. Donagh painted this patchwork quilt twice, once in a self-portrait and again in *Counterpane*. Originally discovered in her mother's birthplace, the quilt references both her female lineage and the victims of the terrorist bombings in Northern Ireland.

Stitchers in time and space:
women in the long eighteenth century

Joanne Bailey

As WITH SO MANY PATCHWORK QUILTS in museum collections, the identity of the designer and maker of the exquisite 1797 'Sundial coverlet' (pl.1, cat no.16) remains a mystery. Yet it may have much to tell us about the life and home of its maker. The form and design of the 'Sundial coverlet' suggest that it was the product of a genteel household with access to financial and cultural resources. The diverse printed cottons that were used were fashionable commodities of the day, and the pieced and embroidered patches surely represent the interests and pursuits of its maker. Given the variety of personal objects included in the design, we may conclude that it was probably created by a woman. These range outwards from her tools for self-expression (needle, thread, scissors and pincushion) to her sphere of influence in home, garden and society (plates, birds, butterflies, flowers, fans and cards) and to the wider world reflected by the maps at each corner.

Why does time stand at the coverlet's centre in the device of the sundial? We cannot know the personal significance of the exact time stitched on it, but we can follow the clues that this patchwork offers us to discover how the maker may have spent her time in the long eighteenth century. The intricacy, complexity and dimensions of a coverlet suggest the female maker had expansive free time to devote to its construction, and control over sufficient space in which to piece together its large final form. Its domestic and decorative function hints that its maker – like the coverlet – was confined to the private sphere. Yet by reading the same features of the coverlet in conjunction with current research into women's lives, these assumptions can be challenged. Instead of free time and space, what emerges is the patchwork of qualities that marked even aristocratic women's daily activities: busyness, versatility and patience, and a continual blurring of the boundary between public and private.

For many married women, their hands were never empty, never still. Their diaries and correspondence reveal that they directed female servants in the daily activities that ensured a successfully functioning home. Since getting and keeping servants was rarely easy, at times such women undertook some of these heavy labours themselves. In addition they bore and raised children, carried considerable responsibilities for their moral training and education, and shouldered the burden of caring for ill and indisposed family members. Thus the availability of time in the home was unpredictable and dictated by the demands of their household.

Though privileged enough to have time for leisure, genteel women's personal recreations, such as needlework, had to be suited to picking up and putting down as necessary (pl.2). As so many images of women indicate, needlework was combined with the other activities of family life (pl.3), such as childcare and sitting by a sickbed, or with social pursuits such as communal reading (where one of the party read aloud to the rest) or receiving and visiting friends. Patchwork projects were ideal, since they could be carried out in short bursts over a lengthy period of time and undertaken in different parts of the home, according to the separate, cumulative stages of design and assembly. Indeed, their portability is indicated by their accessories: the sewing basket and work-table, both of which could be moved to suit where they were working. Similarly, eighteenth-century room use changed during the day with the rearrangement of furniture altering the function of the room,

1 Bedcover. Cotton patchwork. English, with initials MCB, dated 1797. V&A: T.102–1938

2 Diana Sperling, *Mum S at Work in the minor hall – Dynes Hall – Brisk near her dozin'*. Watercolour. English, 1812–23

3 John Harden, *A Mother Sewing*. Pen and pencil on paper. English, *c*.1800–47. Abbot Hall Art Gallery, Kendal, Cumbria

4 John Harden, *Family Group with Dog*. Pen-and-ink wash on paper. English, 1826. Abbot Hall Art Gallery, Kendal, Cumbria

providing the space needed to complete a patchwork's final piecing together.

The 'Sundial coverlet' was a domestic article, but just as it brings together objects from the household and the natural and humanly constructed worlds, so we can see in its design that neither it nor its maker was confined to the private sphere, for the wider world (depicted at its corners) was equally part of their experience. Indeed, private and public were not separate spheres. The domestic environment shaped the lives and personae of genteel English men, as well as women. Before the more rigid separation of work and home that occurred in the second half of the nineteenth century, homes could include spaces where men too carried out work and built their

public reputation (pl.4). Thus life in the home had significance far beyond its walls, for both individuals and households. As Hester Chapone advised her female readers in *Letters on the improvement of the mind, addressed to a young lady* (1773), 'The neatness and order of your house and furniture is a part of Economy which will greatly affect your appearance and character.' The 'Sundial coverlet' advertises these accomplishments, reflecting a keen eye for symmetry and colour harmony and for the rigorous organizational skills required to piece it together. But it had wider meaning still, contributing to the household's public credit, since a well-ordered, attractive abode signalled to others the well-being, taste and status of all its inhabitants.

Jacqueline Riding

His constant Penelope: epic tales and domestic narratives

Retire, oh Queen! Thy household task resume,
Tend, with thy maids, the labours of the loom;
The bow, the darts, and arms of chivalry,
These cares to man belong, and most to me

There in her chamber as she sat apart,
Revolv'd his words, and place'd them in her heart.
On her Ulysses then she fix'd her soul.
Down her fair cheek the tears abundant roll,
'Till gentle Pallas, piteous of her cries,
In slumber clos'd her silver-streaming eyes.[1]

From Homer, *The Odyssey of Homer*, translated by
Alexander Pope, 1760

T HE 'GEORGE III COVERLET' (pl.1, cat. no.23), with its 41 independent scenes, is an object that should be read, as much as appreciated for its complexity and technical skill. Images of warfare interlink with scenes of domestic life, as if *The Iliad* and *The Odyssey* had been updated and Britain was the new Ithaca. For 20 years the Ithacan Queen Penelope awaits the return of her husband Odysseus (or 'Ulysses', to the Romans) from the Trojan Wars. For three years she repels the aggressive attention of her suitors by weaving and then unpicking her father-in-law's shroud, on the completion of which she has promised to marry. Modern Penelopes, as described by Anne Elliot in *Persuasion*, 'live at home, quiet, confined, and our feelings prey upon us', while the Odyssean captains Wentworth and Harville 'are always labouring and toiling, exposed to every risk and hardship. Your home, country, friends, all quitted. Neither time, nor health, nor life, to be called your own.'[2] The unknown maker faithfully records these two separate worlds not on a sampler or wall hanging, but on a coverlet.[3] As the final layer over a bed – a place of comfort and safety – this coverlet and its tales assume an intensely personal significance.

The dominant feature of the coverlet is the central medallion (pl.2). It contains a military scene, but not of a battle. It is a heroic representation of George III reviewing volunteer troops in Hyde Park on his birthday, 4 June, in 1799. The composition comes directly from a print after John Singleton Copley (pl.3).

This seemingly inconsequential and unheroic event was in reality a vital display of domestic military strength during a period of perpetual threat of invasion. In 1799 Britain had been at war with France for six years. This was nothing new in itself. However, after the French Revolution of 1789, Britain was no longer fighting a monarchy, but a republic. Increasingly, therefore, British patriotism was centred upon the King himself, as symbolic of Britain's liberty and particular brand of constitutional monarchy. The scene at Hyde Park represented not just the physical protection of the King and his subjects against French aggression on home soil, but the preservation of the British settlement and body politic. As the *General Evening Post* reported, 'So large a body of men thus standing forward to surround his Majesty's person, and on the anniversary of his birth to manifest their resolution to maintain his rights as well as their own, was certainly the most superb spectacle.'[4] In focusing on the person and position of the King, the nation rose above such divisive concerns as party politics and united, doughty and steadfast.

Placing this image at the heart of the composition, the maker emphatically engages with the patriotic sentiments that this morale-boosting event served to engender. And this palpable sense of pride and patriotism in Britain, its monarch, armed forces and people continues throughout. The following three key narratives or strands alternate along the entire border: military, naval and domestic or 'home front'. Broadly speaking, the military scenes appear to refer to events long past, generic images of officers or the allegorical. For example, the scenes at the top edge (second from left) and (second from right) are derived from Edward Penny's *Marquis of Granby giving alms to a sick soldier and his family* (1764) and his *The Death of Wolfe* (1763, mezzotints by Richard Houston after Penny being published in 1769 and 1772 respectively). Both are heroic in different ways: Granby for the conspicuous care of his troops and their dependants, General Wolfe for his ultimate sacrifice during the victory at Quebec against the French in 1759.

In contrast, the naval scenes represent very recent events and one officer's heroics in particular. For example (left, fourth from bottom), the dying Captain Hood receives the sword of

1 Coverlet. Patchwork of printed cottons. English, 1803–05.
V&A: T.9–1962

1 Homer (1760), vol.V, book XXI, pp.82–4, lines 377–80, 383–8

2 Austen (1818), vol.4 (vol.II), pp.262, 264

3 It is clear from the positioning of the images around the border and the off-centre location of the medallion that this object was intended to be placed over a bed, with the left, right and bottom edges draped over the respective sides. The key view is therefore from the bed's foot towards the bedhead.

4 *General Evening Post* (London), 4–6 June 1799, no.10402, p.1, col.3. This is an astonishing reflection of George III's recovery – both in health and in reputation – from his 'madness' only a decade before, which had brought his reign and the monarchy itself into crisis.

the defeated Captain L'Hériter in 1798 (possibly after an engraving by James Daniell); of three officers on deck (right, fourth from top), the middle has his empty right sleeve pinned up and a bandaged head wound, followed by (top, fourth from left) an admiral, his head bandaged, again the empty right sleeve pinned up, Britannia seated on a plinth beside him and a sea battle raging behind. The last two scenes almost certainly depict Horatio Nelson during and after the Battle of the Nile of 1798. Nelson famously lost most of his right arm during the Battle of Santa Cruz de Tenerife in 1797 and received a head wound during the Battle of the Nile, returning to direct the battle after the wound was bandaged). An engraving by Daniel Orme after his own imaginary scene of Nelson on the deck of the *Vanguard* was published in 1800.[5] Nelson's full-length portrait was painted by Leonardo Guzzardi while he convalesced at Naples, showing him in a rear-admiral's full dress uniform with the prominent star of a Knight of the Bath, as echoed in the coverlet image. Neither the Battle of Trafalgar in 1805 nor Nelson's death at the moment of victory is represented – an extraordinary omission if the coverlet remained incomplete in late October of that year. Thus far the dated sources do not extend beyond 1801. The scene (bottom, fourth from right) of two Greenwich Hospital pensioners is derived from the Robert

2 Detail of the central medallion. V&A: T.9–1962

3 Charles Turner after John Singleton Copley, *His Majesty Accompanied by the Prince of Wales and the Dukes of York and Gloucester. Reviewing the Volunteer Corps of London and its vicinity, in Hyde Park, on the 4th June, 1799*. Published by J. Scatcherd, 18 November 1799. National Army Museum: 1974-04-20

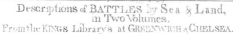

Descriptions of BATTLES by Sea & Land,
in Two Volumes.
From the KINGS Library's at GREENWICH & CHELSEA.

4 Robert Dighton, *Descriptions of Battles by Sea & Land*. Hand-coloured etching, published March 1801. National Maritime Museum: PU4733

5 Detail of stitched scene based on *Descriptions of Battles by Sea & Land*. V&A: T.9–1962

5 National Maritime Museum BHC0514
6 This popular image was replicated in a variety of contexts, including creamware jugs and plates; see National Maritime Museum AAA4489 and AAA4490
7 Dibden [1790?], p.3

Dighton print, *Descriptions of Battles by Sea & Land* (March 1801) (pl.4). This, coupled with the dating to about 1790–1800 of the textiles employed, suggests that the coverlet's creation – and therefore its iconography – was inspired by the British successes during the Wars of the French Revolution, with reference to previous wars and victories, and, perhaps more specifically, by the termination of hostilities with the Treaty of Amiens signed on 25 March 1802.

Yet the battles themselves are only part of the coverlet's narrative. Almost half of the scenes depict women in domestic interiors or landscapes, playing instruments, spinning, reading, writing or simply walking. This 'other side' of warfare creates a contrast in pace to the action scenes: home life continues, a 'normality' is maintained, as the women wait patiently for the men to return. These images may derive from contemporary publications or, unlike the military or naval scenes, from the maker's own experience. The images that bridge these distinctly masculine and feminine worlds are those that include a male

and female figure, usually a sailor or Tar and his lover or spouse. At least one (bottom edge, fourth from left) derives from an engraving (pl.7)[6] inspired by a popular sea-song of *c.*1788 entitled 'Poor Jack' by Charles Dibden. The last verse reads:

> D'ye mind me, a sailor should be every inch,
> All as one as a piece of the ship,
> And with her brave the world without offering to flinch,
> From the moment the anchor's a-trip,
> As to me in all weathers, all times, sides, & ends,
> Nought's a trouble from duty that springs,
> My heart is my Poll's – and my rhino* my friends
> And as for my life – 'tis my king's;
> E'en when my time comes, ne'er believe me so soft,
> As with grief to be taken a-back –
> That same little Cherub that sits up aloft,
> Will look out a good birth for Poor Jack.[7]
> [* slang for money]

For Dibden's audience, Jack encapsulated all the swagger and unblinking patriotism of the common sailor/adventurer, with his priorities simply and succinctly itemized. Like a mock-heroic Odysseus, he circles the globe in pursuit of the French, fame and fortune and – despite the inevitable lapses – will always, God willing, return to his constant Penelope. To reflect this hoped-for conclusion, the maker includes a scene of a family reunited (left, second from base).

The coverlet therefore reflects heroism and sacrifice from all ranks, and indeed from all Britons – a very personal contribution to the war effort. The maker has painstakingly recorded, stitch-by-stitch, deeds and incidents that occurred in distant lands and seas, and the impact of these significant national and international events upon those who remained at home. In itself, there is a Homeric quality to the endeavour. It is clear that the maker had access to a vast array of engraved images and used their compositions creatively – either reflecting them exactly or modifying them for their own purposes. This would not be unusual during the period, but for the prominent inclusion in the design (top, centre) of a printing press – perhaps the family papers of a printer or print seller will one day reveal the maker's own story.

6 Detail of stitched scene based on *Poor Jack*. V&A: T.9–1962

POOR JACK.

7 After Robert Dighton? *Poor Jack*, an illustration of the song 'Poor Jack' by Charles Dibdin (*c*.1788). Mezzotint, *c*.1790. National Maritime Museum: PAJ4029

Catalogue

1 The domestic landscape

1 Set of bed hangings

Maker unknown
Possibly London
1730–50
Made to hang on a bed approximately
248 x 144.5 x 195cm
V&A: 242-F–1908
Given by Major Harlowe Turner

Patchwork bed hangings in a clamshell design with patches of cotton, linen, fustian and silk, some of Indian origin. The hangings include two large foot curtains, two small head curtains, a lower valance in three parts and an upper valance. There is no surviving headcloth or coverlet. The fabrics are both dress and furnishing, and are decorated with a variety of techniques, including block-printing, painting, resist-dyeing, stencilling and embroidery. Each of the patches has a linen rather than paper reverse. These individual patches are worked into a larger design of scallop-edged diamonds edged with green silk tape. The repetition of prints within each diamond is completely symmetrical. Although many of the prints appear to be similar, most have been used exclusively within one diamond, meaning that there is very little duplication. Each of the large curtains has 1,960 pieces and each of the smaller curtains has 784. The right and left lower valances have approximately 196 each, and the foot valance approximately 172. The upper valance has 368. Each object is lined with white linen.

This is the only set of chintz bed hangings from this period that survives in a public collection. They would have been created for a fashionable middling or aristocratic household. The original use of the word 'chintz' was for Indian cotton cloth on which a pattern was produced by hand-drawing and dyeing with mordants and resists. While there was immense enthusiasm for chintz among British consumers in the late seventeenth century, there were also many opponents to the imported Indian goods, including the weavers of wool, linen and silk. In a bid to protect British manufacturing, a law was passed in 1701 to forbid the import of dyed or printed cottons and silk from India into Britain, except for re-export.

Despite this ban, the overwhelming fashion for these light, colourful textiles led the writer Daniel Defoe to comment that it had 'crept into our houses; our closets and bedchambers, curtains, cushions, chairs and at last beds themselves were nothing but calicoes and Indian stuffs, and in short almost everything that used to be made of wool and silk'.

According to a diary written by a the donor's ancestor (Baptist Noel Turner, 1739–1826), these spectacular chintz hangings were thought to have been worked on the Bedford School Estate, London, at a time when 'the whole neighbourhood quilted on account of the Duke of Bedford's claim'. The Bedford School Estate was around 13 acres (5.2 hectares) of land in the parish of St Andrew, Holborn, London. Proceeds from the estate funded the Bedford School, and were also given as alms to the poor and to aid the marriage of poor women. Although difficult to prove, such narratives suggest how the histories handed down with each intricately pieced patchwork are often as cherished as the cottons and silks that document its textile history.

2 Cot cover

Probably Priscilla Redding
Deal or Dover
1690s–1720s
109 x 102cm
V&A: T.615–1996
Given by Ann Thomas

Quilted patchwork cot cover created from a variety of silk velvets, satins, silver and silver-gilt tissues and other complex-weave silks. The central panel is an early brocade of silver-gilt thread on a blue, brown and white striped ground. The remaining silks are arranged in concentric borders around this brocade. Most of the textiles date to between 1660 and 1700. It is quilted in a design of geometric shapes that follows that of the patchwork in some areas, and heavily wadded with wool. The reverse is an English or Dutch block-printed cotton of red and purple flowers on a white ground. It is bound at the edges with pink silk, and was probably intended for a child's bed.

This cot cover probably was made by Priscilla Redding (1654–1723), probably in either Deal or Dover (see pp.52–5). Fashionable silks were readily available in nearby areas, particularly in the attractive city of Canterbury, which the maker visited for her marriage in 1691. In her tour of 1697, Celia Fiennes described Canterbury as 'a flourishing town' with 'good tradeing in ye weaving of silks'. During the Anglo-French wars of the 1690s, illegal traders brought French silks and Flemish lace into the area, carried inland via Deal's intricate alleyways.

In conversation with the Continent, the entire area was a heady mix of sought-after goods, manufactured both locally and abroad. The geographical mobility of fabrics provided the avid shopper with the chance to introduce a piece of the desirable, and sometimes the illicit, into the home.

Priscilla Redding was the daughter of Captain Samuel Tavenor. Tavenor was a Baptist preacher and for a short time governor of Deal Castle. Priscilla kept a diary that reveals both the personal and political life of her family. She charts the 'great persicution and truble' of her father for 'not conforming to the worshipe of the nation'. This political testimony sits alongside poignant accounts of her family: from the birth of her first child to the distressing loss of her only son.

3 Pincushions

Makers unknown
Hampshire
1740s
15.5 x 15.5 x 5cm, 18 x 18 x 5cm
V&A: T.37–1969 and T.38–1969
Given by Mary A. Edmonds

T.37–1969: circular pincushion of cream silk satin. The top is flat quilted with cream silk thread. A central circle contains a rosette and the remainder of the ground is divided into a grid of small diamonds. The circumference is decorated with a frill of cream satin, the edges of which are scalloped and pinked; within each scallop are three punched holes. The frill matches that of the child's corresponding basket (T.36–1969).

T.38–1969: square pincushion of cream silk satin. The top is flat quilted with cream silk thread. A square is set on point in the centre, and the remainder of the ground is divided into a grid of small diamonds. Within the central square are a circle and four squares, all further divided with geometric patterns. The centre of the squares originally contained pins, but these are all missing. The edges are trimmed with a silk fringe and fly braid.

Pincushions in the eighteenth century were both functional and decorative. They had been in general household use from at least the sixteenth century, and were popular as courting and wedding presents, christening and New Year's gifts. Pins at this point were made by hand and were relatively expensive items.

These particular pincushions formed part of a set owned by Amy Burningham (1708–77), and were used for the birth of her firstborn son, Henry, in 1741. They were then passed down to the firstborn son of every generation, finally coming into the possession of Henry's great-great-granddaughter, Mary. The original home of the Burningham family was Hussey's Farm in the village of Upper Froyle, Hampshire.

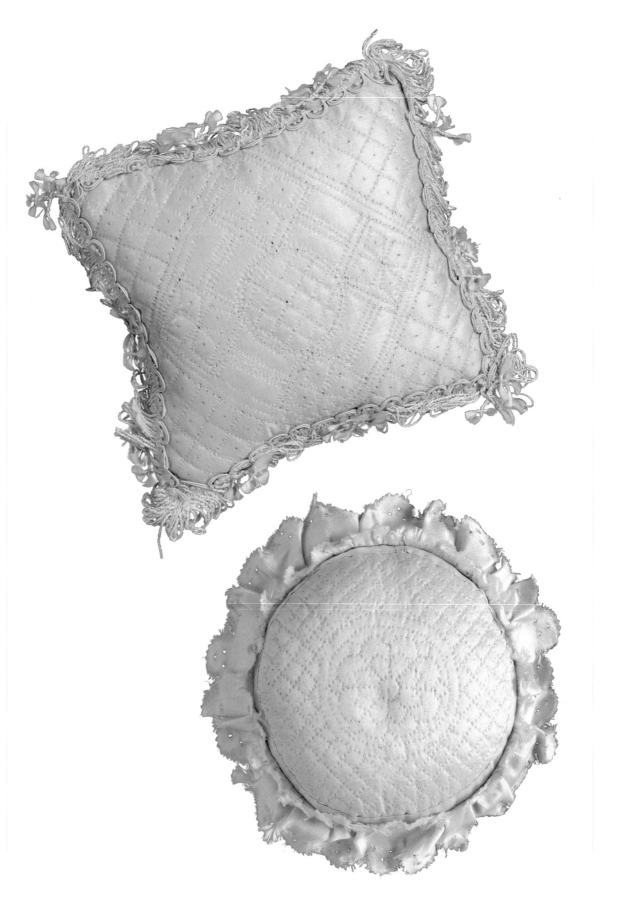

4 Pincushions

Makers unknown
Britain
1788 and 1784
13.5 x 9 x 5.5cm, 11.7 x 16 x 5.3cm
V&A: B.4–2009 and B.3–2009

B.4–2009: pincushion of cream silk satin with tassels of silk thread at each corner. The front of the pincushion is stuck with hand-made pins to show an inscription and a star-like flower within a circle of linked rings. The pincushion is further decorated in pins with a straight line around each edge and arranged into the words 'MP/ Welcome Dear Babe/ 1788'. The back of the pincushion is plain.

B.3–2009: pincushion, of ivory cotton twill woven with a self-coloured stripe. The front of the pincushion is stuck with hand-made pins to show an inscription, with a pair of voided hearts and an enclosed crown above, a tree to one side, and a flower and a coronet beneath, accompanied by two sets of initials and the date. The pincushion is edged with matching cotton fringing, and has a plain back. Pins are arranged into the words 'Health to the Little Stranger/ MH 1784/ TH'.

Pincushions like these were once customary presents to a new mother. They were often given after the baby arrived, as there was a superstitious belief that they could increase the pain felt by the mother during birth: 'For every pin a pain' and 'More pins, more pain' were two of the traditional sayings. And at a time when many problems could arise during childbirth, the pins were often arranged to show good wishes, sometimes in verse. The messages shown here include 'Health to the Little Stranger': a coy way of referring to an unborn or newborn baby. **NM**

5 Cot cover

Maker unknown
Britain
Dated 1703
102 x 88.5cm
V&A: 1564–1902

Quilted and embroidered linen cot cover. In the middle is a quilted and embroidered circular medallion containing a two-handled vase. The vase contains carnations, lilies and other flowers, embroidered in silk threads in shades of pink, blue and green. In each corner of the quilt is a flowering plant, embroidered in the same colours. The ground is quilted in running stitch and backstitch in white cotton thread, in a design of flowers, small squares and circles. The quilted border shows scenes including a griffin, flowers, a house front, a woman holding flowers, rabbits beneath an oak tree, a mermaid with a comb (see pp.162–3), fish, a duck, a three-masted ship, a castle, a camel and a coat of arms with the initials ES and the date 1703.

Little information was available on this quilt when it was acquired in 1902, but the size suggests that it was created for a baby or small child. The quilted and embroidered pattern was probably drawn out by the maker. From as young as eight, the maker might have created samplers and practised her drawing techniques. Mythical figures such as the mermaids shown here were popular subjects. Another motif hints at the presence of quilted fashion garments at this time. The woman at the top edge is wearing a quilted petticoat: a popular item for informal dress.

6 Cot cover
Maker unknown
Britain
1750–1800
11.5 x 87cm
V&A: T.429–1966
Given by John Fowler

Quilted cot cover created from a textile with woven stripes of white linen and yellow silk. The same fabric has been used on both the quilt top and the reverse. The central quilted design is a stylized flower within a round medallion. Quarter medallions of the same design are set in each corner. It is quilted with yellow silk thread and wadded with uncarded and unspun wool. The ground is quilted with a grid of small diamonds, and the wide border at the edge is quilted with a pattern of zigzags and stylized flowers.

This cot cover was probably created in the later part of the eighteenth century, and may have been recycled from dress materials. The reuse of textiles was a common activity, particularly given the economic investment in valuable fabrics. It is possible that the family created this small quilt for the arrival of the newborn with a piece of silk readily available in the home. Measures of silk were also stocked by traders describing themselves as mercers, linen drapers, haberdashers and milliners.

7 Cot cover and curtains

Maker unknown
Britain
1725–50
Designed to fit a cot approximately
93 x 60 x 90cm
V&A: Circ.531&A–1923

Cot cover and two curtains of cream linen embroidered with cream and polychrome silk threads. Both the cover and the curtains are flat quilted with a small, all-over diamond pattern in cream silk thread using very fine backstitch. The embroidery shows trailing flowers in a chintz-inspired design. It is lined with cotton and bound with green silk tape.

This set would have been an expensive item, drawn out by a professional pattern drawer and embroidered in a workshop. The two curtains may have been joined together at a later date, possibly in the nineteenth century when this style of cot curtain became popular.

Children born into middling and aristocratic households grew up among objects that mirrored adult fashions. Ceremonial items such as this cot set tended to be formal, luxurious and rich in appearance, designed to show off both the baby and the status of the household into which he or she had been born. Here, the style of chainstitch embroidery recalls the fashions for chintzes and Indian embroideries that were popular in the late seventeenth and early eighteenth centuries.

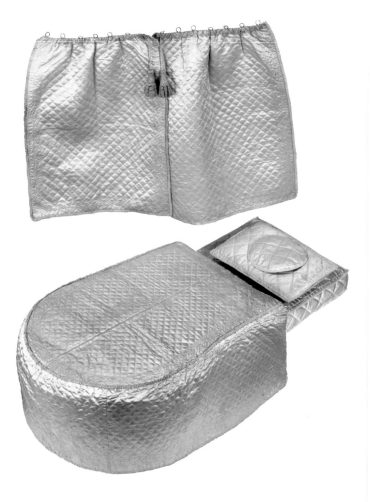

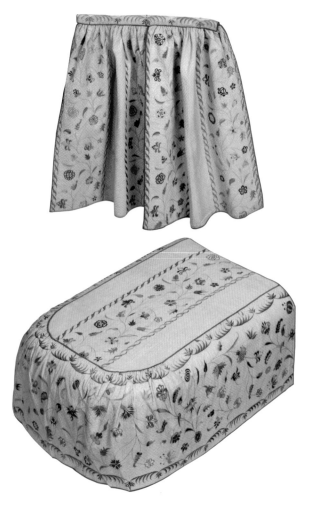

8 Cot set

Maker unknown
Britain
Mid-eighteenth century
Designed to fit a cot approximately
100 x 55 x 87cm
Private Collection

Cot set in six parts. Cream silk satin, flat quilted, with an all-over large diamond pattern, with intricate coils at the edges. The cot cover and curtains are lined with a silk and trimmed with a silk fringe. Large tassels have been used on the curtains. The mattress, pillowcase and circular pillow are lined with linen and have their edges bound with silk tape. The set may have had an upper valance that would have sat above the curtains, but this has not survived with the current set.

Throughout the seventeenth and eighteenth centuries an intricate web of cultural practices surrounded childbirth. It took place in a communal but strictly gendered space.

This small set of objects would have been used as a presentation device for the new baby, providing a focus for the intense euphoria felt with the safe delivery of both mother and child. The V&A also cares for a quilted satin bed-jacket and bedcover, which were probably used by the mother of the child. At a time when expectations hinged on the production of a male heir, objects associated with birth were highly prized and laden with meaning. Sets such as this could be created exclusively for a particular family or birth. Their expense restricted them to wealthy middling or aristocratic households.

This layette set is thought to have belonged to the Hynde Cotton family of Madingley Hall near Cambridge.

9 Bedcover and single curtain
Maker unknown
Britain
Mid-eighteenth century
270 x 270cm (bedcover),
260 x 88cm (single curtain)
V&A: T.386&A–1970
Given by G.H.G. Norman

Bedcover and single curtain of white linen, flat quilted with yellow silk thread in fine backstitch. The design of the bedcover has a central oval medallion, semicircular corner pieces and wide borders all containing large, curved feather/leaf motifs; the remainder of the ground is filled with thick scroll-shaped motifs that interlink to form a wave-like effect. The lower corners of the bedcover are designed to fit around the post ends of the bed. The curtain is decorated with a vertical panel of feather motifs in the centre and with borders of interlaced feathers and scrolls. These objects would probably have been part of a larger set that would have included three further curtains, but these have not survived. Both objects are lined with white linen.

This bedcover and curtain were owned by the Hynde Cotton family. An inventory of Madingley Hall in 1734 shows that 36 rooms were furnished to the height of luxury and fashion. The bedrooms were named according to the colour of their textiles.

The Hynde Cottons were a wealthy and well-connected family. Sir John Hynde Cotton was a noted MP. In 1724 he married Margaret Trefusis, who brought with her a substantial dowry that included real estate, £17,000 of capital, as well as her personal jewels and plate.

10 Panel
Probably made by a member of the Haines family
Britain
Dated 1786
65 x 57cm
V&A: T.20–1938
Given by G.M. Major

Unlined patchwork panel of printed cottons in various colours. At the centre there are eight triangles arranged in what is now known as a 'windmill' design, alternately floral on a white ground and floral on a purple ground. This is surrounded by two patchwork borders of printed cottons and a broad band of cotton embroidered in black wool with stylized sprigs and crowns. The outermost border has been created from printed cotton triangles. Embroidered 'Henry/Iane/Haines/ September the 17 1786 HIH born'.

This small, unlined piece of patchwork may have been made to form part of a cushion cover or larger bedcover or screen. No information concerning its history was available when it was acquired in 1938, but the embroidery announcing the birth of a child, suggests that the panel was prepared to mark the birth or christening of the baby. Originally thought to represent the names of the parents ('Henry' and 'Jane'), it is now believed that the piece gives the full name of the child: Henry Iane Haines.

The central panel is embroidered freehand with black wool in chainstitch, a technique whose popularity was stimulated by the import of Indian embroideries. Six different but fashionable cottons have been used, and the blue stripes in one selvedge indicate that the maker has used English cottons manufactured after 1776. Some patches have been created from tiny pieces, suggesting their limited availability to the members of this household.

11 Bedcover

Maker unknown
Possibly Exeter
1690–1750
230 x 216.5cm
V&A: T.201–1984

Quilted, patchwork bedcover made from a wide
variety of silk velvets and plain and complex-
weave silks. The patchwork design of the quilt
includes a sun-like motif at the centre,
surrounded by several borders of trailing leaves,
clamshells, flowers and various geometric
patterns. The quilting in most areas follows the
design of the patchwork. At the head of the
quilt is a coat of arms showing a lion rampant in
silver-gilt thread. Most of the textiles date to
before 1700, including a green silk dominated by
a silver ground, and a blue silk with brocaded
pomegranates and flowers in silver and silver-gilt
thread, both thought to date from the 1690s.
There is also a late seventeenth-century yellow
silk that is possibly Chinese, and a silver-gilt tissue
with brocaded flowers that seems to be of
Persian design. At the lower edge of the quilt
there are split sides for fitting around the post
ends of a bed. It is wadded with wool and lined
in a green and cream striped silk, and a plain
cream silk.

This bedcover would probably have been
made professionally, and would have been an
expensive commission. The arms at the head of
the quilt suggest a strong connection to a family
of high status, possibly the Bedfords. The arms
would have been created by a heraldic
embroiderer, and could have been made
specifically for this quilt or recycled from
another object. At this point it was not unusual
for a family to declare their love for their king or
a patron through domestic objects such as this.

According to the oral history that
accompanied this quilt when it was acquired in
1984, it was created in the late seventeenth or
early eighteenth century for a property now
known as 'Bishops' Court': a medieval manor
house at Clyst St Mary near Exeter. The Bedford
family owned the house until the onset of the
Civil War, when it was acquired by Peter Beavis,
the son of a wealthy Exeter merchant. The
property remained in the Beavis family until
1801.

12 Winter/Male and Summer/Female

Jo Budd
Suffolk
2010
'Winter/Male': 320 cm x 170 cm,
'Summer/Female':170 cm x 314 cm
'Winter/Male': V&A: TBC, 'Summer/Female':
collection of the artist

Diptych of hand-dyed silk organza, silk chiffon, silk Crepaline, Habotai silk, cotton organdie, silk organdie, plain weave silks, synthetic fabrics and mixed over dyed cottons, appliquéd to a canvas backing.

Jo Budd is a maker firmly rooted in her sense of place. This diptych responds to the rhythms of water and time that play out across the Suffolk water meadow surrounding her studio. The two sets of colours here represent the different seasons, charting through cloth the enormous timescale involved in the act of making.

The pieces are at once personal and universal. The tall, vertical format of 'Winter/Male' relates to the more formal, geometric structures and strong tonal contrasts that Budd aligns with a masculine aesthetic. But it is also partly a portrait of her partner and their relationship to the land, the garden and the studio that they have built together. As Budd remarks, 'At its centre is a green heart, there is the dark mysterious water, blocks of colour flowing in different directions that interlink'. In contrast, 'Summer/Female' is paler in tone, with a less rigid composition and a palette of pinks and reds. Garment shapes introduce curves and diagonals to the piece, while softened edges and veiled layers of sheer fabrics give a more delicate feel.

Formally trained as a painter, Budd started to work with textiles after graduating from Newcastle University, dyeing her own fabrics and experimenting with the potential of stitch. She describes the pleasure of feeling the thread in tension, where:

beneath the surface it manipulates and pulls the fabric, anchoring it to a canvas backing, an underpinning scaffold of criss-cross stitches, barely visible, but emphasizing the tactile qualities of each fabric. Occasionally the stitch appears on the surface, or is used to create a ripple effect, but as a way of breaking up light, not as an embellishment, It is like a kind of Braille – inviting the eye, if not the hand, to touch.

13 Bedcover

Possibly Mary Parker
Possibly Crediton, Devon
Mid-eighteenth century
223 x 196cm
V&A: T.19–1987

Quilted patchwork bedcover of plain- and complex-weave silks. Most of the silks are ribbons dating from the 1720s to 1740s, including some stamped examples. The triangular patchwork borders are quilted in a linear pattern, and divided by wide borders of silk satin. These plain borders are quilted with a pattern similar to that seen on eighteenth-century petticoats, with a sun-like motif and trailing leaves and flowers. It is wadded with wool and lined with two printed fustians.

According to the oral history that accompanied this bedcover when it was acquired in 1987, it was made for the marriage of Mary Parker in 1770. The textiles used appear to be significantly earlier, but it is possible that they were acquired early in the century and pieced at a later date. The lining is also from the 1730s or '40s, and may have been recycled from women's gowns.

The maker was thought to be a resident of Crediton, and the ribbons would have been available in the nearby town of Exeter, where highly skilled weavers were producing and trading in silks and ribbons throughout the eighteenth century. Several Parker families were resident in the area at the time. In 1723, the entire adult population of Crediton trooped before the authorities to sign an oath of allegiance to King George I. A Parker family appears on these Oath Rolls.

A cream favour with a crown has also been used in several triangles. Favours such as these were created for the coronation and wedding of reigning monarchs, and were a popular means of declaring loyalty through everyday items.

14 Casket

Maker unknown
Norcott Hall, Hertfordshire
1660s
20 x 35.5 x 26cm
V&A: T.114–1999
Accepted by HM Government in lieu of Inheritance Tax from the estate of Elizabeth Loxley, and allocated to the V&A

Wooden casket with silk panels, embroidered in silk threads. The scenes are taken from the Bible, but have been updated to include Stuart dress. Those around the sides include episodes from the story of Tobias and the Archangel Raphael, while Rebecca and Eliezer appear on the lid. It is fitted with a variety of drawers and secret compartments.

Caskets such as this one were used to house a young girl's most treasured possessions, including her needlework tools and tiny keepsakes. The panels of the casket would have been worked by a young girl of about the age of 11 or 12, as the culmination of her needlework education, which would have begun with samplers and the decoration of small objects such as pincushions. She would embroider a series of small panels drawn or printed with pictorial scenes, which would then be sent to a cabinet-maker to be made up into a casket, the edges bound with braid.

This casket came originally from the Smart family of Norcott Hall, Hertfordshire. Family history associates the casket with a visit to the house by Charles II. It passed by inheritance to Elizabeth Smart, who married John Loxley in the nineteenth century.

15 Coverlet

Maker unknown
England
1700–20
191 x 138cm
V&A: 1475–1902

Patchwork coverlet made up of silk velvets and a combination of plain- and complex-weave silks. The front comprises almost all silk fabrics, but there are a small number of block-printed cotton patches over-printed with gold. The majority are appliquéd or embroidered with silver and silver-gilt thread and silk threads. Some of the patterned silks date from the 1680s and '90s. The patches have been pieced using polychrome silk threads, including green, yellow and pink. The central monogram is worked in silver and silver-gilt thread on a black silk-velvet ground, and was probably inserted in the late eighteenth century. The paper template is still intact.

This patchwork of silks and velvets would have been made as a bedcover or screen. The original design incorporates small embroidered panels or 'slips', and a wide variety of plain and patterned silks. A less technically accomplished hand has added figurative embroidery and appliqué to many of the patches after the completion of the piecing. The additional embroidery shows a wide range of popular needlework subjects, including four chinoiserie figures and a scene from Aesop's fable 'The Fox and the Vase'.

No information concerning the provenance of the coverlet was available when it was acquired, but when the later lining was removed for conservation, it revealed an early eighteenth-century paper template. Newspaper cuttings relating to the trial of Titus Oates and an advertisement for a proprietary medicine date the template to around 1705. Plain paper has also been used in several areas. Because paper was an expensive consumer item, it was common practice in even the wealthiest households to recycle it. Alongside the range of silks, this suggests an affluent household with access to a range of luxury consumer goods. In 1709 the *Female Tatler* described the exciting experience of shopping for such goods: 'The shops are perfect gilded theatres ... As people glance within their doors, they salute them with – Garden silks, ladies Italian silks, brocades, tissues, cloth of silver or cloth of gold, very fine mantua silks, any right Geneva velvet, English velvet, velvet embossed.'

16 Coverlet

Maker unknown
Britain
Dated 1797
279 x 302cm
V&A: T.102–1938

Coverlet made from a wide range of block-printed cottons of the 1780s and '90s. The small prints are typical of those used for gowns of the period. The maker has used pieced, appliqué and embroidery techniques, and the complex design includes a wide variety of references to the domestic, built and geographical landscape. A printed cotton showing birds and butterflies has been used directly in the top left and right of the object, and as the design template for the two pieced birds and for several butterflies in the garden scenes. All of the non-figurative panels (comprising geometric patterns) are symmetrical, both in design and in the textiles used. It is lined with a plain-weave white linen. Pieced with the initials M/C/B and dated 1797.

This object was probably created as a decorative bedcover for a fashionable middling or upper-class household. The bedroom was one of the main spaces in which women could demonstrate their knowledge of the latest fashions through the careful coordination of upholstery and furnishings, and this piece may have been shown to visitors as they were led from room to room to admire the decor.

The leisure pursuits of such women were fashioned by various categories of trade, time, space and travel. Nowhere is the collusion between these more apparent that on this patchwork coverlet, where the maker has created a microcosm of her world in cloth. Surrounding the central timepiece are domestic tools, including a pincushion, needle, thread and scissors. As the borders extend outwards, the references move outside the home into the garden, where there are ducks, birds, butterflies and trailing honeysuckle. At the far left and right of the coverlet, the maker has pieced two vases similar in shape to neoclassical examples of the late eighteenth century. The four corners extend out to the far corners of the world, where the maker has drawn on map samplers as the inspiration for England and Wales, Scotland and the Eastern and Western Hemispheres.

With more than 40 patches in some of the small figurative scenes, the maker of this object would have required access to an extensive range of textiles, either by involvement in the trade or through conspicuous consumption. The detailed composition and considerable size of the piece also suggest the luxuries of time and space. (see pp.152–5)

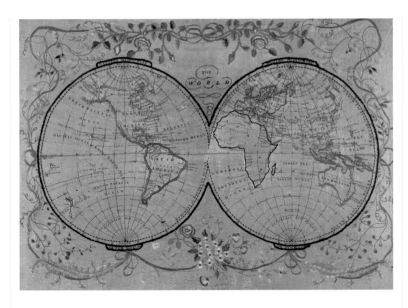

18 Between Counting

Nicola Naismith
Norfolk
2009
DVD 1 minute 43 seconds
Collection of the artist

Throughout her career, Nicola Naismith has explored the relationships between hand-skills and technical processes. Recently she has been researching the historical and contemporary nature of needle manufacturing, using macro photography to explore notions of scale and video to present initially ambiguous images. The needles used in her research come from a manufacturing facility in southern India, where they produce between 25 and 30 million hand sewing needles per week.

Centred around the 'between' needle, this piece explores the connection between the industrial and the hand-made: a manufactured object which enables hand-skills. Using video to create a new level of intimacy, the piece encourages the viewer to recognize the quilter's needle as something other than a solitary tool.

Presenting a thousand or so needles en masse, 'Between counting' explores bodily dexterity. As the activity develops, the imagery becomes increasingly recognisable, with an intimacy developing as the cold steel of the needle is warmed and manoeuvred by the hand. As Naismith comments, 'Traditional (needles) and technological (video) tools are combined to offer an insight into what happens before the needle punctures the surface of the cloth and how the body can be viewed as its own site specific'. The hand and the body become the points of transition: the connective tissue between the needle's history of mass production, and its role as the individual tool of the maker.

17 Map sampler

Maker unknown
Britain
Late eighteenth century
45 x 64cm
V&A: T.44–1951
Bequeathed by I.M.C. Robinson

Silk satin ground with a printed design showing a map of the two hemispheres. Embroidered with silk in running, outline, split, stem, satin and long and short stitch. Inscribed 'The World', 'Eastern Hemisphere/Old World' and 'Western Hemisphere/New World'.

Early samplers were reference points for embroiderers, showing 'samples' of how to achieve particular stitches or patterns. By the seventeenth century they were being created by young girls as part of their education in needlework, and by the eighteenth century map samplers such as this one were particularly popular. Pupils were encouraged to demonstrate an engagement with the world around them, ranging from the field layout of a nearby estate to the globe, or even the solar system. Such complex maps as the two hemispheres were almost always undertaken on printed grounds, which were effectively sampler kits, although generally left with bare borders to allow for some personalized decoration. Map samplers like this would have been framed like pictures and displayed, and provided a source of inspiration for further projects, such as the patchwork examples used in the corners of T.102–1938 (cat. no.16).

The popularity of map samplers among young girls in the eighteenth century was part of a more widespread interest in cartography. Parading an international outlook while also displaying elegant drawing techniques, the paper map-making trend was pursued by many gentlewomen.

19 Coverlet
Possibly made by a member of the Kershaw family
Middleton, Greater Manchester
1804–1811
268 x 268cm
V&A: T.382–1960
Given by Alice B. Kershaw

Unlined white cotton coverlet of block-printed and glazed cottons, most of which can be dated to the years 1804–11. Techniques include piecing, appliqué and *broderie perse*. A square central compartment contains a printed peacock. Further square compartments contain flowers, chinoiserie vases and other fashionable printed cottons. The outer border of the coverlet has a red ground printed in black, with a classical design of urns alternating with a group containing eagles and lyres.

The red and black neoclassical border of this coverlet was printed for George Anstey, a leading London linen-draper, in 1804. The Chinese vases are from two fabrics printed at Bannister Hall in 1805 and 1806. The little zigzag border surrounding the central panel was also printed for Anstey in 1805, and the palm tree with white blossom at the base in 1811.

Bannister Hall near Preston was one of the leading print works for woodblock chintzes in England in the early nineteenth century, producing innovative and constantly changing designs. Many of these were created by leading designers of the day, made exclusively for leading suppliers.

According to the donor, this coverlet was made in the Greater Manchester area by a member of the Kershaw family. The Kershaws owned a medical practice in Middleton in the early nineteenth century, and later moved to Wales.

20 Coverlet
Ann Randoll
Somerset
Dated 1802
375 x 300cm
V&A: T.32–2007
Given by the Coate family in memory of
Randoll Coate

Patchwork coverlet of a wide range of printed
cotton and linen dress fabrics. The central panel
shows a pieced and appliquéd flower created
from printed cottons. This is surrounded by a
circular border of small appliquéd panels
embroidered with various flowers, including
forget-me-nots, and several dense patchwork
and appliqué borders. The patchwork designs
include clamshells (see pp.56–7), hexagons,
flowers and triangles, and the textiles include
woven, block-printed, embroidered and resist-
printed designs. Most of the textiles date to
between 1780 and 1820. It is lined in linen with a
woven yellow stripe. Embroidered 'Ann
Randoll/ October 27 1802'.

The range of textiles suggests that they
were collected over a significant period of time.
During this period, the market was flooded with
a new range of printed cotton goods that could
be used to create light, bright cotton covers for
the bedroom. A short story from the early
nineteenth century (*The History of Polly Patchwork*,
1815) suggests that tailors and dress-makers
were capitalizing on this growing trend by
offering cuttings and fragments for sale: 'She
went sometimes to Bristol to buy meal and salt,
and she took the opportunity of going to a
great many dress-makers, from whom she got a large
packet of cuttings, which were too small for
general sale.'

According to the donor's family history,
the maker of this coverlet was Ann Randoll,
a resident of Somerset in the late eighteenth
and early nineteenth centuries. The inscription
at the centre is significantly earlier than some
of the textiles, suggesting that it may
commemorate a personal event in the
maker's life.

2 Private thoughts, public debates

21 Coverlet
Probably Elisabeth Chapman
Kent
*c.*1829
183.5 x 161.5cm
V&A: T.428–1985
Given by Gwendolyn Baker in memory of her
husband, Stephen Baker

Unlined patchwork coverlet of a wide range of block-printed cottons in the repeating pattern now known as 'jockey's cap'. Most of the prints date from the first quarter of the nineteenth century. A block-printed central panel shows flowers tied with a blue ribbon, with the inscriptions 'Wellington' and 'Vittoria'. The panel was printed to commemorate the last battle of the Peninsula War in 1813. The printed

cottons include coral-like shapes, stripes, spots and flowers. The tacking stitches and paper template are still intact. Under the central motif is a panel of plain white linen, on which is embroidered in dark-blue silk the following verse:

> O luck husband blest of heav'n
> To thee the Privilege is given
> A much lovd wife at home to keep
> Caress touch talk to – even sleep
> Thrice happy mortal envied lot
> What a rare treasure thou hast got
> Who to a woman can lay claim
> Who s [sic] temper ev ry [sic] day the same

Also embroidered in cross-stitch are the names 'John and Elisabeth Chapman' and

'September 19 1829'. The maker has used a slightly different shade of blue silk, and their placement suggests they were added after the completion of the verse.

The central inscription on this coverlet is taken from an epitaph written by William Grove and published in various formats in the late eighteenth and early nineteenth centuries, including *The Gentleman's Magazine* of 1793. The epitaph was dedicated to Mary Van Butchell, who – at the request of her husband – was embalmed after her death in 1775 and put on display in the family home in London. In choosing this verse, the maker may have been alluding to the scandalous story that captured popular imagination, or she may simply have selected it as a charming and witty inscription for her coverlet. The range of dates in the

coverlet, including papers dating from the 1790s and a central commemorative panel produced in 1813, suggests that it was worked on over a number of years, but never finished. The fabrics are thought to have been sourced near Rochester, as some of the receipts in the template relate to commercial premises in the area. (see pp.124–9)

According to the donor, this object was created for the marriage of John and Elisabeth Chapman, residents of the village of Twitton in Kent. The papers still visible in the reverse of the unlined coverlet were thought to be love letters between the two, but the template reveals a typical range of papers available in the middle-class home: ledger books, children's copy books, advertisements, newspapers and receipts.

22 Punctuation

Sara Impey
England
2009
126 x 126cm
V&A

Quilt with a cream silk background, free machine quilted in polyester threads. Quilted with the words:

SEE YOU SUDDENLY ONE DAY/ AT/ THE GAP
BETWEEN THOUGHTS/ OR IN/ THE COLOUR OF
SPEECH/ OR ALONG/ THE DASH OF THE STITCH/
OR BEYOND/ THE PINPOINT OF FOCUS/ OR
AROUND/ THE CURVE OF THE QUESTION/ OR
ON/ THE BRINK OF OMISSION/ OR UNDER/ THE
IMPRINT OF FOOTNOTES/ OR THROUGH THE
TEXTURE OF SCRIPT/ OR ABOVE/ THE SHOUT
OF THE SURFACE/ OR INSIDE THE WEB OF
CROSS-REFERENCE/ OR BEFORE/ THE LILT OF
THE COMMA/ OR AFTER/ THE FINAL FULL-STOP/
NEVER DID LIKE/ PUNCTUATION/ SEE YOU
SUDDENLY ONE DAY

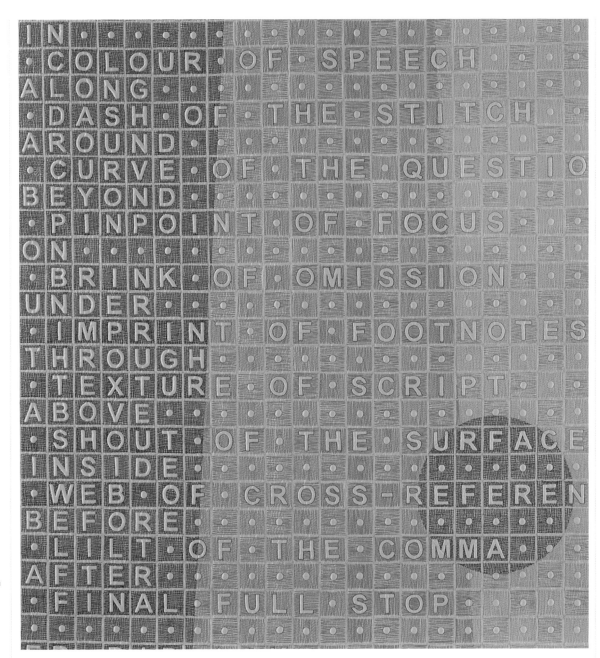

Delicately unravelling a web of mythologies, 'Punctuation' explores the ways in which text can inspire acts of quiltmaking. Captivated by 'the narrative that imbues every quilt', 'Punctuation' was born out of a fractured love story, based on a letter that came to light whilst Impey was searching her mother's belongings after her death. The letter was kept for many years in a chest of drawers containing bottles of perfume and bath essences, and hints at a former relationship between her mother and a family friend. In conversation, Impey speaks of the suprise of discovering a hidden, intimate history, stowed away yet treasured amongst personal possessions. She also notes the enduring power of this story to resurrect itself, its will to survive, and the perpetual allure of the words on the page. She chose two phrases from the letter to work with: 'see you suddenly one day' and 'never did like punctuation'. Without its full stop, the sentence resists closure, instead presenting the possibility of endless renewal. These phrases in turn inspired the rest of the text, and 'Punctuation' explores the emotions that arise when a seemingly complete chapter of experience is reopened, and redefines the present.

Impey's work is a palimpsestic layering of cloth and stitch; a gentle and sometimes unsettling reworking of past events through needle and thread. Trained as a journalist, Impey views words and narrative as implicit to quiltmaking: often constructed over a long period of time, every quilt is imbued with the experience of the maker. By using text, this narrative 'can become explicit as well'.

23 Coverlet

Maker unknown
Britain
1803–05
288 x 288cm
V&A: T.9–1962
Given by Gertrude S. Ferraby

Unlined appliqué and patchwork coverlet made from a wide variety of plain and printed cottons. At the centre is a circular, figurative panel that has been pieced, appliquéd and embroidered, showing the review of volunteer troops in Hyde Park by King George III. The image is taken from a print by John Singleton Copley of 1799. The ground is white cotton with a repeating pieced design of segmented circles in printed cottons. Each circle has a variety of different patterns within it, including stars, squares, crosses, diamonds and flowers. The printed cottons include coral-like shapes, dots, florals, hearts and anchors. Many are block-printed cottons from the late eighteenth century, and some were originally glazed. The central panel may have been inserted after the completion of this patchwork, as it cuts through two pieced representations of the sun and the moon. It suggests that the two may once have been separate patchwork projects, although they may have been worked by the same hand. The border comprises 40 appliqué vignettes, alternately circular and oval in shape, showing patriotic, domestic and naval scenes taken from contemporary prints and paintings. The number of patches per scene ranges from around 23 to 45. Additional embroidery has been added to the central panel and border, worked with polychrome silks in chain, satin and long and short stitches. There is also evidence of drawing, and some areas have been stamped with black ink, such as the small birds in the central medallion. Several small embroidered inscriptions appear within the border vignettes, including 'I am sorry to inform you there must be another campaign' on a soldier's letter, and the Lord's Prayer being read by a mother to her child.

This patchwork coverlet was worked during a period of intense naval euphoria. British naval power was seen as crucial to winning the war against Napoleon, and this coverlet draws on many of the patriotic prints circulating at the time. (see pp.156–61)

Prints of Britannia ruling the waves were immensely popular, as were aspirational prints, including fashion plates that showed the public a desirable, modern world. One of the border vignettes depicts a woman at a spinet, which has been taken from *The Lady's Magazine* of 1798.

24 Bedcover

Maker unknown
England
*c.*1810
243 x 211cm
V&A: T.25–1961
Given by Elizabeth Clarke

Quilted patchwork bedcover of printed cottons.
At the centre is a ready-printed basket of
flowers, including lilies, carnations and daffodil
buds. The basket is flanked by the rose and
thistle, and a cluster of shamrocks appears
beneath it. The panel commemorates the
golden jubilee of George III, and is inscribed
'G 50 R'. Most of the printed cottons date from
the early nineteenth century but the floral
border is a later addition. The maker has used
both appliqué and piecing techniques to create
the patchwork design, which includes the design
now known as 'tumbling blocks'. The reverse is
white cotton. The bedcover was originally
quilted with an all over chevron pattern. An X-
ray of the bedcover revealed an earlier quilt at
the centre, used for the wadding. The
construction of the quilt top suggests that some
of the patches were applied directly to this
earlier quilt rather than pieced together. When
the new top was added, a secondary quilting
pattern of interlocking circles was carried out.

The central panel shown here was one of
several printed textile designs that could be
used to declare allegiance and loyalty to the
state. This particular textile commemorates the
first recorded Golden Jubilee of a British
monarch, King George III. The V&A has two
other examples of the jubilee print, including
one that has been incorporated into another
bedcover.

25 Coverlet

Joanna Southcott, 1750–1814 (reputedly)
London
c.1808
249 x 225cm
RAMM 13/1974/2
Collection of the Royal Albert Memorial
Museum
Given by Lily Bucket on behalf of the Southcott
Society 1974

Unlined patchwork coverlet. Block-, plate- and
roller-printed and resist-dyed indigo cottons,
linens and chintz. It has no wadding and has not
been quilted. The hourglass pattern is made by
piecing triangles together, in this case using a
combination of light and dark fabrics. In the
centre panel a piece of canvas with 'Joanna
Southcott 1808', embroidered in hair, has been
added. This canvas piece may have come from
another piece and been added at a later date.
On the back a paper label tacked on reads:
'Frances Taylors quilt June 18th 1810'.

This coverlet was reputedly made by Joanna
Southcott. The panel at the centre is said to
have been stitched using her own hair, and the
emblems such as the star motif were thought to
have been among her favourites. On the reverse
is the name Frances Taylor: the daughter of one
of Joanna's former employers. It is possible that
the coverlet was created for Frances.

Born near Ottery St Mary, Devon, in 1750,
Joanna Southcott became renowned for her
visions and prophecies. In around 1792 she first
heard an inner voice, which she named the Spirit
of Truth. Joanna published her first book,
Strange Effects of Faith, in 1801 and moved to
London a year later. She was satirized in
contemporary publications and failed to gain
official recognition from the Church and the
state, but continued to publish her visions and
prophecies, which by the time of her death
totalled 65 books. At the height of her fame she
had around 14,000 followers, who had all
purchased her 'seal' as a passport to Heaven.
She had many other supporters, including
members of the Church who had not been
'sealed'. In 1814, aged 64, she announced that
she was pregnant with the new Messiah, a child
who would be called 'Shiloh'. When Joanna
died on 27 December 1814, there was no
evidence of a baby. Her followers, such as the
Panacea Society, believe that the child was born
ethereally on 25 December. A chest reputedly
containing Joanna's writings and prophecies is
in the care of the Panacea Society, and can only
be opened at a time of future distress and in the
presence of 24 bishops. **PM**

26 Bedcover

Maker unknown
England
*c.*1838
271.5 x 274cm
V&A: T.196–1965
Given by F.N. Armstrong

Quilted patchwork bedcover of roller-printed cottons. In the centre is a square panel from a commemorative textile, showing two repeats of the coronation of Queen Victoria. The cotton includes the royal coat of arms at the head of each repeat, plus representations of the rose, thistle and shamrocks. The panel is surrounded by a series of seven wide patchwork borders of printed cotton dating from the first half of the nineteenth century. The reverse is cream cotton. Quilted in cotton thread with interlacing circles, leaf shapes, chevrons and other geometric patterns.

The textile at the centre of this quilt celebrates the coronation of Queen Victoria that took place in 1838. It shows the scene in Westminster Abbey when the crown was placed on her head.

From the time of her coronation, the image of Queen Victoria captured the public imagination. Her portrait could be found throughout the country: in magazines and advertisements, and on commemorative textiles such as this one.

Victoria's youth (she was crowned at the age of 19) and charm were perceived by many as a new start for the monarchy. After witnessing the throngs of people that turned out for her formal procession, Queen Victoria wrote:

*many as there were the day I went to the City, it
was nothing – nothing, to the multitudes, the
millions, of my loyal subjects who were
assembled in every spot to witness the
Procession. Their good-humour and excessive
loyalty was beyond everything and I really
cannot say how proud I feel to be the Queen of
such a Nation.*

27 Bedcover

Maker unknown
Possibly Brecon, Wales
c.1820
264 x 239cm
F73.122.2
Collection of St Fagans: National History
Museum
Given by Emeritus Professor William Rees

Quilted patchwork bedcover made from a range of printed dress cottons arranged in triangles. A printed central octagonal panel contains a portrait of Queen Caroline, consort of King George IV, with the inscription 'Her Most Gracious Majesty, Caroline Queen of England'. The quilting pattern consists of a central roundel containing a star within a circle and four-petalled flowers. Two narrow inner borders feature spirals and triangles; the outer border contains spirals within triangles. The quilting does not follow the lines of the patchwork. The reverse is white linen. The wadding is carded wool.

Very little is known about the exact origins of this object. According to the donor, it came from Brecon in Wales, but the name and occupation of the maker are unknown.

Printed commemorative panels were very popular during the early nineteenth century. They were often used as focal points for pieced frame coverlets and quilts, enabling the maker to build the quilt outwards until the cover reached the required size. This central panel contains an image of Caroline of Brunswick, who reigned as consort from 29 January 1820 to 7 August 1821. The V&A has a printed cotton handkerchief in its collection that is almost identical to the panel (V&A:1739–1913).

Queen Caroline gained much public support during her ill-fated marriage to the Prince Regent, later George IV. As early as 1813 Jane Austen declared: 'Poor woman, I shall support her as long as I can, because she is a Woman, and because I hate her Husband.' She was famously refused entry to Westminster Abbey for the coronation service on 19 July 1821 and was never crowned as queen. Every sordid detail was reported in the popular press in a way that foreshadows the modern cult of celebrity. **EP**

28 Bedcover

Possibly made by a member of the Evans family
Possibly Wales
1800–50
234 x 204cm
V&A: T.124–1937

Quilted patchwork bedcover made from a range of block-printed, discharged and roller-printed cottons, including floral prints. Most of the cottons were originally glazed. The central section shows two large-scale printed designs: one of red flowers against a yellow ground (cut into an octagon to form the central piece), and one of red birds and palm trees against a blue ground. Both date from 1815–20. The most recent cotton, a repeating rosebud pattern on a black ground, dates from the 1840s. There are 156 patches in total, and the design is largely symmetrical, with the exception of an area designed for the pillow at the head of the bed. It is quilted in cotton thread in a design which includes coils, ram's horns, leaves and repeating twists. The name 'Evans' is written in ink on a hand-stitched label on the reverse (possibly a laundry mark). It is lined with cream cotton and wadded with cotton.

This bedcover was owned by a family from Pwllheli, Caernarfonshire. It is not known if this is where it was made, but the family believed that it may have had a Welsh provenance. The cottons are typical of those used for furnishings, such as curtains, and many have been recycled from fabrics available in the home.

There is very little information on domestic patchwork and quilting from this period, but Ellen Stock (née Weeton), a Lancashire governess, left behind a detailed account of early nineteenth-century life. Among her correspondence are letters to her daughter, describing the importance of reusing textiles available within the home. When sending a parcel of patches and ribbon for use in patchwork, she urged her daughter to practise measuring, cutting and sewing, while also acknowledging the monetary value of textiles, 'for you will never be fit to be a housekeeper unless you know the value of most things in daily use'.

29 Bedcover

Maker unknown
England
1810–45
268 x 270cm
V&A: T.17–1924
Given by Maude Marchant

Patchwork and quilted bedcover, made with a wide range of printed cottons dating from the first half of the nineteenth century, with some from the first two decades. At the centre there is an octagonal, ready-printed panel of pink roses. The quilt is interlined with a coarse woven woollen fabric and is quilted in cotton thread in a design of repeating squares. The reverse is a brown printed cotton. Other prints include shaded stripes, checks and spotted fabrics.

No information was available on the provenance of this quilt when it was donated to the Museum in 1924, but the huge range of printed cottons hints at the use and recycling of textiles in this early nineteenth-century household. One large square in the top left-hand corner was cut from a printer's end: the remnant at the end of a roll of printed cotton that is usually discarded. These fragments were available directly from the factories, as well as via warehouses, pedlars and drapers.

The ready-printed panel at the centre is typical of those fashionable in the first quarter of the nineteenth century, although many were stowed away and treasured, to be used in projects at a later date. The central panel of T.428–1985 (cat no.21), for example, was printed to commemorate the Battle of Victoria in 1813 but sits alongside textiles from the 1830s.

30 Bedcover

Maker unknown
England
1830s
259 x 251.5cm
V&A: T.154–1964
Given by A.M. Johns

Quilted patchwork bedcover, worked in the design sometimes referred to as 'mariner's compass', using various printed textiles dating from the early nineteenth century. Many of the cottons were originally glazed. The inner borders include one of triangles, and one in the design now known as 'jockey's cap'. The outermost border is a patchwork design of interlocking triangles. The quilt has a reverse of cream cotton and is quilted with various designs, including clamshells and a star in a circle. The widest border is quilted in a running feather pattern. The quilting also follows the design of the patchwork in other areas. It is wadded with thick wool. There are 1,128 patches in total.

This bedcover was created during a period in which the domestic production of quilted patchwork increased in both working- and middle-class homes. Women were keen to produce items that signalled their aspirations towards gentility, as suggested by George Eliot in *The Mill on the Floss*:

> *Oh, dear, oh, dear, Maggie, what are you thinkin' of, to throw your bonnet down there? Take it upstairs, there's a good gell, an' let your hair be brushed, an' put your other pinafore on, an' change your shoes, do, for shame; an' come an' go on with your patchwork, like a little lady.*

The choice of textiles typifies the fashion for dense patterns and bright colours in the second quarter of the nineteenth century. Many of the cottons date from the 1820s. The pieced patterns shown here also grew in popularity in the nineteenth century and were later given names such as 'jockey cap' and 'mariner's compass'.

31 Quilting Point
Clio Padovani
Winchester
2010
DVD – six-minute loop
Collection of the artist

'Quilting Point' takes as its inspiration the techniques of appliqué and patchwork, digitally layering fragment over fragment. Describing her inspiration, Clio Padovani reflects on the ability of digital technology to replicate the processes of patchwork:

> I was drawn to explore how to reference quilting techniques with fragments of moving images, how to structure and organize a textile media narrative. Just like the scraps of fabric traditionally used to make a quilt possess an intimacy born of everyday personal and family use, I wanted the video clips to have the feel of public and private – to reflect images we might see everyday, with our eyes, or in our mind.

The work is also a commentary on a shared, collective past, with particular reference to the quilting bee. She describes how

> the shaped movie clips pulse and breathe on the screen, enlarging, contracting, constructing a collective dialogue: the blocks of images change and transform into patterns organized by the framework of personal experience. The story of the fabrics becomes individualized, structured by the pattern. The voice is the thread: it connects and constructs, it pieces together this sequence or story, this kind of cloth.

The subtle voices and whispers are designed to stimulate thoughts which, like thread, bind together the pictures on the screen.
    Trained as a weaver and captivated by the mark of the hand, Padovani speaks of both a metaphorical and material 'point' at which cloth, text and dialogue connect.

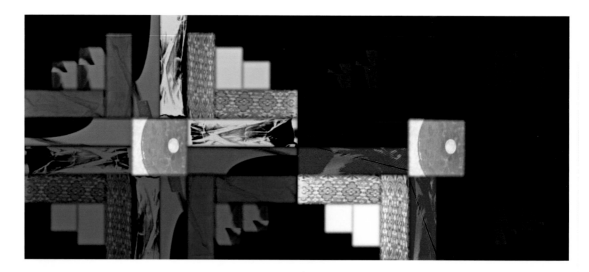

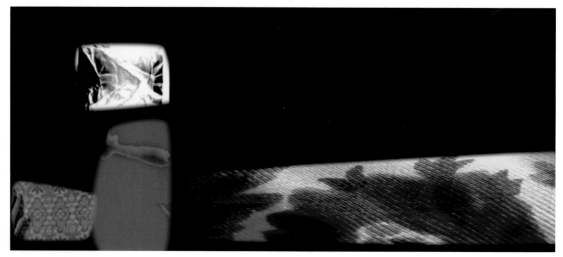

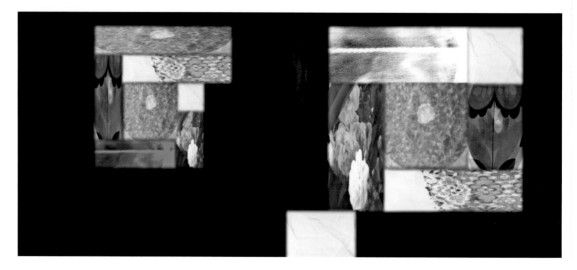

32 Bedcover

Maker unknown
Britain
1800–40
255 x 250cm
V&A: T.340–1977
Given by Hugh Lee

Quilted patchwork bedcover of printed cottons in a number of small-scale patterns. Some are dress fabrics that date from the 1820s to 1840s. There are 1,690 patches in total. It is quilted in cotton thread in what is now known as the 'wine-glass' pattern (overlapping circles). The reverse has been constructed from eight separate pieces of cotton and linen. It is wadded with cotton.

This quilt was created at a time when the expansion of the textile industry improved the supply of cottons to consumers. The repeal of the Excise Duty in 1831 made most goods for home consumption 30–40 per cent cheaper. Radical new textile designs were developed, with the emphasis placed on 'novelty' – such as the four large square pieces of printed cotton resembling patches of fur seen here. Such designs were popular throughout the 1830s.

The wider availability of cottons had an impact on the creation of patchwork by both the working and middle classes. In *Sylvia's Lovers* (1863) Elizabeth Gaskell describes the domestic arrangements in a retired farmhouse in the North of England, where:

*the united efforts of some former generation
of the family had produced patchwork
curtains and coverlet; and patchwork was
patchwork in those days, before the early Yates
and Peels [textile manufacturers] had found
out the secret of printing the parsley-leaf.
Scraps of costly Indian chintzes and
palempours were intermixed with commoner
black and red calico in minute hexagons; and
the variety of patterns served for the useful
purpose of promoting conversations as well as
the more obvious one of displaying the
workwoman's taste.*

33 Box
Diana Harrison
London
2010
215 x 165cm
Collection of the artist

Diptych of pieced and quilted silk, with an
interfacing layer and a cotton backing. Machine-
and hand-stitched.

Diana Harrison's work is intimate and
quietly intense. While referencing the tradition
of quiltmaking through its techniques, this piece
gently questions the perceived function of the
quilt as a vehicle for comfort, warmth and
solace. This diptych centres on the function and
form of the box: a structure designed to contain
and protect its contents. Opened out and
flattened, its function is questioned and the
contents released, leading to an overriding sense
of vulnerability. The final construction of this
'quilt' appears unstable. The open seams,
curving and falling flaps suggest disintegration
and fragility.

Harrison creates pieces which reflect the
roles of women as custodians of their local and
domestic environment, frequently collecting as
her inspiration the weathered fragments from
both urban and rural landscapes: the washed-up
debris of the Kentish coastline, or the flattened
cardboard discarded in urban centres.

In this instance, the surface printing suggests
the worn and discarded quality of paper and
card found in street litter, alongside many boxes
salvaged from the regular piles put out for
recycling each week from local shops. The
process of transformation is long and labour-
intensive: the cloth is dyed black, the shapes are
prepared and layered, and then machine-
stitched. Each piece is washed, shrunk and dried
before screen overprinting with a bleaching
agent. This is followed by washing and finishing
before construction starts by hand-stitching.
Through this process, surfaces are reworked and
transformed to become something new: a
reflection on the role of stitch to move the
maker beyond the everyday. For Harrison, the
process reflects the potential of stitch to create a
space for contemplation beyond the
distractions of day-to-day life.

34 Bedcover

Maker unknown
Penparc, Cardigan, Wales
1860s
209 x 188cm
Collection of Jen Jones

Quilted patchwork bedcover of wool flannel in the pieced design known as 'strippy', with a reverse of plain wool flannel. It is quilted in an all-over design that includes coils and leaves. The rectangular central panel is a paisley shawl, with an appliquéd design of silk satin that includes hearts and a butterfly.

According to the oral history accompanying this bedcover, it was made in Penparc on the Cardiganshire/Pembrokeshire borders. The design takes as its starting point the strippy quilt, constructed by stitching together strips of contrasting fabrics.

The bedcover is created almost entirely from wool flannel, which is likely to have been carded, spun and woven in Wales. It documents the everyday, domestic activities of those working in local textile manufacturing. The design is unusual in that an additional layer of charm and individuality has been added with the appliquéd design at the centre, using a shawl border and small pieces of silk satin. Shawls were valuable and desirable items, completing the fashionable woman's ensemble from around 1780 to 1870. As well as the imported woven Kashmir shawls, printed and woven examples were created by British manufacturers, including those based at Paisley – a place that has now become synonymous with the description of these objects. The use of a shawl border here suggests its preciousness and value to the maker.

3 Virtue and virtuosity

35 Coverlet or hanging
Ann West
England
Dated 1820
244 x 221cm
V&A: T.23–2007
Acquired with the support of the Contributing
and Life Members of the Friends of the V&A

Inlaid patchwork and appliqué hanging or
coverlet of plain- and twill-weave wools.
Appliqué and embroidery have been widely
used, with many of the textiles manipulated to
give the impression of three-dimensional
garments draped over the human figures. A
central panel shows Adam in the Garden of
Eden, surrounded by scenes taken from the
Bible, including 'The Death of Abel' (Genesis
4:15), 'Jacob's Dream' (Genesis 4:12) and 'Daniel
in the Lion's Den' (Daniel 7:16). The maker has
included 54 smaller panels at the top and
bottom showing scenes from early nineteenth-
century life, which include 'Milk Maid',
'Sportsman', 'Coach man', 'Gardener', 'School
Boy', 'Auctioneer', 'Cryer', 'Sweeps' and 'An old
woman selling nets etc'. Many of the scenes are
titled in either ink or stitch, and the pieced
panels have been outlined in a decorative
chainstitch. The lower edge is decorated with
hand-painted felt silhouettes of marine life. It is
edged in scalloped dark-brown wool, with small
yellow and red dots appliquéd in the centre of
each scallop. It is lined in red cotton. Other
embroidered details include 'Ann West's work,
1820', 'Remember me' and 'Forget me not'.

With its scenes of both biblical and secular
life, this cover or hanging may have been
intended as an educational device for children.
Patchwork projects were often started at school,
and the scenes shown here are typical of the
religious and historical instruction that British
schoolchildren would have received at this time.

The piece also offers a glimpse into the
public debates simmering in the early
nineteenth century. One panel, entitled 'Negro
Servant and Master', refers to slavery, which was
not formally prohibited in the British Empire
until 1833 (see pp.88–91).

Ann West was a common name which
makes it difficult to establish for certain the
maker of this cover. However, a milliner called
Ann West, listed at High Street, Chippenham, in
Pigot & Co's *National and Commercial Directory* of
1829, may have been its maker.

36 Cover or hanging
Maker unknown
Britain
1875–85
161.3 x 118cm
V&A: T.200–1969
Given by R. Wood

Cover or hanging of dark-blue wool with
appliqué decoration of plain- and twill-weave
wools, silk velvets and a small patch of fur. Each
panel shows a scene relating to a love story, with
figures in costumes of the late 1870s to early
1880s. The scenes are embroidered with the
titles: Admiration, Beauty, Cupid, Doves, Eyes,
Flowers, Guardian, Hopes, Introduction,
Jealousy, Kisses, Love Letters, Matrimony,
Nonsence [sic], Offers, Papa, Quaking, Refusal,
Spells, Tiffs, Uncle, Valentines, Wedding,
Xpression, Yes, Zingari. The figures are created
from appliquéd and inlaid wool, with
embroidered detail in silk thread. The border
consists of 30 squares of black felt, outlined with
thin borders of beige felt. Further figures and
motifs have been applied to each border square.
The seams of the pieced design have been
outlined in a decorative cross-stitch. It has a
reverse of blue wool. The object shows
evidence of at least two hands.

The central panels of this cover or hanging
depict the various rituals and emotions
associated with courtship, moving from
'Admiration' to 'Zingari' (an archaic term for the
Romany community). These images are framed
by a border that references an array of cultural
figures and symbols, including fairground
favourites such as Mr Punch, and gaming cards
in the four corners. Coupled with the size of the
object, these references suggest that it may have
been created in relation to a card game. Textiles
with playing-card motifs became particularly
popular in the 1880s and '90s.

It was common to associate love and
gambling at this time. In George Eliot's novel
Daniel Deronda (1876) games of chance are
played both around the gaming table and with
the heart. The gestures of the central figures on
the cover also suggest the widespread appeal of
melodrama. Prints, plays, novels and the music
hall all helped to popularize the form and many
of its associated characters.

This cover was probably made between
1875 and 1885, given the fashionable dress of its
central figures. According to the donor, it was
worked by an ancestor on a long sea voyage.

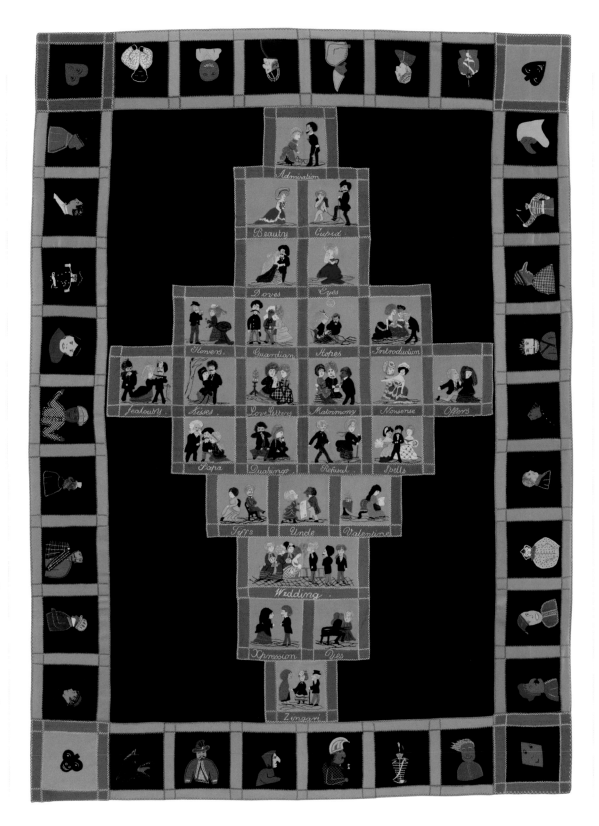

37 How many times do I have to repeat myself

Caren Garfen
London
2010
300 x 200cm
Collection of the artist

Hand-stitched and quilted patchwork bedcover. Silkscreen-printed cotton, hand-embroidered in silk thread. Wadded with a reverse of cotton.

'How many times do I have to repeat myself' is a domestic art work that combines text and stitch to offer a layered statement. For Garfen, the title reflects the three main components of quilt production: the time invested in creating the piece, the repetitive nature of quilt-making, and the sound of a woman's voice. Combining intricate hand embroidery and silkscreen printing, Gafen's exquisitely wrought flowers and leaves are painstakingly worked in the tradition of the needlewomen who carried out professional work within a domestic context. Here, in a reflection of the modern interior, they are embedded in the consumables and white goods that define the modern domestic landscape: washing machines, sofas, kettles and computers. In some cases, the patches have been printed with illustrations taken from the covers of contemporary women's magazines. As Garfen comments, 'these were chosen to echo back to the early quilts in which papers cut from penny weeklies were used as backing patchwork shapes in the creation of the quilts'.

The piece is centred around a study of women, the workplace and the home, compiled from detailed questionnaires and social studies, archival and academic research, as well as fiction and non-fiction relating to women stitching. Following the results, Garfen has created a piece which reflects the shared desire of her interviewees to move away from the workplace. As part of her study, Garfen also asked individual women to identify the most important domestic objects in their homes; these have been labelled with the woman's career, creating an intricate matrix between home and work. The painstakingly hand-stitched text adds a layer of humour that thinly veils a stark social statement: 'She had the weight of the world on her shoulders' accompanies an image of weighing scales, while 'She was programmed to do it all' sits alongside a television set.

The artist also asked women to contribute materials to the quilt, following the historical precedent of the quilting bee. In this case Garfen requested the 'fluff' residue from the inside of domestic clothes driers, explaining the importance of it to her concept:

> 'A bit of fluff' has been used as a description given to women by men. Small pieces of fluff are trapped within the quilt in the same way as women are trapped into working due to financial pressures when in reality they would prefer to remain at home.

The names of these contributors have been sewn onto a long 'care label'. Acknowledging countless generations of unnamed makers, Garfen's piece offers recognition for those contributing fluff to her quilt: 'the recognition which was lacking for their foremothers stitching their quilts.'

comfortable furniture

38 Cover
Maker unknown
Poole Keynes, Gloucestershire
1892–5
194 x 182cm
Geffrye: 21/1940
Collection of the Geffrye Museum

Embroidered patchwork and appliqué cover in the design known as a 'crazy' patchwork. There is evidence of at least two hands, and the cover was probably worked in panels. A figurative scene at the centre shows a church. A wide variety of fabrics have been used, including silks, velvets and wool suiting fabrics. It is embellished with a wide range of both hand-stitched and machine-stitched embroidery. Motifs include birds, moths, flowers, frogs and sewing tools. It is inscribed 'Poole Keynes Rectory 1892' and 'S.W. A.D. 1895'.

In the 1880s 'crazy' patchwork became immensely fashionable. It took its name from the seemingly random placement of brightly coloured velvets, satins, twills and other fabrics used in the design. Many makers exploited the vivid and eye-catching colours that flooded the market with the introduction of chemical dyes. Crazy patchwork was employed for numerous household articles, including quilts, cushions, piano covers, table covers and sofa pillows, and for small articles such as theatre and work bags. Magazines such as *Weldon's Practical Guide to Needlework* and *The Englishwoman's Domestic Magazine* (edited by the husband of the noted cookery writer Mrs Beeton) illustrated examples of what was alternatively termed 'Japanese' or 'kaleidoscope' patchwork. Embellishment, appliqué and embroidery were all promoted as the height of taste and fashion, contributing to an opulent and luxurious interior.

Crazy patchwork was also widely used for fund-raising activities. This particular object is thought to have been created by women affiliated with the Rectory at Poole Keynes, possibly as a collaborative project, because there is evidence of more than one hand. The design of elaborate botanical motifs, including beautiful moths and extravagant peacock feathers, was highly fashionable during the 1890s.

39 Whispers
Nina Saunders
London
2010
63 x 131 cm
Collection of the artist

Nina Saunders works with a variety of media,
including textiles, furniture and found objects.
Subverting any notion of the pastoral, domestic
idyll, her work is emotionally challenging and often
provocative. Saunders is drawn to acts of tension:
both at a material level through the controlled
manipulation of fabric, and at an emotional level
through the viewer's response to it. Her primary
technique is upholstery, carefully stretching fabric
to radically subvert notions of the everyday.
Saunders' inspiration for this piece is based on the
stories of maternal love and loss within the
context of the Foundling Museum. She was
particularly moved by the trinkets and pieces of
fabric pinned to babies – tokens of recognition
should the mother ever be financially able to
reclaim and support her child. Saunders' explores
the tension of this parting within the context of
the Victorian class structure.

In conversation, Saunders speaks of a place
where the old and new can merge. As a starting
point for this piece she has taken a nineteenth-
century workbox and vintage textiles. Saunders
challenges the original function of the workbox,
which would have traditionally contained
precious tools, possessions, secrets and keepsakes.
Here, the workbox ceases to be a symbol of
Victorian middle-class feminine virtue, expressed
through the art of stitching. Instead it acts as a
vehicle for remembrance; the tiny baby fists act as
a memorial to a lost childhood both physically and
metaphorically. Undermining any notion of
containment, the piece interrupts the comfort
and familiarity of the domestic sphere to question
how we view and use the objects that have
become part of our everyday space.

40 Coverlet

Maker unknown
Britain
c.1851
214 x 240cm
V&A: T.86–1957
Given by E.A. Hunt on behalf of the West Kent
Federation of Women's Institutes

Appliqué coverlet of printed-cotton silhouettes
on a cotton ground, including both animate and
inanimate objects: houses, socks, men on
horseback, trees, scissors and a range of animals.
At the centre is an octagonal ready-printed
cotton showing flowers against a pale-yellow
ground. On either side of the panel are
appliquéd silhouettes of *The Greek Slave* (1844) in
a printed cotton. It is lined with plain-weave
white cotton.

One of the most popular American statues
of the second half of the nineteenth century,
The Greek Slave portrays a Greek girl captured by
the Turks and put up for sale in a Middle Eastern
slave market. The sculptor said of his work:

> As there should be a moral in every work of
> art, I have given to the expression of the Greek
> slave what trust there could still be in a Divine
> Providence for a future state of existence, with
> utter despair for the present, mingled
> somewhat with scorn for all around her …
>   It is not her person but her spirit that stands
> exposed.

The statue became one of the most
recognizable and widely discussed figures of the
second half of the nineteenth century,
popularized through ballads, prints, satire,
journalistic commentaries and engravings. It was
exhibited in the American Section of the Great
Exhibition in 1851, and miniature copies were
available for the rest of the century; 'so
undressed, yet so refined, in sugar-white
alabaster, exposed under little glass covers in
such American homes as could bring
themselves to think such things right,' as the
writer Henry James remarked.

Little is known about the history of the
coverlet but it came to the attention of the WI
at an exhibition of needlework in East Kent
(c.1920–22). It was subsequently purchased by a
Miss Rowe and donated to the V&A in 1957.
Prior to acquisition, it was assessed by the quilt
historian Avril Colby, who suggested that the
striped 'fencing' border and range of animals

may indicate 'rural family life on a farm'. With
the identification of the central silhouettes, it is
now thought that the coverlet is a more active
engagement with the contemporaneous
debates and a wider culture of exhibition and
display.

41 Coverlet

Maker unknown
Britain
1850–1900
196.5 x 170cm
V&A: T.67–1970
Given by HM Queen Elizabeth II

Unlined patchwork and appliqué coverlet of printed cottons and linen. Most of the printed cottons date from before 1850, but one or two pieces date from after 1860. The appliqué decoration includes printed cotton flowers. 15 rectangles of linen have been applied to the cover. All of the rectangles are embroidered with a series of inscriptions worked with red and blue cotton in fine cross-stitch. The passages are taken from the Bible and alternate with short prayers. The inscriptions include John 3:16, Revelation 1:5 and 1:6, John 9:25 and 9:26, and the First Epistle of St Paul to the Thessalonians 4:16 and 4:17.

'Scripture coverlets' such as this were popular throughout the nineteenth and early twentieth centuries. Their production was encouraged by organizations and institutions to offer spiritual comfort and guidance during times of duress. Churches, Sunday schools, Bible classes, Temperance groups, ladies' sewing circles, hospital wards and asylums all advocated the benefits of recording Christian scripture while engaged in the act of stitch. *Hobbies* magazine in 1899 suggested that 'invalids find considerable pleasure in such coverlets … The words are sometimes arranged upon the coverlets that the occupants of neighbouring beds can read inscriptions upon the part that hangs over the edge.' This design principle is evident here.

Most examples, such as this one, date from the mid- to late nineteenth century. While some were made for the maker's own use, others were created as objects to be sold at church fairs and auctions. This example has embroidered panels, but others used ready-printed textiles, such as those promoted by Robert Mimpriss: an entrepreneur and textile printer born in 1797.

42 Right to Life

Grayson Perry
Britain
1993
250 x 250cm
Collection of the artist

Quilt of red, white and black velvet rhombuses in the 'tumbling block' design, embellished with computer-controlled embroidery in rayon thread. It is edged with a wide border of turquoise velvet.

For Perry, the potential of the quilt lies in its ability to act as a vessel for powerful and emotionally charged messages. At first glance this piece seems to follow the design known as 'tumbling blocks': the rhythmic repetition of rhombus shapes to create a *trompe l'oeil* effect. But closer inspection reveals an intricate design of rotating foetuses embroidered onto vivid velvets. Inverting the assumed role of the quilt as a domestic object of warmth and comfort, Perry creates a vehicle for an unsettling commentary, in this case the American abortion debate of the 1990s.

The quilt has been designed by the artist and professionally stitched by computer-controlled embroidery. It follows in the long tradition of quilt designers who marked out the quilt top, but sometimes outsourced the stitching. The sense of the hand is employed, but in a very different way.

In conversation, Perry – who is drawn to the collective meaning of quilts – speaks of the bed as a site of danger: the place traditionally associated with both birth and death. The quilt itself takes on the patina of age: the stains of the site in which we truly love and live.

43 Valance or cover

Maker unknown
England
1775–1825
264 x 69cm
V&A: T.312–1977
Given by V. Stenhouse

Unlined linen valance or cover, appliquéd with printed cottons. The ground is formed from three panels of linen that have been seamed together. All except one of the applied cottons are block-printed. One or two pieces show the dark grounds and mossy trails of the late eighteenth century. 'JD yds 21' is embroidered in cotton thread on the linen underneath one of the appliqué triangles, and is probably a linen-maker's mark. Four tucks have been created down the central fold of the object.

This small valance or cover was displayed at the *Naval, Shipping and Fisheries Exhibition* at Earl's Court in 1905 to commemorate the centenary of the Battle of Trafalgar, with a hand-written note stating: 'Nelson's quilt, was on Nelson's bed on board the *Victory* at Trafalgar'.

Viscount Horatio Nelson (1758–1805) was a British naval commander in the wars with revolutionary and Napoleonic France. He was celebrated as a national military hero, and the euphoria surrounding his success was on a scale rarely witnessed in Britain. Nelson was portrayed as not only a military but also a romantic hero and on his death, he was deeply and publicly mourned by both men and women. Relics associated with him were much prized.

44 Cover or hanging

James Williams
Wrexham, Wales
1842–52
234 x 203cm
35.632
Collection of St Fagans: National History Museum
Given by the maker's son, Mr R.J. Williams

Unlined, inlaid patchwork cover or hanging made from 4,525 separate pieces of fulled woollen cloths. The background is a pieced composition of small diamond patches, chevrons, squares and rhomboids. At the top centre is a crown, and in each respective corner is a rose, a thistle, a leek and a shamrock – the emblems of the constituent nations of the British Isles. The remainder of the coverlet is composed of figurative motifs, including Thomas Telford's Menai Suspension Bridge (completed in 1826), a Chinese pagoda, a black man hunting a wild horse, and Cefn Viaduct near Wrexham, complete with a crossing steam train. Other scenes include several biblical motifs: Jonah and the whale, Cain and Abel, Noah's Ark with a dove bearing an olive branch, and Adam naming the animals. Details are picked out through embroidery in silk thread.

This cover or hanging was made by James Williams, a master tailor from Wrexham in North Wales. According to family history, the tailor spent a decade completing the piece, the work being done in his leisure hours. The coverlet became an exhibition piece; it was displayed at the *Art Treasures Exhibition* in Wrexham in 1876, at the Palace of Arts in Wembley in 1925, and, to much public acclaim, at the Wrexham National Eisteddfod of 1933.

Examples of inlaid patchwork found in museum collections are more often than not the work of tailors. The technique requires a high degree of skill and the use of thick cloth to accommodate the over-sewing required. Meticulously pieced, James Williams' coverlet was made by recycling a variety of fulled woollen cloths.

The coverlet reflects a growing sense of national pride in the technological achievements of the day. In Victorian Britain, Telford's Menai Suspension Bridge became an icon of engineering, inspiring countless travelling artists and poets. Souvenir prints and engravings secured the bridge a place in the popular consciousness of the Welsh nation.

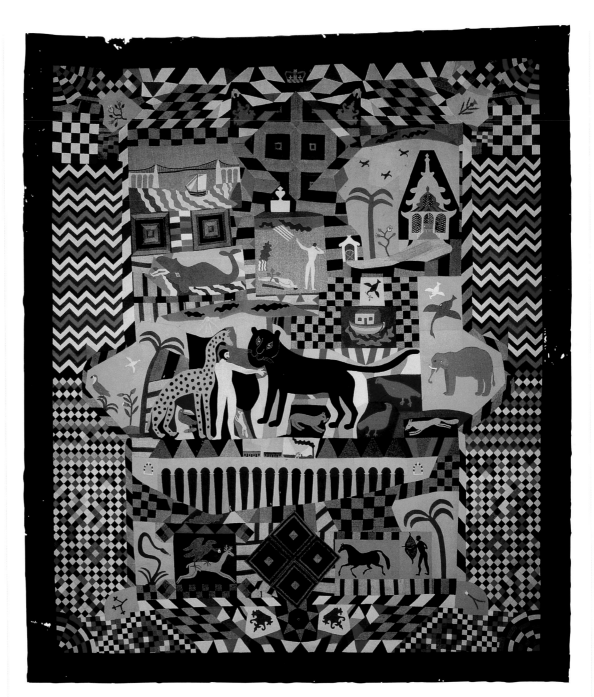

Influenced by military and missionary activities in colonized lands, Victorian Britain also sought knowledge about the wider world, as reflected by the black figure hunting a wild horse and the Chinese pagoda. Visual representations of 'the other' were often used to advertise and embellish products, from tea caddies to bone china. James Williams probably adapted his images from these sources. **EP**

45 Cover (The Royal Clothograph)

John Monro
Paisley, Renfrewshire
c.1830–50
200 x 200cm
E:1979.101
Collection of Culture and Sport Glasgow
(Museums)

Inlaid patchwork cover made using felted tailor's broadcloth with embroidered details worked in silk thread. The main layout has seven panels. Three panels along the top depict a seascape with ships (entitled 'Nelson'), a lion (entitled 'Burns') and a woman, building and ship (entitled 'Pleasure'). In the centre is one large panel with a church, woman and harbour entitled 'Prosperity in Winter'. Along the bottom are three panels depicting a seascape (entitled 'The Chase'), a sailor (entitled 'Britain for Ever') and a ship (entitled 'Elizabeth Brown'). A wide border is embroidered with the names of famous men and a couple of women. At the bottom is an embroidered inscription:

*John Monro The Paisley Artist-Tailor
Born May 16 1811 Author of the Royal
Clothograph Work of Art. This Piece of Art
took 18 years to complete at Odd Hours.
All round the border is the Names of Men
of Learning and Genius. Some before Christ.
To Gain the Grand End. We ought to keep
in Mind 7 words. 1st Push. 2nd Piety. 3rd
Patience. 4th Perseverance. 5th Punctuality.
6th Penetrate. 7th Please. Stop. Man Know
Thyself and others learn to know. Love God
and Man. Amen.*

The maker of this piece, John Monro, was born in Paisley, Renfrewshire, on 16 May 1811. He was a master tailor, who settled at 137 Bridgegate Street, Glasgow, in later life. This cover was made sometime during the 1830s and '40s. It was certainly completed by 1851, because in the Census for that year he is listed as 'Assistant Exhibiter of The Royal Table Cover Exhibiting', lodging in Newton-on-Ayr. It was subsequently displayed on several occasions in Scotland and Ireland, including at a Belfast Temperance Association meeting in 1860. A report in the *Belfast News-letter* on 15 November states that by exhibiting the piece, Monro 'illustrated therefrom what patience and perseverance could accomplish, and urged upon the young men present to practise those

virtues, and in order to do so, they should become total abstainers'. After Monro's death, the cover was auctioned on 8 March 1888 to raise money for his widow, Elizabeth.

The source of the figures and ships in the seven panels are from contemporary prints. The sailor from 'Britain for Ever' closely resembles in pose that of Thomas Potter Cooke as William in *Black-Eyed Susan*, a play written by Douglas Jerrold in 1829. **RQ**

46 Cover or hanging

Maker unknown
Britain
1856–69
250 x 287cm
V&A: Circ.114–1962
Given by Brigadier Johnson

Inlaid patchwork cover or hanging consisting of 61 figurative panels. The materials include a variety of plain- and twill-weave wools, many of the type referred to as 'fulled' or 'tailors' broadcloth', with appliqué decoration of plain and figured woven silks, and silk velvets in a variety of colours. The royal coat of arms is shown in the centre, with figures symbolizing the four continents in each corner. The subjects of the remaining panels include scenes from the Old and New Testaments of the Bible, images of the four evangelists, Queen Victoria and her husband Prince Albert, celebrated French and British military and naval heroes, well-known performers and actors, and episodes and characters from popular plays. The subject of each panel is identified by an embroidered title. The figures are carefully represented with drapery, details of their clothes and accessories embroidered in polychrome silks in chain, satin, back and other flat stitches. The inclusion of Lord Raglan suggests a date of manufacture after the Crimean War (1853–6). At the top of the cover is Theobald Mathew (1790–1856), a leading Irish Catholic Temperance campaigner, suggesting a connection to the Temperance movement. It is edged in a heavy red wool fringe.

The imagery of this piece reflects a patriotic interest in the military prowess of the country. The selection of episodes from plays about Robin Hood and Wat Tyler. and the reference to the Anti-Corn Law League, may also reflect the maker's support for radical politics. Other theatrical images include Jenny Lind as Maria in *La Figlia del Regimento* and John Liston as the busybody character Paul Pry. The prints that inspired these may have been produced by toy theatre printmakers, but the selection of characters is unusual: Liston made his name in Poole's play in 1825 while Jenny Lind made her name in Donizetti's opera about 20 years later.

The creation of intricate patchwork hangings reached its zenith in the second half of the nineteenth century. Master tailors displayed their work at national exhibitions, to the admiration of thousands of visitors. In the *Great*

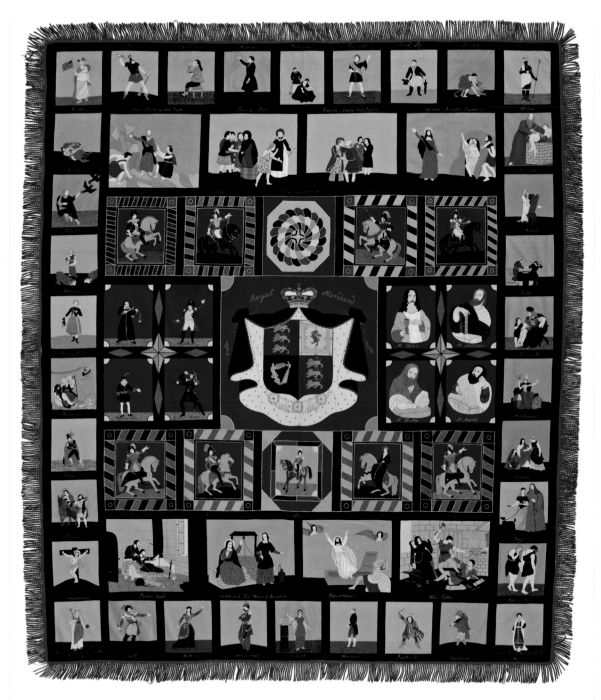

Exhibition of the Works of Industry of All Nations in 1851, held at the Crystal Palace, London, four examples of inlaid patchwork were displayed.

47 Cover or hanging

Possibly Francis Brayley
India
1864–77
238.7 x 238.7cm
V&A: T.58–2007

Patchwork cover or hanging made from Melton wool fabrics of a similar weight and finish to those used for military uniforms. The complex geometric pattern is created using small hexagons, and features six-point stars, large diamonds and larger hexagons. Each individual piece measures 1.5cm in diameter, and is pieced with overcast stitches. It is lined with green damask.

According to the donor's family history, this cover or hanging was thought to have been made by William Brayley. However, archival research suggests it was probably created or purchased by his father, Francis Brayley. It was kept in the family until its acquisition by a dealer and subsequent sale at auction in 2007.

Francis Brayley served as a Private in the 1st/11th foot between 1864 and 1877. During his time in India, Brayley saw no active service. Long periods of inactivity were not uncommon, and the British Government was faced with the challenge of occupying its servicemen. Towards the end of the 1860s, Soldiers' Industrial Exhibitions and professional workshops started to develop, with prizes on offer for skills as diverse as rifle-shooting and embroidery. Families of soldiers stationed out in India were also encouraged to participate, with prize money on offer for winning exhibition entries. They were also a fund-raising opportunity, and officers' wives are known to have purchased some items created in the camps. The professional workshops were promoted as the opportunity to alleviate boredom, while also transferring skills between comrades and to the young family members who were schooled there.

A month after returning to England Brayley married Mary Ann Ash in the Parish of South Molton in Devon, and it may be that this piece was intended as a wedding gift.

48 Billowing Maenads

Dinah Prentice
Worcestershire
2008
380 x 260 cm
Collection of the artist

Silk chiffon backed with polyester voile, heat-fixed dyes and stitched with polyester thread.

For Dinah Prentice, the choice to work with textiles is a deliberate rejection of a patriarchal sphere. Formally trained as an artist, Prentice describes paint as 'too truculent and temporary; too muscular and welded to its own aesthetic. It is like armour or a carapace.' Textiles, on the other hand, represent for the artist a surface to be stretched, repaired and patched: a porous, flexible and forgiving medium which absorbs both memory and meaning. While some of her earlier work explored the violent landscapes and discourses of war, 'Billowing Maenads' returns to the site of the female body. Prentice describes the moment that inspired her *Maenads* series, which was created in a sensory and fluid silk-chiffon gauze:

> I had been looking at Greek art in anticipation of a walking holiday with one of my daughters, when I fell upon a photograph of a small ancient Greek sculpture; a maenad: A mythical figure, she was a Dionysian nymph given to drunken murderous excess. The damaged sculpture embodied for me one of the female identities in the patriarchal unconscious, that is a female out of control and dismembered. In this form she seemed to me to be fiercely courageous and co-operatively adventurous which adds up to an alternative reading of the feminine.

This narrative is born out in the act of piecing. Prentice describes both the unifying and the confrontational potential of patchwork. Drawn to the seams, she delights in a deliberately disjointed vision which allows the 'murderous conspiracy to be revealed', exploring 'the unconscious anxiety that art is supposed to soothe and hide'. Piecing together materials becomes 'a metaphor for compressing unacceptable ideas together'. For Prentice, the process also represents the contemporary condition of feminism: 'the female condition is characterized by fragmentation like it or not. This has always, from the start, been the reason I sew images together'.

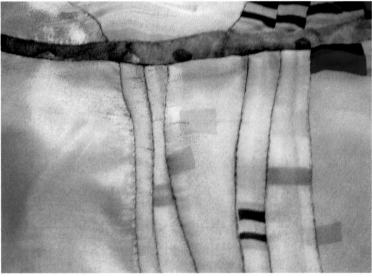

4 Making a living

49 Bedcover
Maker unknown
Backworth, Northumberland
c.1910–20
210 x 233cm
V&A: T.255–1979
Given by E.H. Booth

Quilted patchwork bedcover of cotton sateen.
The design shows an eight-point pale-yellow
star within an eight-point bright-yellow star,
surrounded by four narrow pieced borders and
a wide outer border, alternately pale and bright
yellow. It is quilted within each border in several
designs, including a running leaf pattern in the
two pale-yellow borders, and a cable pattern in
the two bright-yellow narrow borders. The
outermost border has a quilted design of
flowers and leaves. It is quilted with cotton
thread. The reverse is of pale-yellow cotton
sateen.

According to the donor's family history, this
quilt was owned by a resident of Backworth,
Northumberland, in the early twentieth century.
The design is based on the popular 'Sanderson
Star', originally developed by the professional
quilter Elizabeth Sanderson, but much emulated
in the first few decades of the twentieth
century.

Although this quilt cannot be attributed
to Sanderson, the design testifies to the
significance of her role as a designer and teacher.
First apprenticed to the renowned quilter
George Gardiner, Sanderson went on to build
her own formidable career as a quilt-top marker
or 'stamper'. For between 1s.6d. and 2s. she
would mark out a quilt top in blue pencil. This
could then be quilted by either professional or
domestic quilters. At the height of her career
she was marking up to two quilts a day.

Sanderson continued to support the
professional apprentice system. At around the
age of 14, girls would work for her unpaid while
they carried out their training, which usually
took between six months and a year. Sanderson
offered them board during the week, and at the
end of their training the apprentices could be
taken on as professional markers.

50 Applecross Quilt
Pauline Burbidge
Scottish Borders
2007
198 x 206cm
Collection of the artist
Commissioned by Sheffield Galleries & Museums
Trust with the support of the Arts Council
England

Quilt of silks and cottons. Hand-stitched, pleated
and painted, hand- and machine-quilted.

For Pauline Burbidge, the process of stitch is
here concerned with mapping and space. Taking
her inspiration from visiting and studying the
Ordnance Survey maps of Applecross, situated on
the north-west coast of Scotland, Burbidge has
quilted lines and contours to echo the more
physical topography of this area. Through layers of
stitch she explores the strata of rock, sand, reeds
and water: the rugged landscape of this area.
These layers also represent time: the constant
morphing of the landscape in response to the
elements. Like the act of stitching, she brings up
one surface through another, binding together
different chronological layers.

Now rooted in the Scottish Borders,
Burbidge's studio quilts converse with the work of
professional quilters that worked in the area in the
early twentieth century. Exploring how we
unconsciously take note of the spaces that
surround us, 'Applecross Quilt' echoes those
historic quilt-makers whose work was so firmly
entrenched in both the domestic and local
landscape.

Burbidge started her career exploring the
American tradition, experimenting with form to
create intricate yet perfectly repeating designs.
She was amongst a group of artists who helped to
revive an interest in quilting in the 1970s.

51 Bedcover

Miss Nixon
Slaley, Northumberland
1870–80
239 x 216cm
1972–97
Collection of Beamish Museum
Given by Mrs Isabel Nixon of Greenshaw Plain,
Hexham, Northumberland

Quilted bedcover of turkey-red and white
cotton. The design is known as a 'strippy quilt',
with bold stripes of turkey-red and white cotton
pieced and then quilted. The quilting pattern
follows the stripes in a running feather design
(on the red ground), and running diamonds
enclosing a rose, fan and leaf pattern (on the
white ground). Reverse of white cotton.

According to family history, this quilt was
made by Miss Nixon of Slaley, Northumberland,
who ran quilting clubs with her sister to
augment her living. Quilt clubs provided an
important source of income at this time,
particularly among mining communities.
Customers would pay a small weekly sum into
the club, and would be eligible for a completed
quilt only when they had paid the requisite
amount. The clubs became increasingly
important during periods of economic
recession, with women able to take on the role
of main wage earner. Despite the relief that it
provided for many households, the work was
labour-intensive, frequently hurried and poorly
paid: a single quilt would sell for around the
same price as a miner's fortnightly wage.

Miss Nixon's brother married a Sarah Purvis
of The Steel, Hexham, and the quilt was a
present to them for their wedding. The donor
of the quilt and daughter-in-law of the original
owner, Mrs Isabel Nixon said, 'When I came here
64 years ago [1908] my late husband showed it
to me and said it had not to be used.' **RA**

52 Bedcover

Mrs M.E. Shepherd
Amble, Northumberland
1935
254 x 214cm
1980–744
Collection of Beamish Museum
Given by Miss B. Shepherd of Amble,
Northumberland

Quilted bedcover of peach cotton sateen.
The outer border is worked with large shell-like
motifs and, according to the maker, the corner
design is inspired by 'the seat of a bentwood
chair'. The centre is quilted with a circle
enclosing four flowers and a whirl, surrounded
by a cable circle and roses. The ground is quilted
with a diamond pattern. The reverse is of yellow
cotton sateen.

This quilt was made by Mrs M.E. Shepherd,
a resident of Amble, Northumberland. Her
daughter, Miss B. Shepherd, believed it was
made in 1935. It was intended as a wedding gift
for her brother, who in the end never married.
Miss B. Shepherd states:

> the history of the quilt … begins on Coquet
> Island where my mother was brought up.
> My mother received very little education.
> She stayed with her granny at Warkworth
> when another brother or sister was born.
> Her mother died when the seventh was born.
> My mother and sister did all the sewing and
> knitting for the family – underclothing, shirts,
> dresses, mats, socks, fancy work and quilts.
> They sewed for what was then called the
> bottom drawer, which was their preparation
> for marriage. They both married miners.
> Their married life began with a strike, so they
> quilted. Wages were small, so they went on
> quilting to help out. Then my father was
> injured, later deprived of compensation, so
> my mother went on quilting. She had quilting
> clubs taking on 20 [quilts] at a time, completing
> one every fortnight. The patterns were drawn on
> brown paper, then cut out for use. She drew the
> pattern on the material in a day and half,
> improving on them over the years.

Amble is both a fishing and colliery village,
and these two influences seem to play a part in
the making of this quilt. The shell design may
have been inspired by Mrs Shepherd's
upbringing on Coquet Island, off the north-east
coast. **RA**

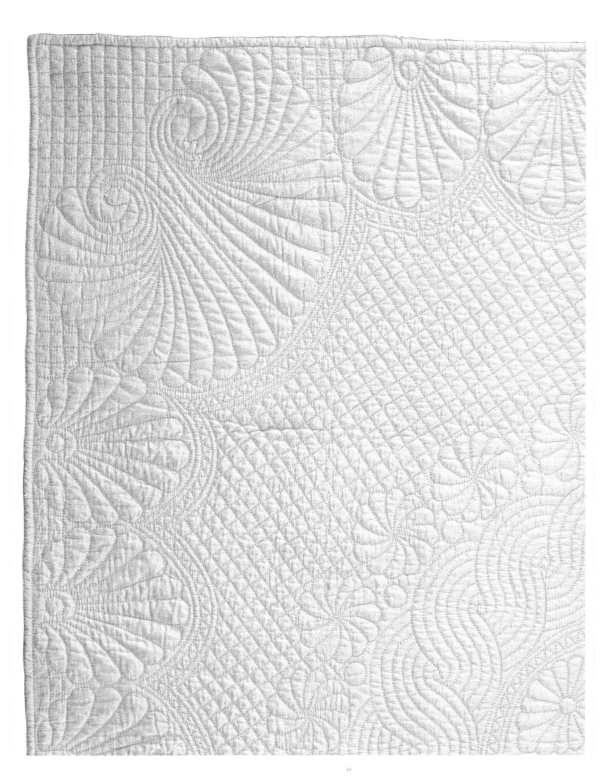

53 A Chinese Dream

Susan Stockwell
London
2010
200 x 200cm
Collection of the artist

Machine-stitched patchwork of new and used bank notes.

Susan Stockwell's beautiful, yet subversive quilt uses paper and paper products to form a visual treatise on the Chinese economy. The quilt has been created from one of the most transferable and anonymous paper objects within contemporary society: money. Through the careful selection of both crisp, newly printed Chinese bank notes, and the slightly weathered notes already in circulation, Stockwell forms a visually arresting piece that is at once a fluid, scale-like surface, and a political statement of the importance of China to the global trade network. Following a recent visit to the country, Stockwell observed 'I realized how productive and fast moving its economy is'. For the artist, the strength and efficiency of this national economy contributes to China's wider global relevance, particularly to the textile trade.

This piece is one of a series of quilts by Stockwell. The last one, 'Imperial Quilt' was made of maps of the world reconfigured with the Middle East at the centre and a swatch of America woven into every continent. Gathered and collected, the materials in all the quilts refer to politics and trade and use of everyday familiar materials. For Stockwell, the continuing relevance of quilts lies in their connection to a 'Make-do-and-mend mentality' where recycling and ecology are an inherent part of the process.

Stockwell chooses these industrial and domestic 'commodity' materials because, in her words, they contain 'stains of existence' and 'act as ready-made signifiers' which she can sculpt and interweave in ways that delicately reveal their obscured politics and hidden beauty.

54 Bedcover
Maker unknown
Britain
1930s
217 x 191cm
Collection of Jen Jones

Quilted bedcover of pale-yellow cotton poplin, with a reverse of pale-pink cotton poplin. Quilted in cotton thread in a design of a large flower within a diamond, and smaller flowers and spirals. The wide outermost border is quilted with a design of leaves and flowers.

This quilt was commissioned in 1932 for the newly renovated wing at the exclusive Claridge's Hotel in London. Designed by Oswald P. Milne, the renovation beckoned a return to British-led design and production. The extension was formally opened to the public for the British Porcelain Ball, in aid of the National Birthday Trust Fund, on Tuesday 24 November 1932.

The quilts were created for the new wing by professional quilters under the jurisdiction of the Rural Industries Bureau, which was established in 1921 by the Ministry of Agriculture. Funded by the Development Commission, the RIB was active throughout the first half of the twentieth century. Influential patrons included Members of Parliament such as Margaret Bondfield: a politician under the Labour government of Ramsay MacDonald and a firm advocate of women's suffrage and employment rights. The RIB was responsible for providing outreach programmes to rural areas to encourage the production of high-quality goods aimed at the luxury market. The organization was known to have sent out lists of quilting designs for potential customers to select from. This may account for the idiosyncratic design of the pillowcases, incorporating both the North Country and Welsh quilting designs.

Further examples of RIB quilts were sold by the Little Gallery in Sloane Street, London, founded by Muriel Rose and Peggy Turnbull in 1928.

55 Bedcover

Porth Quilters
Porth, Rhondda, Wales
1933
193 x 179cm
33.231
Collection of St Fagans: National History
Museum
Given by the Rural Industries Bureau in 1933

Quilted bedcover of beige cotton poplin. The
quilting pattern consists of a central diamond
motif, filled with nine smaller diamonds, on a
square field of double trellis. The central
diamond contains a flower motif; the others
feature alternating four-leafed and double spiral
motifs. The inner border contains diamonds
and triangles, filled with double spirals and
three-leafed motifs. A middle border of double
trellis includes eight squares, each containing a
four-leafed motif. Large spirals fill the outer
border. The reverse is of beige cotton poplin.
It is wadded with a carded wool filling.

This quilt was made under the auspices of
the Rural Industries Bureau. The RIB established a
scheme in 1928 to encourage small craft
industries in economically deprived areas.
Evidence collected during the 1920s by Mavis
FitzRandolph on behalf of the RIB concluded that
the few remaining village quilters in south Wales
were still producing quilted work, but the revival
and improvement of the craft would need to be
led by better materials and financial incentives.

In response, the RIB established several
quilting classes in the industrial valleys of south
Wales, taught by the most accomplished
quilters in the area. Classes were set up in six
centres: at Porth in the Rhondda, Abertridwr,
Merthyr Tydfil, Splott in Cardiff, Blaina and
Aberdare. The RIB paid for the provision of
materials and sourced commercial outlets for
their work, one being Miss Muriel Rose's the
Little Gallery, off Sloane Street in London. Miss
Rose demanded well-designed quilts and
needlework of the highest standard – a
contributing factor, no doubt, in her winning a
commission to supply quilted bedcovers for
Claridge's. The Porth group became especially
well known for the quality of their work, mainly
due to the knowledge and skill of their teacher,
Miss Jessie Edwards.

The RIB scheme ended with the outbreak
of the Second World War in 1939. Although
geared towards a luxury market outside the
locality, the scheme succeeded in raising the
standard of Welsh quilting, producing a new
generation of quilters who were well versed
in the traditional Welsh techniques and
patterns. **EP**

56 Coverlet

Annie O'Hare
Strabane, County Tyrone
1940s
190 x 196cm
UFTM 711.1999
Collection of the National Museums Northern
Ireland (Ulster Folk and Transport Museum)

Unlined machine-pieced patchwork coverlet of
striped printed pyjama cotton.

This coverlet was made in the 1940s by
Annie O'Hare of Strabane, in the west of
County Tyrone. The fabrics were supplied to her
by her sister Margaret, who was working at the
time as a stitcher in a factory at Castlederg,
County Tyrone.

The factory in question had been
established at Main St Castlederg, in 1947, with a
Mr Jack Scott of Londonderry as manager, then
proprietor. Early manufacturing at the site
concentrated on shirts and pyjamas; later
production expanded to include a range of
hospital gowns and shrouds. Jack Scott retired in
1970 and the business continued until 1988,
when it ceased production.

For those working in factories in the area,
there was a ready supply of fabrics. These were
sometimes bought at the factory shop in bags
priced, according to weight, between one
shilling and sixpence and two shillings and
sixpence. **VW**

57 Sides to the Middle, Fingers to the Bone

Jane Whiteley
Fremantle, Australia
2009
235 x 170cm
Collection of the artist

Silk and cotton-gauze quilt. The quilt is designed in layers of indigo-dyed cotton gauze with a central seam and a top layer of silk. Stitched all over in varying directions and densities with running stitch in red silk.

Jane Whiteley's work offers a connection to the domestic practices of post-war Britain: a world that sought to understand and extend the life of cloth. Through exquisitely hand-dyed and stitch layers of gauze, she evokes the 'make-do-and-mend' initiatives designed to prolong the use of domestic textiles, in this instance, the practice of 'turning sheets'. The imprint of the body on the 'worn' areas is stitched in red thread, evoking how both the body and cloth remember.

Born in Britain but now a resident of Fremantle, Australia, Whiteley has experimented with worn and stained bed sheets, tea towels, nappies and bandages that have a strong affinity to the domestic sphere. She reflects on the personal reassurance provided by these everyday textiles as the bearers of highly personal messages. Simultaneously, Whiteley creates a vessel for mass memory, nodding towards the human condition of hardship shared by many in the post-war years. A celebration of experience and memories, this piece is a testimony to the life lived by both people and textiles.

58 Threaded Wrists

Kirsty Fenton
Dundee
2010
100 x 135cm
Collection of the artist

Hand- and machine-embroidered wool felt baby's blankets. The design shows small figures outlined in deep plum, olive green and deep royal-blue stitch in polyester thread. Hand- and machine-quilted. Wadded with cotton backing.

'Threaded Wrists' was the result of a collaboration between the V&A and Duncan of Jordanstone College of Art and Design. Third-year textile students were asked to design a quilt that resonated with one of the five main themes of the exhibition, *Quilts 1700–2010*. 'Threaded Wrists' was the successful entry, designed and created for the exhibition by Kirsty Fenton. While commenting on the contemporary condition of global trade, this piece also gestures towards the beautiful, comforting and often ceremonial historic objects associated with birth and childhood, acknowledging the many unknown professionals who lay behind the production of these objects.

'Threaded Wrists' presents two very different visions of childhood. Working with found and recycled materials, Fenton offers a commentary on the commodification of textiles and the labour involved in producing them. The ground of the piece is a baby's blanket: a beacon to many of the warmth and security of childhood. Scattered with images of infants, the piece at first glance nods towards the role of textiles as vessels for memories, radiating with the emotional warmth of the nursery. But closer inspection reveals a layer of ambiguity: the children are in fact exposed, alone and susceptible, their stitched outline fraying and in some cases unfinished. Threatening to disappear, they are captured in a precarious state of betweenness, their future uncertain.

These ephemeral figures are based on a series of Unicef images. Layered over the recycled blankets, they represent the 246 million children worldwide that share a condition of poverty and hardship; a reality far removed from the comfort and solace provided by the blanket. Their limbs are reminiscent of puppets, with loose threads lacing their wrists. In conversation, the artist speaks of what she terms a 'hidden', unseen aspect of production; an unsettling network of child labour that underpins the creation and circulation of some textiles. Anonymous and voiceless, the thread that joins these children is a thread that binds, looping millions of bodies into a wider network of trade.

59 Coverlet

Elizabeth Magill
Belfast
c.1930
175 x 202cm
UFMT 359:1989
Collection of the National Museums Northern
Ireland (Ulster Folk and Transport Museum)

Patchwork coverlet of a wide variety of plain and
full-weave wool suiting fabrics and dress cottons.
Machine-pieced in a bold geometric pattern that
includes rectangles, squares and triangles.

The coverlet is one of almost 200 made
over a 40-year timespan by Elizabeth Magill.

Magill (née Drennan) was born on 29
October 1888 and grew up at Enniskeen, near
the town of Newcastle in County Down. The
area was well known for the skill of local
embroiderers, employed by agents for the large
linen companies. As a young woman, she was
trained in the stitching of fine white embroidery
on handkerchiefs, as were her sisters. An
informal apprenticeship in dress-making
provided her with a modest income in her late
teens.

At 21 Magill married the son of a local
farmer and they moved to live in Belfast. Living
in a busy urban area in the south of the city, she
had easy access to retailers of remnants from
the many stitching factories. Her knowledge of
dress-making enabled her to undertake work at
home, for friends and neighbours, in order to
help raise her family of seven children. Fabric
offcuts from the light tailoring and dress-making
provided the basis for some of Magill's earliest
projects, machine-sewn from wools and cottons
in mosaic-pieced 'medallion and frame' designs.

Magill continued to make patchwork long
after her family's own requirements had been
satisfied, and when there was no longer a
necessity on her part. She took a keen interest in
the history of local textile industries, and a study
that she made in the 1960s charts the
development of synthetic fibre mixes and the use
of vibrant colours for the domestic linen market
of the time. Her later coverlets, particularly those
from about 1970, exhibit an increasingly
sophisticated approach to design, in a range of
simple strip patchwork examples.

Elizabeth died on 10 October 1987 in
Belfast. The textiles collection of the Ulster Folk
and Transport Museum at Cultra has five
examples of her work, dating from the 1930s to
the mid-1970s. **VW**

60 North and South

Louis Moreau Workshop
London
2010
V&A

Quilted bedcover of hand-printed linen. The linen is printed by the Timorous Beasties design studio using a technique similar to block-printing. The two prints used for the quilt top and reverse are entitled 'Glasgow Toile' and 'London Toile'. They are hand-quilted in cotton thread in a twisted wave design.

Louis Moreau is a north-London workshop that creates bespoke quilts to order and employs women from the London area. The distinctive wave was developed by Victoria Rutter during the course of her professional career, continuing a long tradition of design innovation among the professional quilting community.

The textiles used here are part of a series designed by Timorous Beasties. Founded in Glasgow in 1990 by Alistair McAuley and Paul Simmons, the design studio experiments with both hand-printing and machine production, using textiles as the unsuspecting vehicle for uncompromisingly contemporary scenes. At first glance these appear to mirror the provincial scenes portrayed in eighteenth-century toile-de-Jouy textiles, but closer inspection reveals a nightmarish vision of modernity, where the homeless and dispossessed are depicted against a landscape of tower blocks and graveyards.

5 Meeting the past

61 The Rajah Quilt
The women of the convict ship, *HMS Rajah*
Made onboard the convict ship, *HMS Rajah*
1841
325 x 337cm
Collection of the National Gallery of Australia

Unlined patchwork coverlet of plain and printed cottons. A central panel of white cotton is appliquéd with sprigs of flowers and smaller birds, encircled by four large printed cotton birds. The panel is contained within several narrow borders of printed dress cottons pieced in geometric designs, mostly squares and triangles. The prints are predominantly small flowers, stripes and dots. The outermost border has a design of appliquéd cottons and an inscription worked in silk thread. There are 2,815 pieces in total. Inscribed 'To the ladies of the convict ship committee, this quilt worked by the convicts of the ship *Rajah* during their voyage to van Dieman's Land is presented as a testimony of the gratitude with which they remember their exertions for their welfare while in England and during their passage and also as a proof that they have not neglected the ladies kind admonitions of being industrious. June 1841.'

The 'Rajah quilt' is one of the world's most important textiles. Its story is one of hope and persistence, and has been a central subject of study into colonial life since its rediscovery in 1987. In 1816, Elizabeth Fry, concerned by the plight of women prisoners in Newgate Prison, formed the British Ladies Society for the Reformation of Female Prisoners. One of the many improvements the Society implemented was to offer prisoners active employment such as needlework, to keep them occupied during their incarceration. The Society donated sewing supplies, including tape, ten yards of fabric, four balls of white cotton sewing thread, a ball each of black, red and blue thread, black wool, 24 hanks of coloured thread, a thimble, 100 needles, threads, pins, scissors and two pounds of patchwork pieces (or almost ten metres of fabric).

These provisions were carried by the 180 women prisoners on board the *Rajah* as it set sail from Woolwich, England on 5 April 1841, bound for Van Diemen's Land. When the *Rajah* arrived in Hobart on 19 July 1841, the supplies had been transformed into the inscribed, embroidered and appliquéd coverlet now known as the 'Rajah quilt'. It was presented to the Lieutenant-Governor's wife, Lady Jane Franklin, as tangible evidence of the cooperative work that could be

achieved under such circumstances.

At some stage after its arrival in Tasmania the quilt was returned to England, to be presented to Elizabeth Fry. Whether she knew of it before her death four years after its completion is unknown. **RB**

62 HMP Wandsworth Quilt

Inmates of HMP Wandsworth
HMP Wandsworth, London
2010
195 x 260cm
V&A
Acquired with the support of
the Friends of the V&A

Quilted patchwork hanging of plain-weave
cottons and linens, and plain-weave and twill-
weave wools, embellished with appliqué and
embroidery. Hand-pieced over paper, in a design
based on the floor plan of HMP Wandsworth.
The cottons and wools used are the same
colour and weave as those used for inmates'
uniforms. The pieces show figurative scenes
from early twenty-first-century prison life. It is
lined in cream cotton.

This piece has been created in collaboration
with Fine Cell Work: a registered charity that
teaches needlework to prison inmates. The
charity works to a philanthropic model set up by
its founder, Lady Anne Tree. Volunteers work
with small groups of inmates (around 11 or 12),
teaching embroidery, patchwork, quilting and
various other needlework skills. Each prisoner
involved with the charity carries out his or her
needlework while confined to his or her cell.

The V&A commission has been designed
and made by the all-male quilting group of HMP
Wandsworth. The emphasis of the
collaboration has been on creative expression,
personal reflection and community, centred on
the act of bringing the participants together to
stitch. Many of the hexagons demonstrate a
clear conversation with both the history of the
British prison system and contemporary
discourses on authority. In one, a fingerprint is
surrounded by borders of DNA, suggesting
issues relating to the identification of criminals
and the control of personal freedom. Other
hexagons engage directly with the action of the
probation board, the intricate subculture of
prison life and the tools of the stitcher. The
diversity of these designs demonstrates the
continuing appeal of the needle as a tool of
both subversion and salvation.

63 Coverlet

The Changi Girl Guide Group
Changi Prison, Singapore
1943
188 x 96cm
EPH:9206
Collection of the Imperial War Museum

Patchwork coverlet of plain and printed cottons in the pattern now known as 'grandmother's garden'. A variety of printed dress cottons from the early 1940s including checks, stripes and florals have been used to create 72 rosettes. Each rosette is surrounded by plain white cotton hexagons; the rosettes have been embroidered with the following names:

Nellie Symons
Ossie Handcock
Olga Morris
Theresa Walters
Bessy Sanger
Queenie Smith
Eileen Harris
Cynthia Smith
A. Silberman
Pansy NG
R. Reilley
T. Van Roode
Evelyn Harris
Sheila Summers
Mary Gilfillan
Mary Trevor
Nelly Cummings
Shirley Harris

The coverlet is lined with white cotton. The central rosette has the Girl Guides' insignia outlined in satin stitch.

It was created in Changi Prison, which housed civilians following the Japanese conquest of Singapore in 1942. The conditions in the prison could be harsh and overcrowded, with many elderly men and women as well as young children held in small domestic quarters. Powerful images such as those created by Leslie Cole (a war artist who travelled widely during the Second World War) offer a vivid portrayal of life in the camps, alongside the objects created by the internees, which testify to their endurance.

The coverlet was created by 20 girls aged 8–16 as a surprise birthday present for their Girl Guide leader, Elizabeth Ennis. The Guide group was set up in June 1943, and met once a week in

the corner of the exercise yard. The girls would all wear white dresses as their uniform, and made badges and emblems from other scraps of fabric that they found. This continued until the Japanese guards raided the camp in October 1943. The coverlet was stitched in secret, using any materials available within the camp.

Each patch communicates a story of survival: a girl's endurance, her time passed, and her refusal to disappear from the visual landscape. The patches testify to the hope and independence of individuals through the creation of beautiful objects, seemingly at odds with the difficult conditions in which they were created.

64 The Presence of Absence

Jennifer Vickers
Manchester
2010
243 x 160cm
Collection of the artist

Paper patchwork comprising over 38,000 squares of plain and printed paper, each measuring 1cm x 1cm. Each grid of four squares is assembled by hand, and then machine-stitched into the wider construction.

At the centre of Jennifer Vickers's work is an interest in the representation and collection of memories. She explores notions of identity by examining the connections between individual and collective experiences, seeking to contrast personal and institutionalized memories through the use of forgotten narratives.

This work commemorates military and civilian casualties of the second Iraq War while also prompting a reflection on the way such incidents are reported in the Western media. Civilian deaths are marked using an anonymous square of paper, military deaths with an image of the deceased taken from newspaper documentation. Over 38,000 squares list the sequence of deaths occurring between the start of the war in March 2003 and the 100th British military fatality in January 2006.

Vickers counter-memorial questions rather than solidifies collective responses, beckoning the viewer to personally and emotionally engage with the ways in which we contemplate and record death. Viewed in its entirety, the piece serves as a focus for contemplation on the human cost of war, the escalation of civilian casualties, and the degree of public commemoration. Variations caused by the fading of different squares at differing rates subtly underline the individuality of each life lost. To complete the project, Vickers invited colleagues, family, friends and members of local women's groups with refugee status to assist with the production.

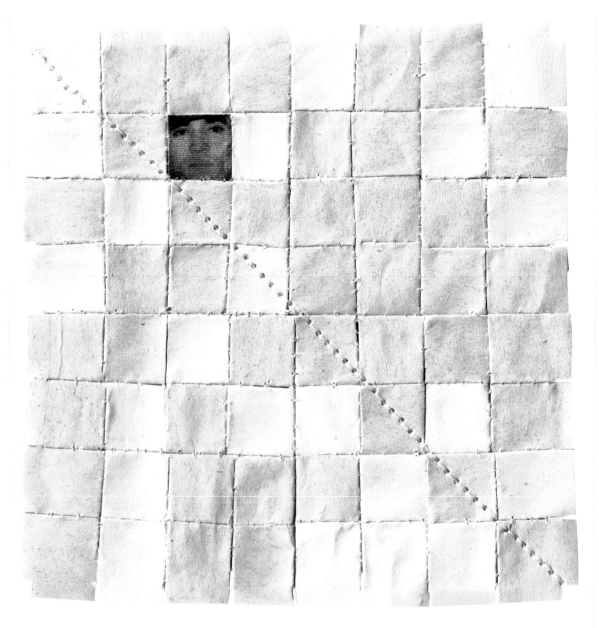

65 Bedcover
Elizabeth Hamilton
Perth, Scotland
1946–7
230 x 196cm
Private Collection

Yellow cotton sateen bedcover with a reverse of cream cotton. It is quilted in yellow cotton thread and wadded with wool. The centre is quilted with a repeating pattern of the maker's own design, while the borders include geometric patterns and vignettes inspired by her time in the Land Army. Figurative scenes include the poultry school and the morning milking. The Women's Land Army insignia is in one corner, with the date '1939' and an unfinished date '19_'.

This quilt was made by Elizabeth Hamilton (1917–2004), a member of the Women's Land Army during the Second World War. The scenes are drawn from her training and regular duties, which included the morning milking and annual harvest. Elizabeth worked as a Land Girl for five years and later became a teacher of art. This quilt was made as part of a post-diploma course at Edinburgh College of Art as a reflection on her time in the Land Army.

The Women's Land Army was established during the First World War to address a shortage of labour in the agricultural sector, and was revived during the Second World War. Many of the men previously working on British farms became part of the armed forces, leaving farms unable to meet the increasing demands placed upon them. As food production became ever more important. with supply ships and trading routes threatened by military action, women were encouraged to join the Women's Land Army. By 1944 there were 80,000 women volunteers working on the land. Around one-third of them moved from Britain's urban centres to get involved with the initiative.

Elizabeth first worked at a farm near Perth, before being assigned to a second farm near Ballingluig.

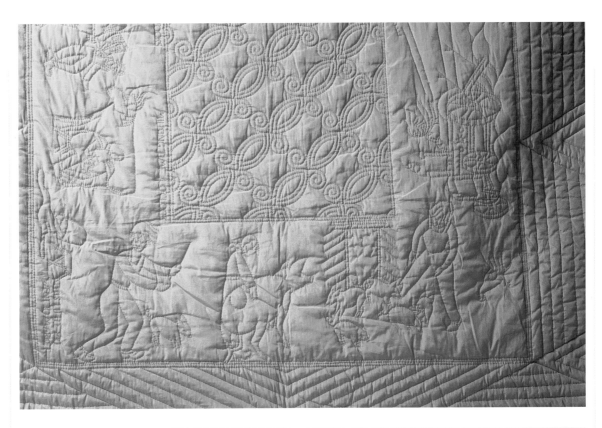

66 At the End of the Day

Natasha Kerr
London
2007
75 x 110cm
V&A: T.43–2008

Transfer printed, silk screen printed, hand painted, hand stitched antique French bed linen pieced into a design reminiscent of a flag. A transfer-printed image at the centre depicts a male figure lying prone on a blanket in a garden with a seated female.

Natasha Kerr creates complex, multi-layered objects that resonate with the hidden histories of family heirlooms and everyday objects. Her work has a softness and warmth that invites an emotional engagement with the personal narrative at the heart of each piece.

'At the End of the Day' takes as its starting point a series of family photographs given to Kerr by her mother. Tucked away for many years in a cupboard below the stairs, these images provided Kerr with what she describes as a 'visual thread', linking her to an otherwise unknown part of her family history. At the centre of this piece is her grandfather, a Viennese surgeon who came to Britain in 1936. Interned during the Second World War, he was released to carry out essential work as a surgeon. The transfer print depicts him lying prone on a blanket in a garden: one of the few images taken of him in repose. Her grandmother sits alongside, shielding her eyes from the sun, and an empty chair completes the picture. The stitched fabric radiates away from the image, reminiscent of a flag. This seemingly quiet, unassuming and somewhat ghostly image is charged with emotional resonance. This is a story of the dispossessed: a man denied a sense of home or belonging. The empty chair is a poignant marker of both displacement and absence: a testimony to the condition of invisibility shared by many during these years. The barren landscape similarly speaks of a place where there is no new life, with nothing rooted to build on.

As an artist, Kerr takes the viewer on these often uncomfortable journeys to reveal something about both a personal and collective past. In 1998, she created an installation entitled *There are Things You Don't Need to Know*. Set in a Victorian townhouse in Battersea London, the installation resounded with the unsettling voice of the past. Incorporating sounds (ticking clocks, a dripping tap and a child's laughter), smells and objects, it evoked the presence of an absence: a somewhat forgotten heritage. For many years, the house had been home to generations of one family, whose last member had died 12 months earlier in the front room. For Kerr, the dilapidated and crumbling nature of the building reflected the tenuous and fractured family relationships at the heart of her work; the peeling paint and wallpaper a symbol of the layers delicately stripped away by the artist to reveal a greater truth.

67 Coverlet

Griselda Lewis
Manningtree, Essex
Late 1940s
238 x 239cm
V&A

Patchwork coverlet of printed cottons and heavy blackout cotton. Most of the patterned prints are of furnishing fabrics and date from the 1930s and '40s. The patterns include a variety of bold floral and novelty prints. It is pieced in a hexagon design, and backed in 'red cotton'.

The maker of this coverlet, Griselda Lewis, was the editor of the *Handbook of Crafts* (1960). Some of the patterned furnishing fabrics were taken from swatches sent to Robert Harling, an editor of *House and Garden* for 28 years, who lived nearby in Wiston by Nayland, Suffolk. The main bulk of the hexagons were cut from old dresses and shirts, in fact anything available. As the coverlet was made just after the Second World War, materials were scarce.

This object testifies to the maker's ingenuity in terms of both materials and design. According to the maker, the material on the reverse is a cotton that was used for Red Cross famine-relief parcels during the Second World War. It was acquired from one of the many army-surplus stores that existed at the time. The black material used for the quilt background has been recycled from the maker's blackout curtains. The quilt took between two and three years to complete, and was worked on mainly in the evenings. This was the only patchwork coverlet she ever made.

68 Bedcover

Maker unknown
Canada
1939–41
207 x 173cm
Private Collection

Quilted patchwork bedcover of printed and brushed cottons. The cottons are dress- and pyjama fabrics, with most dating to the late 1930s. The printed cottons have been arranged in blocks of nine patches, and then pieced into a wider design of 42 blocks against a patterned light-blue ground. It is tuft-quilted with red wool and lined with a brushed cotton in a design of grey, blue and red stripes.

This quilt was made by the Canadian Red Cross Society as part of its initiative to provide relief for civilian victims of the Second World War. The scheme set up a supply network across Canada, whereby women could create quilts from donated materials.

This particular quilt was donated to a child who lived in Bromley, England, in August 1944. The family were on holiday in Wales when their house was demolished during an air raid. After losing most of their material possessions, the family sought out both a building to shelter in and essential goods. The mother of the child found an empty house, and then purchased utility grey blankets, china, saucepans, chairs and a white kitchen table. At some point, the family received three bed quilts from the Canadian Red Cross, of which this is one.

The present owner charts not only the resilience and inspiration of her mother, but also the strong feeling of dislocation that she felt in the wake of the war. She remembers how strange it was to 'sleep in a bed again and a room of my own'. Having slept in a Morrison shelter, the return to a sense of the interior was both welcome and unfamiliar.

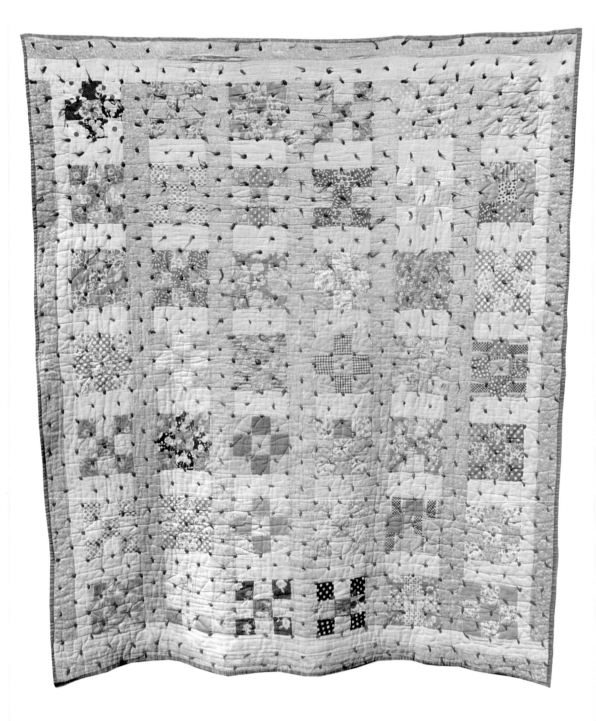

69 Memoriam

Michele Walker
Brighton
2002
236 x 144cm
V&A: T.6:1–2009

Quilt of steel wire wool and transparent plastic. Pieced in a 'crazy' design, with steel wire wool wadding and twisted steel wire wool fringing. See also pp.128–9.

Michele Walker creates multi-layered quilts that unite personal testimony with social commentary. Referencing her mother's struggle with Alzheimer's disease, 'Memoriam' reflects on the fragmentation of personal identity. Walker describes the meaning behind the twisted and knotted wire wool borders of the quilt:

As my mother lost her memory she became obsessive about everyday things, small things that didn't really matter; she would sit and twist and tease her hair. I noticed that many of us obsessively twist our hair without realizing, particularly when lost in thought.

The remaining pieces are sewn with the imprint of the artist's own skin: the delicate envelope that acts as the body's bearer of messages; the means by which we often identify ourselves and others. This pattern is at once both familiar and disturbing; a beacon of our individuality, while also a perpetual reminder of the body's transience and vulnerability.

The ephemeral materials similarly speak of the transience of life while also testifying to a wider culture of memory-loss. 'Memoriam' is the last quilt in a body of work which draws inspiration from the patterns, stitches and ethos of traditional quilt-making – the incorporation of everyday, cast-off scraps and fabrics used to make both decorative and functional bedcovers. Pieced in the late nineteenth century design known as 'crazy' patchwork, 'Memoriam' is an ode to thousands of makers unknown, serving as a poignant reminder of the fading of quilting skills in Britain. Instead of the wool or cotton of traditional wholecloth quilts, 'Memoriam' is wadded with wire wool. Moving against the quilt's traditional associations of safety, this steely aesthetic acts as a metaphor for decay: the wire wool gradually reacts to exposure to the atmosphere. In time, it ages and eventually disappears.

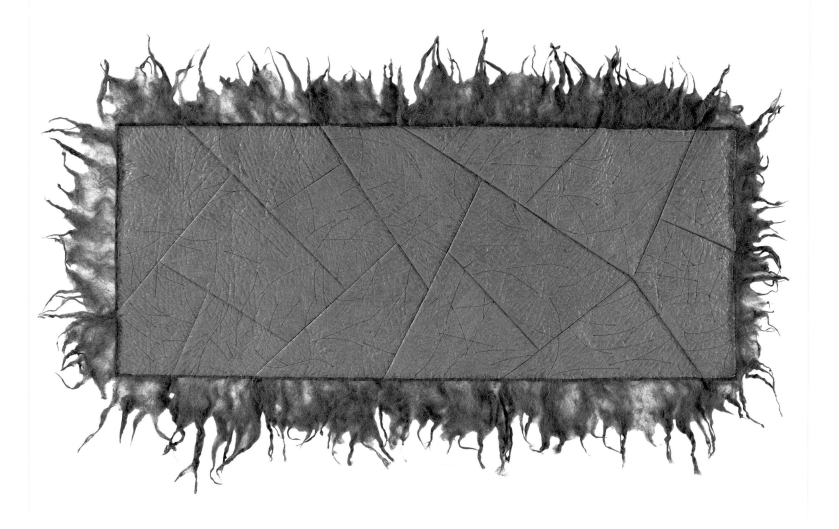

70 Liberty Jack

Janey Forgan
Oxford
2008
165 x 160cm
Collection of the artist

Machine-stitched quilt of printed cottons. Most of the fabrics were printed by Liberty & Co., and date from the 1960s to the present day. The fabrics have been pieced in a repeating design that echoes the structure of the Union Jack.

At the heart of Janey Forgan's work is questioning of what it is to be British. Having worked overseas, Forgan returned to the UK to question her personal and collective heritage through the act of stitch. Taking the Union Jack as her inspiration, her reworking of the flag through densely patterned Liberty prints is underpinned by an understanding that 'we are no longer red, white and blue'.

Quilt-making also fulfils a very personal role for Forgan:

I have always liked fabric – the feel and beauty – and used to play with my mother's fabric drawer as a child, but was never that interested in making clothes. Patchwork, with its combination of colours and patterns, allows me to play with shapes and forms, and represent ideas in a tactile form.

Here, she used the slow, careful and creative process of piecing together fabrics inherited from her mother to build a patchwork of intense diversity. Interested in the joins, the point at which people connect and become a nation, she questions what it is that holds us together with ever greater diversity and devolution.

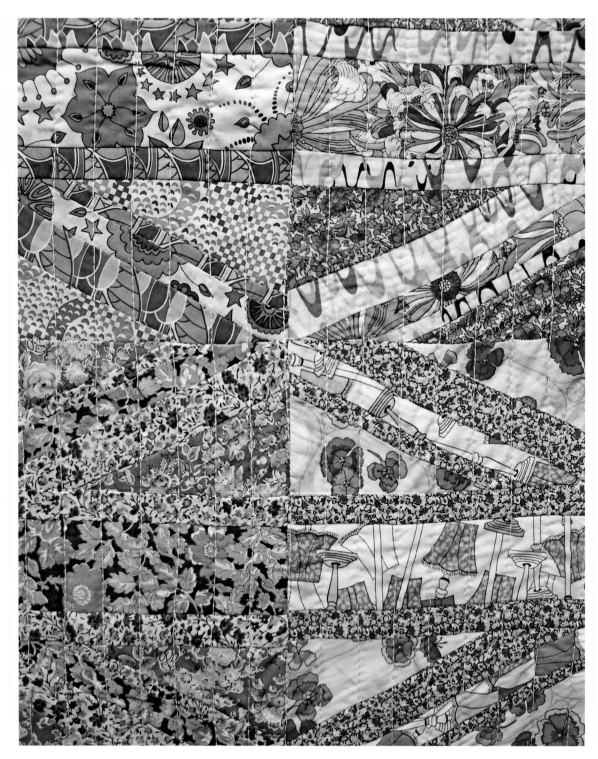

71 To Meet My Past

Tracey Emin
London
2003
Approximately 300 x 170 x 215cm
Collection of the Saatchi Gallery

Multi-media installation of dressed and painted brass bed with sprung mattress. Embroidered and appliquéd blankets and cotton sheets. Materials include printed cottons, cotton velvets and some wool patches and details. The appliquéd text includes: 'I CRY IN A WORLD OF SLEEP' and 'I AM NOT AFRAID'. Embroidered phrases include: 'Why when I was a little girl, why did I not see the world like this, innocent?'

In 'To Meet My Past', Tracey Emin creates a marriage bed of uncomfortable truths. Layered in beautiful floral prints and trailing text, this bed is not restful; it is replete with fragments of memory that take on the appearance of bodily stains, intricately embroidered in red thread across the sheets. Emin explores both the pleasures and pains of the procreative bed, transforming it into a site of fear, danger and betrayal, where nothing is private or reserved.

In particular, as for many quilt-makers, the bed becomes a site of personal testimony. Emin uses embroidery and appliqué as traditional tools of revelation and documentation. The work exposes periods of despair and darkness through stitch, in a manner not dissimilar to historical needlework by women such as Lorina Bulwer and Agnes Richter who were both in asylums in the nineteenth century and documented their lives in stitch. Emin's piece exhibits the same combination of stark emotion and personal testimony, inexorably linked to a historical understanding of the feminine and of childhood. The quilt itself is inscribed 'TO MEET MY PAST'. The piece resounds with a hidden history: an erstwhile unspoken narrative held within the layers of time and fabric. Beckoning the viewer to reflect on his or her own past, Emin's piece epitomizes the role of quilts as vessels for both personal and collective memories.

Notes

Introduction

1 In her letter Ellen Weeton explains that her mother bequeathed the bed to her brother, and sent it to him on his marriage. In a somewhat poignant afterthought she concludes, 'I suppose it is now worn out.' Edward Hall (ed.), *Miss Weeton: Journal of a Governess 1811–1825* (London, 1939), pp.324–5

2 See Jeremy Aynsley and Charlotte Grant (eds), *Imagined Interiors: Representing the Domestic Interior Since the Renaissance* (London, 2006)

3 The British Quilt Study Group (BQSG) was formed in 1998 by the Quilters' Guild of the British Isles; its annual seminars bring together textile and quilt historians and scholars. In 1979 the Quilters' Guild of the British Isles was established to promote the history and craft of patchwork and quilting; it established the Quilt Museum in York in 2008. See www.quiltersguild.org.uk (consulted 10 June 2009)

4 Susan Pearce explores the nature of museums, collections and the reasons why objects are collected in Pearce (1992). For her discussion on the nature of collections as 'souvenirs', see pp.68–73

5 Martin Myrone discusses the development of folk art as an idea in English culture in 'Instituting English Folk Art', *Visual Culture in Britain*, vol.10, no.1, March 2009, pp.27–52

6 See Eddy (2005), pp.6–11

7 See John Styles, 'Patchwork on the Page', pp.48–51

8 Paul Thompson discusses the reliability of oral evidence in Thompson (2000), pp.118–72

9 Styles and Vickery (2006), p.2

10 See Laurence (1996), pp.148–9

11 Edwards (2005), p.72

12 Styles and Vickery (2006), p.9

13 See Kruger (2008); written to accompany an exhibition of the same name, held at Compton Verney 21 June–7 September 2008

14 See Smith (2008)

15 Margaret Tucker, 'The Quiltmakers', in *Quilt Treasures: The Quilters' Guild Heritage Search* (London, 1995), p.145

16 Samuel (1994), p.ix

Chapter 1

1 British Library, Burney Collection 449b, *General Advertiser*, 15 April 1752

2 Starkey (1998), item 9771, p.212

3 *Of Household Stuff: The 1601 inventories of Bess of Hardwick* (National Trust, 2001), p.46

4 Starkey (1988), item 9081, p.184, and item 9182, p.190

5 See Rosemary Crill, 'The Hardwick Hall Bengali Quilt', in Santina M. Levey, *The Embroideries at Hardwick Hall* (National Trust, 2007), pp.389–90

6 Murdoch (2006), p.126

7 Peter Thornton and Maurice Tomlin, *The Furnishing and Decoration of Ham House* (London, 1980), p.166

8 Karin Walton, 'The Worshipful Company of Upholders of the City of London', *Furniture History* VIII, 1972, p.48

9 Murdoch (2006), p.280

10 Ibid., p.181

11 R. Campbell, *The London Tradesman* (London, 1747; reprinted Newton Abbot, 1969), p.213

12 Guildhall Library London, Sun Insurance records 11936, vol.17, p.470

13 Ibid., vol.162, p.81

14 G. Eland (ed.), *Purefoy Letters 1735–1753* (London, 1931), vol.1, pp.99–102; discussed in Clabburn (1988), p.109

15 See Rose (1999); and Rose (2000)

16 Rose (1999), p.108

17 R.W. Blencowe (ed.), 'Extracts from the Journal of Walter Gale, Schoolmaster at Mayfield, 1750', *Sussex Archaeological Collections*, vol.IX (London, 1858), p.190

18 The wealthy Londoner was Ralph Ingram, a merchant tailor (Corporation of London Record Office, Orphans Court Inventory 2513). I am grateful to David Mitchell for this reference.

19 Public Record Office, Prob.3, Bundle 35, pt.I, no.27, 20 March 1736, for Henry Shelley

20 G. Smith, *The Laboratory or School of Arts* (London, 1756), vol.2, p.49

21 John Beresford (ed.), *The Diary of a Country Parson: The Reverend James Woodforde* (Oxford, 1968), vol.III, pp.150, 308; vol.V, p.108

22 See Barber (2001)

Chapter 2

1 Colby (1958), Osler (1987) and Rae (1987)

2 Hake (1937) – West Country; FitzRandolph (1954) – south Wales, Durham and Northumberland; Osler (2000) – North Country; Allan (2007) – Durham and Northumberland; Anthony (1972), Stephens (1993) and Jones (1997) – Wales; Jones (1979) – Ireland

3 Rae (1987) cites one, Mrs Sally Ranson of New Seaham, County Durham

4 Morris (1962), p.63

5 Monro displayed his quilt at a meeting of the Belfast Revival Temperance Association in November 1860. Information provided by Clare Rose and Rebecca Quinton.

6 See Osler (2000), Rae (1987) and Allan (2007)

7 Fred Harrison & Co., Bow Churchyard, and Myerscough of Rawson Street

8 Newton's specification for Erastus T. Bigelow's Counterpane Loom, 1841; Bigelow was an American entrepreneur, inventor and textile manufacturer. National Archive ext. 6/89

9 These include Bury Quilting Manufacturing Co. and Eccles Quilts Ltd.

10 Cited in Hughes (1961), p.27

11 The Rachel B. Kay-Shuttleworth collection is housed at Gawthorpe Hall, which is a National Trust property.

12 The 1851 Census shows that of a population of 10,376 in Clitheroe, Lancashire, 40 per cent of all heads of households were employed in the cotton industry. This does not include spouses or children.

13 *Loan Exhibition of English Chintz*, V&A, May–July 1960, cat.209, p.40

14 The Bannister Hall records were acquired by Stead McAlpin in 1893. The firm is now owned by John Lewis. See Lorna Poole, 'So world wide a reputation', in *The Gazette*, John Lewis staff magazine, vol.75, no.44, 1993

15 Bannister Hall were contract printers – that is, they printed designs for others to sell under their own labels.

16 Hefford (1992), p.158

17 One curtain derived from the set is now in the V&A, together with the note (V&A: T.632–1972).

18 Usually made of the same fabric as the side curtains, watch pockets were used for storing small valuables overnight.

19 *The Workwoman's Guide* (1840), p.197

20 V&A: T.169-169TT–1978

21 Registration no. 87/1135-4. Descendants of the original maker took it to Australia.

22 Austen (1884), letter dated 31 May 1811

23 Made by Jane, Cassandra and their mother. It is housed in the Jane Austen House Museum in Chawton Cottage near Alton in Hampshire, where the novelist lived for her last eight years.

24 Allan (2007), pp.89–95

25 The quilt is assumed to be Welsh because the donor, Miss Margaret Evans, lived in Pwllheli, Caernarfonshire.

26 Furnishing cottons depicting sprigs of rosebuds were particularly popular in the 1840s. A number are included in a collection of textiles from two Oxford Street shops, Miles and Edwards (1821–47) and their successors, Charles Hindley, which are now in the V&A.

27 For further details, see Osler (1987), pp.113–15

28 Ibid.; Allan (2007), pp.45–55

29 The donor, Mrs I. Grimshaw, came from Accrington.

30 My thanks to Joan Marie Hanson for this information.

31 Elizabeth Chapman's wedding quilt of 1829 uses an 1813 centre. (see cat.)

32 The Castle Museum, York, has a small collection of these; see Sheppard (2005), pp.120–1

33 V&A: T.293–1913, T.355–1960

34 Another is owned by the National Museum of Wales at St Fagans.

35 The National Maritime Museum has two fragments of embroidered silk used around Nelson's bed on board ship in 1802; their shape suggests half-valances.

36 A version of this handkerchief is owned by the V&A; V&A: T.1759–1913

37 Most nineteenth-century silks were finished with tin salts to give a more lustrous finish. Unfortunately, in time this rots the fabric.

38 So called because it resembled imported asymmetrical designs from that country. There was also a craze for all things Japanese at the time.

CHAPTER 3

1 Muriel Rose archive

2 Goodenough (1977), p.70

3 *Home and Country*, January 1926, p.6

4 Minutes of the Handicrafts Sub-committee of the Durham Federation of Women's Institutes, 21 March 1929, ref. no.D/WI 1/2/5, Durham Record Office, Durham

5 Holly Tebbutt, *Industry or anti-industry? The Rural Industries Bureau*, V&A/RCA MA thesis (London, 1990)

6 Vacher (2006), p.5

7 *Report of the Rural Industries Bureau, 1929–36* (London, 1936), p.17

8 *Rural Industries*, September (London, 1930), p.3

9 *Rural Industries*, Autumn (London, 1932), p.4

10 Muriel Rose archive

11 Osler (1987), p.150

12 Ibid., p.125

13 Ibid., p.117

14 Helen E. FitzRandolph and M. Doriel Hay (vols I–III), Anna M. Jones (vol.IV), *The Rural Industries of England and Wales* (Oxford, 1916–27)

15 FitzRandolph (1954), p.7

16 Ibid, p.37

17 Ibid., p.164

18 Dorothy Osler, 'Across the Pond: New World Influences on Old World Quilt Traditions', *Quilters Newsletter Magazine*, June 2006, pp.38–41

19 *Fabrics and Fabrication* (2001), pp.20–21

CHAPTER 4

1 Huws studied for two years at Chelsea School of Art, moving in 1927 to the Mural Decoration Department at the Royal College of Art. She worked as a freelance artist before marrying the sculptor Richard Huws in 1931. *Edrica Huws Patchworks*, Oriel Ynys Mon, Llangefni, 17 August–23 September 2007

2 See 'Making pictures from strips of cloth isn't art at all – but it mocks art's pretensions to the core', *The Guardian*, 13 August 2007

3 Edrica Huws, 'Observations on the medium of patchwork', in *Edrica Huws Patchworks* (2007), p.15

4 Gill Perry, 'Visibility, Difference and Excess', in Perry (2006), p.5. Catherine de Zegher was director of the Drawing Center in New York (1999–2006) and edited *Inside the Visible* (1996).

5 Alicia Foster, 'Women Working Now', in Foster (2004), p.171. Organized by Judy Chicago and Miriam Schapiro, *Womanhouse* was both an art installation and performance piece set in a 17-room mansion in Hollywood, California. Each room was transformed into different female environments, including 'Menstruation Bathroom' and 'Womb Room'. First shown in Manchester in 1976, *Postal Event: Portrait of the Artist as Housewife* moved to the Institute of Contemporary Arts in London the following year and explored the difficulties and isolation of women artists; see Su Richardson, 'Crocheted Strategies: A New Audience for Women's Work', in *Women and Art* (London, 1987), pp.37–41. *Women Artists and Textiles: Their Lives and Their Work* was organized by the Women Artists Slide Library at Battersea Arts Centre in 1983.

6 Foster (2004), p.7

7 Ibid., p.198

8 Emin was shortlisted for the 1999 Turner Prize and exhibited her infamous *My Bed*. Her appliquéd blanket, *Hate and Power Can be a Terrible Thing* (2004, ref. T11891), is a personal response to the 72-day Falklands War (1982) between Great Britain and Argentina.

9 Foster (2004), pp.198–9

10 Elliott (2008), p.21

11 Adamson (2007), p.154

12 For a discussion of Emin's 'faux' amateurism, see ibid., pp.158–63

13 Sara Impey, email correspondence with the author, 2 March 2009

14 Ibid.

15 For a discussion of objects and the creation of a national identity, see Ulrich (2002)

16 Faith Ringgold, 'The 1970s: Is There a Woman's Art?', in Ringgold (1995), pp.178–81. Ringgold had protested against the exclusion of black artists in the 1968 Whitney Museum exhibition *The 1930s: Painting and Sculpture in America*; ibid., pp.165–9

17 Diane Waldman, 'At the Whitney', in Holstein (1991), p.29

18 *Abstract Design in American Quilts* (1 July–12 September 1971) proved so popular that the exhibition was extended and ran until 6 October.

19 Holstein (1991), p.50

20 Gee's Bend is a remote black community situated in the Alabama River area. The striking geometric quilts made by generations of women were constructed from recycled work clothes, including denim, feed sacks and dress remnants. For information on the Gee's Bend exhibition schedule, see www.quiltsofgeesbend.com/news/ (consulted 17 February 2009)

21 Anna C. Chave discusses the cultural politics inherent in the *Gee's Bend* exhibitions in Chave (2008), pp.181–96

22 See Parker and Pollock, 'Crafty Women and the Hierarchy of the Arts', in Parker and Pollock (1981)

23 Foster (2004), p.171

24 See, for example, *How to Make an American Quilt* (Amblin Entertainment, 1995) starring Winona Ryder; and *The Simpsons* ('Bart's Dog Gets a F', season 2, episode 16, 1991). Marge, the matriarch of the family, sits down on the couch with her daughter Lisa and shows her the family quilt. She explains that the quilt has been in her family for five generations and that it is now time for the reluctant Lisa to add a patch.

25 Holstein (1991), p.74

26 In 1985 Holstein lent part of his collection to the Sainsbury Centre for Visual Arts, University of East Anglia.

27 Michele Walker in conversation with the author, 17 February 2009

28 *The American Quilt Tradition: An Exhibition to Mark the Bi-Centenary of American Independence*, curated by Shiela Betterton, Commonwealth Institute, London, 1976. Betterton worked as a volunteer steward at the American Museum in Bath from 1963 until her appointment as Textile Advisor, which she held until her retirement in 1993. The American Museum in Bath was co-founded by Dallas Pratt and John Judkyn in 1961.

29 Pauline Burbidge, email correspondence with the author, 24 February 2009

30 Agnes and Kate Walker, 'Starting with Rag Rugs: The aesthetics of survival', in Elinor (1987), pp.27–30

31 Jennifer Harris, 'Introduction' to *Take 4* (1998), p.9

32 Griselda Pollock, 'Framing Feminism', in Robinson (2001), p.210

33 Dinah Prentice, in conversation with Eilean Hooper-Greenhill, in *Take 4* (1998), p.45

34 Dinah Prentice, *Fragments: New Works*, exhibited at the Butter Market, Brindleyplace, Birmingham, 7–30 November 2008

35 Dinah Prentice, email correspondence with the author, 14 February 2009

36 Jo Budd, email correspondence with the author, 18 February 2009

37 Sara Impey, email correspondence with the author, 2 March 2009

38 Whiteley (1999), p.5

39 Ibid.

40 Gail Jones, 'Softness: Four Meditations on the Poetics of Cloth', ibid., pp.7–8

41 Josie Golden, 'And sew it begins, again', *Telegraph Weekend*, 14 February 2009

42 Goldup's findings were developed from a long-term research placement. 'Don't judge an artwork by its maker … A qualitative study into the lives of Young Mothers' combined workshops, group discussions and case-study interviews. The project worked with young mothers with few formal learning experiences.

43 Joanne Hollows, 'Can I Go Home Yet? Feminism, Post-feminism and Domesticity', in Hollows and Moseley (2006), p.98

44 Janey Forgan, email correspondence with the author, 4 March 2009

List of contributors

Joanne Bailey is a Senior Lecturer in History at Oxford Brookes University. She has published on the cultural and social history of conflictual marital relationships and is currently engaged in exploring the history of the family as a set of ideas, practices and experiences in the eighteenth and early nineteenth centuries.

Christopher Breward is Head of Research at the V&A and a Professional Fellow at the London College of Fashion, University of the Arts, London. He sits on the Editorial Boards of the journals *Fashion Theory* and *Journal of Design History*; and on the Advisory Board of the *Journal of Design History*. He has published widely on fashion's relationship to masculinity, metropolitan cultures and concepts of modernity.

Clare Browne is Curator of European Textiles 1500–1800 at the V&A, where she has worked since 1982. She deals with dress and furnishing textiles across a wide range of techniques, including weaving, printing, embroidery, lace and tapestry.

Joanne Hackett graduated with an MS in Art Conservation from the Winterthur/University of Delaware Program in Art Conservation in 1998. After graduating she worked at the Fine Arts Museums of San Francisco and the Indianapolis Museum of Art. She has been a senior textile conservator at the V&A since 2006.

Jenny Lister is Curator of Nineteenth-Century Textiles and Fashion at the V&A. She curated the V&A exhibitions *60s Fashion* (2006) and *Grace Kelly Style* (2010), for which she has also edited the accompanying book. She was formerly a curator at Kensington Palace and the Museum of London.

Angela McShane is Tutor in Graduate Studies (post-1600) for the joint V&A/RCA Masters Course in the History of Design. The 'Chapman coverlet' case study emerged from a seminar on 'objects of emotion' and study days analysing quilts led by the Exhibition Team, with all the MA students, especially Ann Christie and Abigail Turner.

Dorothy Osler is an author, independent scholar, exhibitions curator and consultant specializing in historical British quilts. She is an Associate Fellow of the International Quilt Study Center and Museum at the University of Nebraska–Lincoln. She is an external consultant for the 2010 Quilts Exhibition.

Linda Parry is a textile historian. She worked for more than 30 years in the textile department of the V&A, specializing in the nineteenth century. She has published extensively on William Morris and the Arts and Crafts movement, as well as more wide-ranging histories of embroidery, tapestry and quilt-making. She is an external consultant for the 2010 Quilts Exhibition.

Sue Prichard is Curator of Contemporary Textiles at the V&A and Curator of the exhibition *Quilts 1700–2010* (2010). She curated the displays *Recent Acquisitions 1992–2002: A Decade of Collecting Textiles* (2003–4), *Concealed-Discovered-Revealed: New Work by Sue Lawty* (2005) and *Penelope's Thread: Contemporary Tapestry from the Permanent Collection* (2006). Recent publications include *V&A Pattern: The Fifties* (2009) and *British Textile Design: The Search for a New Aesthetic in Henry Moore Textiles* (2008).

Jacqueline Riding is an arts and heritage consultant, writer and doctoral candidate at the University of York (eighteenth-century British art). She was Director of the Handel House Museum, London, and Assistant Curator of the Palace of Westminster. She is co-editor of *The Houses of Parliament: History, Art, Architecture*. She would like to thank Pip Dodd (National Army Museum), Dr Richard Johns (Curator of Prints and Drawings, National Maritime Museum) and Professor Geoffrey Quilley (University of Sussex) for their help and expertise in preparing her feature spread.

Claire Smith is the Research Assistant for the exhibition *Quilts 1700–2010*. She completed her DPhil at the University of Oxford before joining the V&A in 2007 as Assistant Curator in the Department of Furniture, Textiles and Fashion.

John Styles is Research Professor in History at the University of Hertfordshire. He was previously Head of Graduate Studies at the V&A and developed the historical themes for *The British Galleries 1500–1900* (2001). He specializes in the history of eighteenth-century Britain, especially the study of manufacturing, consumption and design.

Catalogue authors

RA Rosemary E. Allan. Museum Curator, Beamish Museum

RB Robert Bell. Senior Curator, Decorative Arts and Design, National Gallery of Australia

NM Noreen Marshall. Curator of Dress and Nursery Collections, V&A Museum of Childhood

PM Paula Martin. Assistant Curator of Costume and Textiles, Royal Albert Memorial Museum

EP Elen Phillips. Curator: Costume and Textiles, St Fagans: National History Museum

RQ Rebecca Quinton. Curator, European Costumes and Textiles, Culture and Sport Glasgow (Museums)

VW Valerie Wilson. Curator of Textiles, Ulster Folk & Transport Museum

Bibliography

Adamson, Glenn, *Thinking Through Craft* (Oxford, 2007)

Allan, Rosemary E., *Quilts and Coverlets: The Beamish Collection* (Durham, 2007)

Anon., *The Wedding Ring; or, History of Miss Sidney*, 3 vols (London, 1779)

Anthony, Ilid E., 'Quilting and Patchwork in Wales', *Amgueddfa*, no.12, Winter 1972

Austen, Jane, *Letters of Jane Austen*, ed. Lord Brabourne (1884)

Austen, Jane, *Northanger Abbey: and Persuasion*, 4 vols (London, 1818)

Bailey, Joanne, *Unquiet Lives: Marriage and Marriage Breakdown in England, 1660–1800* (Cambridge, 2003)

Baker, Thomas, *Hampstead Heath: A Comedy* (London, 1706)

Baker, Thomas, *Tunbridge-Walks: or, the Yeoman of Kent: A Comedy* (London, 1703)

Barber, Jacq, 'Fabric as Evidence: Unravelling the Meaning of a Late Eighteenth Century Coverlet', *Quilt Studies* 3, 2001, pp.11–32

Baudino, I., Career, J. and Revauger, C. (eds), *The Invisible Woman: Aspects of women's work in eighteenth-century Britain* (Hampshire, 2005)

Brown, Neal, *Tracey Emin* (London, 2006)

Bryden, I. and Floyd, J., *Domestic Space: Reading the nineteenth-century interior* (Manchester, 1999)

Chadwick, Whitney, *Women, Art, and Society*, 4th edn (London, 2007)

Chave, Anna C., 'Dis/Cover/ing the Quilts of Gee's Bend, Alabama', *Journal of Modern Craft*, vol.1, issue 2, 2008, pp.221–54

Clabburn, Pamela, *The National Trust Book of Furnishing Textiles* (London, 1988)

Colby, Averil, *Patchwork* (London, 1958)

Colby, Averil, *Patchwork Quilts* (London, 1965)

Colby, Averil, *Quilting* (London, 1972)

Dancyger, Irene, *A World of Women: An Illustrated History of Women's Magazines* (Dublin, 1978)

Dibden, Charles, 'Poor Jack; or, the Sweet Little Cherub', in *Poor Jack's garland, containing several excellent new songs* (Newcastle-upon-Tyne, [1790?])

Eddy, Celia, *Quilted Planet: A Sourcebook of Quilts from Around the World* (London, 2005)

Edrica Huws Patchworks (exhibition catalogue, Aberystwyth, 2007)

Edwards, Clive, *Turning Houses into Homes* (London, 2005)

Elinor, G. et al., *Women and Craft* (London, 1987)

Elliott, Patrick, 'Becoming Tracey Emin', in *Tracey Emin 20 Years* (Edinburgh, 2008)

Fabrics and Fabrication (exhibition catalogue, Ulster Folk and Transport Museum, 2001)

Fenwick Smith, Tina et al., 'The 1718 Silk Patchwork Coverlet', *Quilt Studies* 5, 2003, pp.24–109

Ferguson, Carolyn, 'A Study of Quakers, Convicts and Quilts', *Quilt Studies* 8, 2007, pp.35–64

FitzRandolph archive, Mavis, Archive of Art and Design, V&A, London

FitzRandloph, Mavis, *Traditional Quilting: Its story and its practice* (London, 1954)

FitzRandolph, M. and Fletcher, F.M., *Quilting, Traditional Methods and Design* (London, 1968)

Flather, A., *Gender and Space in Early Modern England* (Suffolk, 2007)

Foster, Alicia, *Tate Women Artists* (London, 2004)

Freeman, June, *Quilting, Patchwork and Appliqué 1700–1982: Sewing as a Woman's Art* (London, 1983)

General Evening Post, 4–6 June 1799, no.10402, p.1, col.3

Goodenough, Simon, *Jam and Jerusalem* (Glasgow and London, 1977)

Hake, Elizabeth, *English Quilting Old and New* (London, 1937)

Harrod, Tanya, *The Crafts in Britain in the Twentieth Century* (New Haven and London, 1999)

Hefford, Wendy, *The Victoria and Albert Museum's Textile Collection: Designs for printed textiles in England from 1750 to 1850* (London, 1992)

Henderson, Frances, '"Swifte and Secrete Writing" in Seventeenth-Century England, and Samuel Shelton's Brachygraphy', *Electronic British Library Journal*, 2008, article 5

Hillyer, Lynda, 'Adhesives Yesterday: The use of adhesives in textile conservation at the Victoria and Albert Museum', unpublished paper from the Canadian Conservation Institute/V&A/British Museum adhesives workshop, held at the V&A and British Museum, April 2002

Hollows, Joanne, *Feminism, Femininity and Popular Culture* (Manchester, 2000)

Hollows, Joanne and Moseley, Rachel (eds), *Feminism in Popular Culture* (Oxford, 2006)

Holstein, Jonathan, *Abstract Design in American Quilts: A Biography of an Exhibition* (Kentucky Quilt Project, 1991)

Homer, *The Odyssey of Homer*, trans. Alexander Pope, 5 vols (London, 1760), vol.V, book XXI, pp.82–4

Hughes, Ann, 'Thornton, Alice (1626–1707)', *Oxford Dictionary of National Biography* (Oxford, 2004); www.oxforddnb.com/view.article/38063 (consulted 24 March 2009)

Hughes, Therle, *English Domestic Needlework 1660–1860* (London, 1961)

Jones, Jen, *Welsh Quilts* (Saint-Etienne de Montluc, 1997)

Jones, Laura, *Irish Patchwork* (Kilkenny, 1979)

Kruger, Kathryn Sullivan, 'Clues and Cloth: Seeking Ourselves in "The Fabric of Myth"', in Kruger, Harrison and Young (2008), pp.10–31

Kruger, K.S., Harrison, A. and Young, J., *The Fabric of Myth* (Compton Verney, 2008)

Lambert, Miles, '"Small Presents Confirm Friendship": The "Gifting" of Clothing and Textiles in England from the Late Seventeenth to the Early Nineteenth Centuries', *TEXT: For the Study of Textile Art Design History* 32, 2004, pp.24–32

Landi, Sheila, *The Textile Conservator's Manual*, 2nd edn (Oxford, 1992), pp.121–30, 188–90

Laurence, Anne, *Women in England 1500–1760: A Social History* (London, 1996)

Menderson, Sara Heller, 'Stuart Women's Diaries and Occasional Memoirs', in Mary Prior (ed.), *Women in English Society: 1500–1800* (London, 1985)

Morris, Barbara, *Victorian Needlework* (London, 1962)

Murdoch, Tessa (ed.), *Noble Households: Eighteenth-Century Inventories of Great English Houses, A Tribute to John Cornforth* (Cambridge, 2006)

Old Bailey Proceedings Online, 1674–1913: see www.oldbaileyonline.org (consulted 8 March 2009)

Osler, Dorothy, *North Country Quilts: Legend and Living Tradition* (Durham, 2000)

Osler, Dorothy, *Traditional British Quilts* (London, 1987)

Parker, Rozsika, *The Subversive Stitch: Embroidery and the making of the feminine* (London, 1996)

Parker, Rozsika and Pollock, Griselda, *Old Mistresses: Women, Art and Ideology* (London, 1981)

Parry, Linda (ed.), *A Practical Guide to Patchwork from the Victoria and Albert Museum* (London, 1987)

Parry, Linda, *The Victoria and Albert Museum Textile Collection: British Textiles from 1850–1900* (London, 1993)

Pearce, Susan M., *Museums, Objects and Collections: A Cultural Study* (Leicester, 1992)

Perry, Gill (ed.), *Difference and Excess in Contemporary Art: The Visibility of Women's Practice* (Oxford, 2006)

Ponsonby, M., *Stories from Home: English domestic interiors 1750–1850* (Aldershot, 2007)

Prichard, Sue, 'Precision Patchwork: Nineteenth-Century Military Quilts', unpublished conference paper, Military and Textile Conference, University of Copenhagen, 20–22 May 2008

Rae, Janet, *The Quilts of the British Isles* (London, 1987)

Rae, Janet and Tucker, Margaret, 'Quilts with Special Associations', in *Quilt Treasures: The Quilters' Guild Heritage Search* (London, 1995), pp.170–77

Redding, Priscilla, *Her Booke April 24 1678* (1678–1723); permission to reproduce extracts kindly given by Professor Richard P. Brent

Ringgold, Faith, *We Flew Over the Bridge: The Memoirs of Faith Ringgold* (Boston, 1995)

Robinson, Hilary (ed.), *Feminism-Art-Theory: An Anthology 1968–2000* (Oxford, 2001)

Rose archive, Muriel, Crafts Study Centre, University College for the Creative Arts, Farnham, Surrey

Rose, Clare, 'Exhibiting Knowledge: British Inlaid Patchwork', in *Fabric Intarsia in Europe from 1500 to the Present Day* (exhibition catalogue, Museum Europäischer Kulturen, Staatliche Museen zu Berlin, 2009), pp.87–98

Rose, Clare, 'The Manufacture and Sale of Marseilles quilting in eighteenth-century London', *CIETA Bulletin* 76, 1999, pp.104–13

Rose, Clare, 'Quilting in Eighteenth-century London', *Quilt Studies* 2, 2000, pp.11–30

Samuel, Raphael, *Theatres of Memory* (London, 1994)

Sheppard, Josie, *Through the Needle's Eye: The Patchwork and Quilt Collection at the York Castle Museum* (York, 2005)

Smith, Claire, 'Doing Time: Patchwork as a Tool of Social Rehabilitation in British Prisons', *V&A Online Research Journal*, no.1, Autumn 2008; www.vam.ac.uk/res_cons/research/online_journal/journal_1_index/doing_time/index.html

Starkey, David (ed.), *The Inventory of King Henry VIII: The Transcript* (London, 1998)

Steinbach, Susie, *Women in England 1760–1914: A Social History* (London, 2004)

Stephens, Christine, *Quilts* (Cardiff, 1993)

Styles, John, 'Lodging at the Old Bailey: Lodgings and their Furnishing in Eighteenth-Century London', in Styles and Vickery (2006)

Styles, John and Vickery, Amanda (eds), *Gender, Taste, and Material Culture in Britain and North America, 1700–1830* (New Haven and London, 2006)

The Subversive Stitch (exhibition catalogue, Whitworth Art Gallery, Manchester, 27 May–29 August 1988, and Cornerhouse, Manchester, 27 May–17 July 1988)

Swain, Margaret, 'Search the Scriptures', in *Figures on Fabric: Embroidery Design Sources and Their Application* (London, 1980), pp.38–51

Swift, Reverend Dr, *Directions to Servants in General* (London, 1745)

Take 4: New Perspectives on the British Art Quilt (exhibition catalogue, Whitworth Art Gallery, Manchester, 11 September–15 November 1998)

Thompson, Paul, *The Voice of the Past: Oral History*, 3rd edn (Oxford, 2000)

Tracey Emin, I Need Art Like I Need God (exhibition catalogue, South London Gallery, 16 April–18 May 1997)

Tracey Emin 20 Years (exhibition catalogue, National Galleries of Scotland, 2008)

Trimmer, Mrs Sarah, *The Oeconomy of Charity*, 2nd edn, 2 vols (London, 1802)

Ulrich, Laurel Thatcher, *The Age of Homespun: Objects and Stories in the Creation of an American Myth* (New York, 2002)

Vacher, Jean (ed.), *Muriel Rose: A Modern Crafts Legacy* (Farnham, 2006)

Vickery, Amanda, *The Gentleman's Daughter: Women's Lives in Georgian England* (New Haven and London, 1998)

Walker, Michele, *The Complete Book of Quiltmaking* (London, 1985)

Weiner, Annette B. and Schneider, Jane (eds), *Cloth and Human Experience* (Washington, DC, 1989)

Weldon's Encyclopaedia of Needlework (London, n.d. [c.1954])

White, Cynthia M., *Women's Magazines 1693–1968* (London, 1970)

[Whiteley, Jane], *From Within: Jane Whiteley, Works in Cloth* (exhibition catalogue, The Moores Building, Fremantle, Western Australia, 1999)

Women's Institute, *Textile Treasures of the WI* (London, 2007)

['A Lady'], *The Workwoman's Guide* (London, 1840)

Zegher, Catherine de, *Inside the Visible: An Elliptical Traverse of Twentieth Century Art, in, of and from the Feminine* (Cambridge, MA, 1996)

Glossary

Aniline dye The first artificial dye used for cloth; the colours were very bright but fugitive, fading into a beige/brown sludge with extended exposure to light. The first aniline, a mauve, was discovered by William Perkin in 1856 while experimenting with quinine in an attempt to find a treatment for malaria. This led to new crimsons, violets, blues and reds, all colours that were fashionable at the time. By the mid-1860s a wide range of colours was available.

Appliqué The application (usually by means of embroidery) of shaped pieces of fabric to a ground material in order to create a design.

Block-printing One of the oldest methods of printing; each colour (except those to be 'pencilled') was applied with a separate block of wood, carved to leave in relief the pattern for that particular colour. Registration of the design was regulated by means of 'pins' at the corners. The printer grasped a shaped hand-hold or leather strap at the back of the block, pressed its face to a taut cloth saturated with dye or mordant, which his assistant had prepared above a tub of the substance to be printed, then positioned the block by means of the pins and struck it with a mallet to make a smooth transfer of the printed matter. If finer details were required than could be carved in wood, metal strips and pins were inserted in the block.

Block quilt A quilt made from a series of pieced or appliquéd block units, usually square.

Blue thread By an Act of 1774 all-cotton cloth could legally be sold and printed for use in Britain, but three blue threads had to be woven in the selvedges of cotton of English manufacture, to identify it for payment of duty. This condition was dropped in 1811.

Broderie perse A form of appliqué in which individual motifs, such as flowers or birds, are cut from printed fabrics and then stitched onto a larger piece of fabric to create the design.

Calico Unbleached cotton cloth.

China blue An English invention, known as *bleu d'Angleterre* in France, this fine indigo-blue technique overcame the problem of indigo oxidizing and becoming insoluble on the way from dye-vat to cloth. By printing the indigo as a paste with iron sulphate and a suitable thickener (such as gum arabic), the desired shade of blue could be obtained by dipping the cloth alternately in baths of lime and iron sulphate. As this technique could not be used with the many processes that were necessary to produce all the other chintz colours, it tended to be favoured for plate-prints.

Chinoiserie A form of decoration influenced by Chinese ornament and decoration, aimed at the European market.

Chintz Printed furnishing cotton, often with a glazed finish.

Chrome yellow Chromate of lead. The first of the chrome dyes was invented in 1819 by Koechlin of Mulhouse; chrome orange and chrome green followed. John Mercer produced a chrome yellow in England in about 1823.

Clouds In England, the name given to a textile with a pattern printed on the warp, or on the warp and weft, before weaving, thereby producing imprecise outlines.

Corded quilting The technique of threading cord or wool through the space created by double lines of stitching through two layers of fabric.

Coverlet Usually an ornamental (pieced, embroidered or appliquéd) cloth cover for a bed, without wadding or backing. The term is widely used for unquilted but backed bedcovers, such as chintz appliqué coverlets.

Crazy patchwork Patchwork made with irregularly shaped pieces of silk, brocade and satin, randomly stitched on top of a large piece of fabric. The edges where patches join or overlap are usually embellished with decorative embroidery stitches, such as herringbone or feather stitch, worked in brightly coloured threads. In the centre of pieces of plain satin or silk, flowers, birds or insects are sometimes embroidered.

Cretonne Printed cotton, which from the 1870s superseded chintz as a fashionable furnishing fabric. Cretonne is unglazed and has a heavier, more textured ground than traditional chintz.

Cylinder-printing Thomas Bell is credited with this invention in 1783: the cylinders used in Britain were at first of copper plate hammered to shape and joined by brazing; as these joins tended to open, later cylinders were bored from solid metal. As broad as the cloth to be printed, the early cylinders were restricted in circumference, not being large enough for pictorial furnishing prints until about 1815. Despite this, the new technique, so much faster than printing by hand, led to a strike by journeymen printers as early as 1790, and Livesey, Hargreaves, Anstie, Smith and Hall (who, according to Charles O'Brien, had had some 600 or 700 cylinders cut and pinned) were threatened with arson in 1786 if they did not stop working their 'Machines for Printing'. The design is engraved on copper rollers (one for each colour), which revolve around a central stationary roller; the engraving is

filled with colour and the cloth pressed onto it. The entire width of the cloth is printed. Best-selling designs are usually roller-printed, as the cost of engraving the rollers is high and large quantities of cloth have to be printed and sold to recoup the initial outlay. This is a quick patterning technique: one machine can print thousands of yards of fabric in one day.

Demy chintz In the mid-eighteenth century 'half-chintz' was composed of red, blue and yellow, which could be overprinted to produce other colours, but lacked the extra reds and purples of 'whole chintz'. By the early nineteenth century the term 'demy' or 'demi-chintz' had a more restricted range (fewer than five colours) and was often used to denote the 'drab' style, with no reds.

Discharge Discharges were not widely used until the early nineteenth century, though they were being advertised in the late 1780s. Printed on the cloth after dyeing or mordanting, they made the colour either colourless or soluble, so that it could be washed out, leaving a white figure to receive other colours.

Fancy machine-ground The elaboration of roller-prints in the 1820s and '30s led to increasing use of fancy ground covers as alternatives to plain or coloured grounds. Those engraved by the firm of Joseph Lockett were particularly intricate.

Fent A remnant or damaged piece of cloth.

Flat quilting A single or double line of stitching, worked into a pattern through two layers of fabric with no wadding in between.

Framed quilt A quilt with a central panel or pieced or appliquéd centre, around which a series of borders is sewn. The borders can

be pieced, appliquéd or of a single fabric; they may increase in width towards the outer edges of the quilt. During the nineteenth century ready-printed panels gained popularity and were used as quilt centres. Framed quilts are also commonly referred to as 'medallion quilts'.

Fulling A finishing process in the manufacture of woollen cloth, in which the newly woven or knitted cloth is felted or compressed, causing it to shrink in both directions.

Fustian This name was used for several different fabrics – sometimes a twilled cotton or cotton and linen, sometimes with a nap. When printed, fustian was usually a plain-weave cotton weft on linen warp, and was legal for printing in Britain from 1736 to 1774, at which time all-cotton cloth was banned in deference to the silk and woollen industries. Some dyes took differently on cotton and linen, producing a speckled effect.

Glazed cotton Cotton with a shiny surface, which is achieved by various chemical or physical finishing processes. Many cottons lose this sheen when laundered.

Inlay patchwork A technique similar to appliqué, whereby cut-out fabric shapes are set or inlaid into an identical cut-out space in another fabric.

Lapis style Before the invention of 'resist red', the different processes for printing red and blue necessitated a white or black outline between the two colours. A resist for the blue dye, which at the same time contained a mordant for madder, made precise juxtaposition possible from 1808. The style was developed on the Continent at Mulhouse, and in England by James Thomson at Primrose, Lancashire.

Madder colour Pinks, reds, purples, brown and black could be dyed from the madder plant by using different mordants.

Mordant A substance that bonds certain dyes to cloth so that they cannot be washed out. Cloth printed with different mordants – such as iron, tin and alum – would emerge in shades of brown, black, red and purple from one dye-bath. Iron, which was used for blacks and browns, tended to eat away the cloth.

Mosaic patchwork A type of patchwork in which geometric shapes are joined together in an overall mosaic design. The patchwork shapes are usually first pieced over paper templates. This type of patchwork is also called '"English" pieced patchwork' because of the popularity of the style in Britain. See also **Paper template**.

Paning The joining up of pieces of fabric of different types or colours, applied to bed furnishings from at least the early sixteenth century. Paned bed hangings and bedcovers were a precursor to what became known as patchwork in the eighteenth century, in their juxtaposition of different-coloured and patterned textiles, for visual effect, in a geometric arrangement.

Paper template Most commonly used when making mosaic or 'English' pieced patchwork. Paper is cut up into the shape required for a patchwork pattern and same-shaped fabric pieces are then tacked over it.

Passementerie A French term used collectively to denote all kinds of lace and ribbon, especially the decorative trimmings that were used for dresses.

Patchwork A patchwork or 'pieced work' is a form of needlework that involves sewing together pieces of fabric to form a flat design.

Pencilling In the early eighteenth century it was impossible to print indigo because of problems with oxidization. However, it was discovered that dye held in the bristles of a paintbrush could be protected from the air long enough to be painted or 'pencilled' onto the cloth, producing an uneven and not-always-fast blue. Weld (to make green with the blue) was sometimes also pencilled rather than mordanted, and then was not fast.

Piecing The method of sewing cut-out shapes of fabric together.

Plate-printing Copper plates up to 36 inches (91 cm) square, with finely engraved designs, were used for printing monochrome pictorial designs in the second half of the eighteenth century, after the invention in Ireland in 1752 of thickeners suitable for printing dyes and mordants. Handkerchiefs and other items printed earlier from copper plates were in ordinary printers' ink that could not be washed. After roller-printing became common in the early nineteenth century, copper plates were used only for handkerchiefs.

Polychrome A work of art executed or decorated in many colours or a collection of many colours.

Printer's end The end of a length of block- or roller-printed cotton, which shows various makers' stamps and written codes made by the printer as working documents. They tend to appear on early productions of patterns and are kept at the factory as information for later printings.

Quercitron The bark of the yellow oak, which is native to North America. When mordanted, it made yellow with alum, 'drab' with iron, and olive with a mixture of the two. An American chemist,

Edward Bancroft, patented its use in October 1775, and printers had to use it under licence from him. In 1779 a sale of print works in Surrey advertised 'a large Quantity of American yellow bark which, if not superior, is an excellent Substitute for Wold' (weld). When patent restrictions were lifted at the end of the eighteenth century, the general use of quercitron helped to promote the drab style.

Quilt (1) A bedcover made of two layers of fabric with a layer of padding (wadding) in between. (2) To stitch together a fabric top, padding (wadding) and back (or lining); the stitches are usually based on a design or pattern, although the three layers can be held together with ties.

Quilt marking/stamping Drawing a quilt pattern; this may be done with a pencil, crayon, chalk, chinagraph pencil or blunt needle.

Rainbow style Invented by the paper-stainer Spoerlin of Vienna and developed at Mulhouse, this was at first a block-printed style that was adapted for roller-printing. The principle was to provide different colours from parallel troughs, to be merged by brush or roller at the edges after application to the cloth.

Resist-printing Creating a pattern by applying a paste composition that will resist dyeing. After the fabric is dyed, washing removes the resist from the printed areas leaving a white pattern. A different colour may be applied in the resist paste.

Roller-printing See **Cylinder-printing**, **Fancy machine-ground** and **Surface roller**.

Satin (1) A warp-faced weave that is constructed to give an unbroken, lustrous surface; the close warp covers the weft. (2) A fabric made by satin-weave. Originally satin was

all-silk, but it is now made from silk, cotton, rayon and other fibres.

Shumac (sumac) An astringent agent that assists the dyeing process like a mordant, and also adds a yellowish tone.

Strippy quilt A quilt made from broad, alternating coloured strips of fabric, usually cotton or cotton sateen, sewn together lengthways. Most strippy quilts are quilted with patterns that follow the stripes.

Surface roller Wooden rollers, cut in the same way as woodblocks, were used for areas of solid colour, to supplement the fine engraved lines produced by the metal rollers. A 'union' or 'mule' machine to combine the two kinds of roller was invented in about 1805 by James Burton of Church, Lancashire.

Tea-ground A pale, weak colour much favoured for the grounds of colourful chintzes between 1805 and 1825, after which it became less popular than the finely engraved fancy grounds.

Template A cardboard or metal shape used as a pattern for cutting out quilt papers and fabric.

Trapunto A plain-ground fabric layered with a loose-weave backing, which is backstitched to create enclosed motif pockets that are stuffed from the back with thread or batting, by teasing apart the loose weave or slitting it with a small cross before sewing it back up, producing a relief (or raised) surface design.

Turkey red A fine, bright red based on madder, first dyed on cotton cloth by Koechlin of Mulhouse in 1810. The style was very popular with discharge work for handkerchiefs and export goods. There was a very large turkey-red industry in Scotland.

Velvet A close-cut, warp-pile fabric; the cut ends of the fibre form the fabric surface. Originally the term was applied only to silk fabrics that were the most expensive on the market.

Velveteen A close-cut, weft-pile fabric; the cut ends of the fibre form the fabric surface. It was particularly popular for furnishings in the late nineteenth and twentieth centuries.

Wadding The filling used between two pieces of fabric.

Warp pattern A form of cloth in which the pattern is printed directly onto the warp (lengthwise yarn) prior to weaving. It is a complex and delicate procedure and relies on accuracy in printing, setting up the loom and weaving the finished cloth.

Wholecloth A wholecloth quilt is made from a single fabric, strips of which are seamed together to make up the quilt top. Before 1950 most North Country wholecloth quilts were made from cotton or cotton sateen.

Acknowledgements

Quilts 1700–2010: Hidden Histories, Untold Stories has been five years in the making. This publication and the exhibition it accompanies would not have been realized without the assistance and support of a great number of people, not all of whom can be mentioned here.

I would especially like to thank my Assistant Curator Claire Smith. Claire's extraordinary research skills, tireless dedication and commitment to the project, together with her immense good humour and personal support have made her an invaluable member of the team.

We are extremely grateful to The Friends of the V&A who generously sponsored the exhibition, with further support from Coats Crafts.

The exhibition would not have happened without Rosie Wanek and the exhibitions team and the V&A Textile Conservation Studio. Joanne Hackett, our lead conservator, has been steadfast in her support of the project, researching, analysing and pushing the boundaries of quilt conservation. Thanks also to Lynda Hillyer, Sarah Glenn, Jennifer Barsby and Gretchen Guidess from the Winterthur/University of Delaware Program in Art Conservation. The skill and expertise of the V&A Photographic Studio is reflected in the detailed and exquisite photography of all the Museum's objects and the work in progress of contemporary artists. Many, many thanks to Richard Davis, Pip Barnard and Peter Kelleher.

We have worked closely with colleagues across the Museum, whose knowledge and advice have proved invaluable in helping to realize the project. I am enormously grateful to Christopher Wilk for his encouragement and support. Additional thanks to: Jo Ani, Amelia Calver, Olivia Colling, Rachel Fenn, Cathy Flanagan, Nadine Fleischer, Zoe Franklin, Cathy Hale, Rhian Harris, Debra Isaac, Annabel Judd, Andrew Kirk, Emma Laws, Karen Leatham, Andrew Lewis, Elizabeth Miller, Lesley Miller, Susan Mouncey, Carrie Rees, Naomi Saffery, Sarah Sevier, Mor Thunder, Lucy Trench, Mike Wheeler and Cassie Williams.

I would also like to acknowledge the assistance of Lydia Beanland, Clare Borthwick, Maya Rae Oppenheimer and Olivia Quigley.

I am eternally grateful to our creative and dynamic exhibition design team: Celine Dalcher and Adriana Ferlauto from the V&A, Frith Kerr and Amy Preston from Studio Frith and Zerlina Hughes from ZNA. Thanks also to Sor Lan Tan and Keith Flemming from Flemming Associates for managing the project.

I am also indebted to colleagues in both national and international museums for engaging so positively with this project. Their generosity in providing access to their collections has been matched only by their hospitality. I wish to thank the following individuals: Rosemary Allen of Beamish Museum, Simon Chaplin of the Royal College of Surgeons, Joanne Davenport of Upton House, the Bearsted Collection (National Trust), Pip Dodd of the National Army Museum, JoAnne Gloger of the Forge Needle Museum, Alex Goddard of the Geffrye Museum, Antony Griffiths of the British Museum, Diane Lees of the Imperial War Museum, Paula Martin of Rougemont House, Elen Phillips of the National History Museum, St Fagan's, Rebecca Quinton and Jeff Dunn of Glasgow Museums, Ron Radford and Robert Bell of the National Gallery of Australia, Valerie Wilson of the Ulster Folk and Transport Museum and the Quilters' Guild of the British Isles.

Many thanks also to the many private collectors and individuals, some of whom wish to remain anonymous, who have been so generous with their time and hospitality including Philly Adams of the Saatchi Collection, Annette Gero, Jen Jones, Griselda Lewis, Anna Mansi and Ron Simpson.

Great admiration and huge thanks to all the artists and practitioners who have given so generously of their time, creativity and inspiration to this project: Jo Budd, Pauline Burbidge, Kirsty Fenton and the tutors of Duncan of Jordanstone College of Art, Dundee, Janey Forgan, the volunteers of Fine Cell Work and the men of HMP Wandsworth, Caren Garfen, Diana Harrison, Sara Impey, Natasha Kerr, Nicola Naismith, Clio Padovani, Grayson Perry, Dinah Prentice, Victoria Rutter of Louis Moreau, Nina Saunders, Susan Stockwell, Timorous Beasties, Jennifer Vickers, Michele Walker and Jane Whiteley.

Special thanks are due to the V&A Publishing team without whom this publication would not have been possible: Mark Eastment, Frances Ambler, Laura Potter, and to copy editor Mandy Greenfield and book designer Nigel Soper. My sincere thanks also to all those who have contributed to this publication (listed on p.232), who have so generously shared their knowledge and expertise, not least Dorothy Osler and Linda Parry who had the additional role as external consultants to the exhibition.

Words cannot express how much I appreciate my family's patience, love and understanding: Graham, Charlotte and Emily all deserve much more than a simple thank you.

SUE PRICHARD

Picture credits

Index